The Monetary Turning Point

Joseph Huber

The Monetary Turning Point

From Bank Money to Central Bank Digital Currency (CBDC)

palgrave
macmillan

Joseph Huber
Berlin, Berlin, Germany

ISBN 978-3-031-23956-4 ISBN 978-3-031-23957-1 (eBook)
https://doi.org/10.1007/978-3-031-23957-1

This Palgrave Macmillan imprint is published by the registered company Springer Nature Switzerland AG
The registered company address is: Gewerbestrasse 11, 6330 Cham, Switzerland

Contents

Abbreviations and Glossary

AI	Artificial Intelligence
Bank money	Bank-account balances in the form of sight deposits (aka demand deposits, overnight deposits) as well as savings and time deposits
BIS	Bank for International Settlements
Cash equivalents	Includes near-money such as certificates of deposit, as well as short-term securities such as treasury bills, bank acceptances, commercial paper, repos
CBDC	Central Bank Digital Currency, digital central-bank money
CC	Complementary Currency
Central-bank money	Money issued by central banks, in the form of notes, reserves, and soon also CBDC. Coins are mostly still treasury money, but circulated via the central banks, too
CPI	Consumer price inflation
Digital Token	Token money in the form of digitised currency units
DC	Digital Currency
DCEP	Digital Currency Electronic Payment System (China)
DeFi	Decentralised Finance, generic term for peer-to-peer financial services
DLT	Distributed Ledger Technology, or decentral blockchain technology
ECB	European Central Bank
FASB	Financial Accounting Standards Board
Forex	Foreign exchange
GAAP	Generally Accepted Accounting Principles

GDP	Gross Domestic Product
IASB	International Accounting Standards Board (EU and UK)
ICO	Initial Coin Offering (cryptocurrencies)
ID	Identity, e.g. referring to a money user's identification code
IFRS	International Financial Reporting Standards
IMF	International Monetary Fund
IPO	Initial Public Offering (stocks)
IT	Advanced Information and Telecommunications Technology
MMF	Money Market Fund
P2P	Peer-to-peer (directly, without intermediation)
PSP	Payment Service Provider
QE	Quantitative Easing, meaning expansive policy of "loose money"
QT	Quantitative Tightening, meaning contractive policy of "tight money"
Reserves	Banks' central-bank account balances, serving as the means of payment in interbank cashless transactions
RTGS	Real-Time Gross Settlement (central-bank payment system)
TARGET	Trans-European Automated Real-Time Gross Settlement Express Transfer System (ECB payment system)
TIPS	TARGET Instant Payment Settlement
TLTRO	Targeted Longer-Term Refinancing Operations
tps	Transactions per second
Twh	Terawatt hour

List of Tables

List of Boxes

CHAPTER 1

Core Points for Introduction

The monetary system is at a turning point. Hitherto dominant types of money are going down, while new types of money are on the rise, competing for becoming the next dominant type of money, that is, the prevailing means of payment to determine the functioning of the monetary system.

Today's by far dominant money is the balances on current bank accounts, known as sight deposits or demand deposits, hereafter referred to as bank money, as distinct from central-bank money. Cashless payment with bank money has become system-defining and made central-bank money subordinate. For creating bank money under conditions of business as usual, banks only need a small payment reserve in cash and central-bank reserves.

Cash (coins and notes) has long since passed its zenith. Its share in the money supply is now often only in the single-digit range and a considerable part of it does not even circulate but serves as a dormant safety cushion. Contrary to what cash payment of small amounts suggests, the actual role of cash is no longer of systemic importance. The importance of central-bank reserves in relation to bank money has also declined. One should not be deceived in this respect by the glut of central-bank reserves as a result of the crisis policies of Quantitative Easing (QE) in the 2010s.

J. Huber, *The Monetary Turning Point*,
https://doi.org/10.1007/978-3-031-23957-1_1

By contrast, bank money is at its zenith, even though it is likely to have passed it by now. From a present-day perspective, it hardly seems conceivable that bank transfers could become obsolete. But that's what is likely to happen over time. Bank money, on a small base of central-bank reserves, has become ever more dominant because central banks and governments actively support bank money and come to the banking sector's rescue from one crisis to the next. Otherwise—as a purely private means of payment without state warranty—bank money would have perished long ago, as private banknotes did in the past.

Meanwhile, there is another reason for the gradual decline in bank money. Bank money is book money, just like central-bank reserves, used for cashless payment by way of transferring account balances among banks. What undermines book money is the rise of digital tokens as a new and technically superior type of money. In a way, digital tokens are a kind of digital cash. The tool for receiving, storing and paying out digital tokens are e-wallets in succession to purses, billfolds and current accounts. The tokens are transferred directly from the e-wallet of the payer into that of the payee (P2P), like cash from hand to hand. This leaves out bank money, as well as intermediary interbank payments in reserves.

Unlike cash, digital tokens are denominable like book money. Certain varieties of digital tokens promise to be easier to handle, faster, less expensive and even safer than conventional bank transfers. On top, digital money opens up the possibility of being programmable, including smart contracts and their fulfilment, an additional function to which book money cannot be upgraded. Digital tokens thus offer themselves as an alternative to traditional solid cash as well as to bank money and central-bank reserves, and thus as a successor to them. Just as cashless payment with book money displaced traditional cash, digital money will gradually take the place of book money, that is, of bank money and central-bank reserves.

Over the last three and a half centuries, the structural composition of the money supply has experienced three epochal turning points, and the fourth is emergent right now. Technically, the development went from metal coins to paper money and then to book money. Until after the middle of the seventeenth century, money was sovereign coin made of silver and copper, partly of gold. Overall, there was too little coinage to meet the needs of growing populations and economies. So the coin base was then complemented, and replaced to a degree, by paper money, issued as private banknotes or as government treasury bills. During this period, the issue of banknotes and treasury bills was largely unregulated. In Europe this resulted in recurrent over-issue of paper money, depreciation and acceptance problems. The then governors of the later United States (U.S.) were more considered and successful with the issue of their colonial bills.

In response to the problems, European countries gradually introduced the banknote monopoly of the central banks since around the middle of the nineteenth century. This was the second monetary turning point. The banknote monopoly was based on the gold standard, which was supposed to act as an artificial limit to the money supply. However, the gold standard was not consistently successful, due to the unprecedented growth pressure resulting from industrialisation and urbanisation.

As a result, a third monetary turning point occurred. The centuries-old banking practice of mutual clearing of claims and liabilities led to the spread of book money in the form of central-bank reserves and bank deposit money, involving cashless payment by transferring current account balances, and becoming more broad-based in the decades around 1900. This gave rise to the bank money regime, more firmly established in the course of the 1920–1970s. It again led to recurrent over-issue of money, over-crediting and over-indebtedness. Debt and currency crises, banking and financial crises were becoming more frequent worldwide. The effectiveness of monetary policy diminished, money creation got largely out of control, and the bank money regime looks set to approach a state of ungovernability.

Put another way, a fourth monetary turning point is now imminent in order to get a grip on the present problems. The change occurs by way of another recomposition of the money supply, with new types of money emerging and competing for future dominance, while bank money, still dominant today, is about to losing importance, and traditional cash (coins and notes) disappearing altogether.

One candidate in the competition for the dominant position has already been confirmed: Central Bank Digital Currency (CBDC). Other candidates may well include the one or other cryptocurrency, be it monetarily uncovered or in the form of a stablecoin, that is, a cryptocoin stably pegged to the US dollar or another reserve currency unit at a ratio of 1:1. Such stablecoins have potential beyond the current teething troubles of that new type of money. By contrast, uncovered and unwarranted cryptocurrencies such as Bitcoin today are too slow, energy-consuming and expensive to prevail against the competition. Others like Ether based on a proof-of-stake process may fare better. From today's perspective, it is still open to what extent cryptocurrencies may succeed in playing an important role as a regular and truly universal means of payment, or whether they are bound to remain a special-purpose instrument for special user groups.

CBDC, as well as the one or other cryptocoin, will assert pressure on bank money, not right away, but over the years and decades. Moreover, the challenge also affects central-bank reserves. From a technical point of view, both bank money and central-bank reserves are the same type of book money. The monetary difference is that reserves only act as a fractional base for bank money, while they have never been made available to the public. If this remains the case, reserves will lose their function together with bank money. This is a decisive reason for central banks to plan CBDC issuance. Otherwise, in the absence of an important quantity of central-bank money in general public use, central banks not only risk sliding into irrelevance, but also losing their nations' monetary sovereignty.

The People's Bank of China has officially launched its digital currency on the occasion of the Winter Olympics in February 2022. The digital yuan contributes to improving the national payment system and strengthens the central bank's position vis-à-vis large corporate providers of e-money (Alibaba, Tencent). It may also be intended as a first step towards changing the international monetary setup.

In addition to the digital yuan, there was in 2019–2022 Facebook's failed attempt to launch a corporate global stablecoin called Libra, later rebranded Diem. Both events—the digital yuan and the Libra/Diem plan—have helped to accelerate the move of central banks everywhere to CBDC. A good dozen central banks are already carrying out extensive pilot projects, and most other central banks are by now exploring CBDC.[1] By and by all central banks will introduce CBDC. It is just a matter of time. People will then pay even less or not at all with cash, less often with bank money, and increasingly with CBDC, for example digital dollars, or other digital tokens denominated in the home currency of a respective central bank or treasury.

Thus, a situation is emerging in which CBDC is on the rise and even cryptocurrencies may for a while be vying for supremacy, while bank

[1] Atlanticcouncil.org/cbdctracker.

money is striving to assert itself against both. This applies to the Western world, not to China where cryptocurrency transactions have been banned in September 2021, thus barring any digital competition to the digital yuan within China.

One will ask why banks should not also issue digital money, as a tokenised variety of bank book money. However, this would be tantamount to a throwback to the eighteenth and nineteenth centuries, when the banks issued their private banknotes, just as royal and princely treasuries in Europe issued paper bills of their own, fraught with various difficulties in circulation, until private and treasury paper money was replaced in the course of the nineteenth century by the central-bank note monopoly. Although central banks act primarily as "bank of the banks" today, they are unlikely to tolerate such a throwback.

Hypothetically, banks cooperating in a sector-wide syndicate could certainly act as issuers of a stablecoin. However, this would make them subject to pertinent regulation. In all likelihood, regulation to be expected will stipulate full coverage in other types of money and cash equivalents, rather than still granting the current status of bank money based on fractional coverage in central-bank reserves. From today's perspective, this is not attractive for a bank. By contrast, for non-bank financial institutions, stablecoins are definitely of interest, for example for shadow banks and various web and IT corporations with hundreds of millions of customers.

As digital currency spreads and the share of bank money declines, banks will once again become financial intermediaries, that is, loan brokers and investors using CBDC and probably also cryptocurrencies and stablecoins. The status of banks as *monetary* financial institutions, as creators of bank money, will diminish accordingly. However, a diminishing role of bank money, possibly its distant demise, does not mean the end of banking. Credit and banks have existed since early antiquity. Today, in a monetarised and financialised world, banks remain indispensable. It is just that they evolve with the times. Currency exchange services and PSP, money lenders, investment institutes and a multitude of other financial institutions will conduct their business with CBDC, cryptocurrencies and stablecoins just as they have with all previous types of money.

At present, banks are still in a privileged position. They alone are eligible for refinancing with the central bank. Bank money is allowed to circulate on the basis of only a small fractional reserve. This in turn involves extensive central-bank support and state warranty for the existing stock of bank money—and thus for the banking sector itself. As a result, systemically relevant large banks and their bank money have acquired para-state status.

However, this too has just begun to change. The near-monopoly of bank money in public payment transactions is going to dissolve due to the rise in CBDC and private digital monies. In addition, non-bank financial institutions and government budgets are now being refinanced by central banks indirectly. Some central banks even contribute to government spending in direct ways. This is declared to be about temporary unconventional measures, but it looks more like a new normal is taking hold here.

The range of monetary and financial services provided by banks and non-monetary financial institutions has evolved a great deal. In earlier times, there was no financial sector beyond the banks (except for insurance companies). The banks were the financial sector. In the meantime, new PSP as well as shadow banks in the form of new credit institutions and investment agencies have joined the traditional banks in large numbers. With the spread of CBDC and private digital monies, and the accompanying relative decline in bank money, the differences between the traditional banking sector and those non-bank financial institutions are likely to even out.

The new developments are changing the relationship between central banks and previous non-bank financial institutions. For example, central banking is no longer just about refinancing banks. Central banks have by now effectively assumed responsibility for the weal and woe of the entire financial sector, for the stabilisation of shadow banks and financial markets as well as for the indirect refinancing of public debt. At 40–60% of GDP, government budgets represent an integral part of the financial economy. Basically, this has never been different, although on a smaller scale. At any rate, treating private and public finances as worlds apart is unworldly. They surely form two different sectors with partly different modes of operation, but they are intertwined and interdependent.

In response to the financial crises in recent decades, central banks have begun taking into account the extended scope and interconnectedness of banking, private and public finances. This is not about a retrograde merging of monetary, financial-market and fiscal responsibilities. Rather, it is about the necessary realignment of the division of these functions through reassessing the role of monetary policy for both financial markets and public finances. In the face of possibly overshooting financial interests, whether from the private or public sector, central banks must be able to assert themselves as an independent monetary authority, equipped with a systemically decisive supply of CBDC that acts as a strong policy transmission lever. Only from such a position are central banks able to conduct monetary policy as balanced and effectual as possible, as creators of the primary money base and as lenders of last resort for the banking sector, non-bank financial institutions *and* the state.

Changes are also in the offing as far as the accounting of money creation is concerned, starting with the traditional practice of accounting for central-bank money as a liability of the central bank. This is a strange anachronism from those long ago times when "real" money consisted of silver coin and bullion. At least on the balance sheets of central banks, money should always be present for what it is: a liquid monetary asset of safe stock, the money base of a nation or community of nations. Even if money is created in connection with extending credit, money and credit are two different things. "Credit money" or "debt money" are handy metaphors, especially in a world of book-money banking, but they insinuate a false identity of money and credit.

The following chapters at first provide an overview of the functional hierarchy of the current types of money, followed by a historical time lapse of the rise and fall of modern types of money to date. This condenses into a model of monetary turning points in the composition of the money supply and an associated paradigm of dominant money.

The future relationship between CBDC and bank money is currently envisaged by central banks and governments as a peaceful coexistence rather than a competitive struggle for dominance. Equally, both central banks and banks do not yet see cryptocurrencies, including stablecoins, as true competitors. But the real-world version of this story is likely to be one of competition and conflict.

CHAPTER 2

Three-Tier Monetary System. Types of Money, Their Creation and Circulation

2.1 Three-Tier Taxonomy of Money

The taxonomy of money as shown in Table 2.1 rests on two aspects. One is the technical form of money (metal coins, paper notes, book money, digital money). The other aspect refers to the money issuer, such as the treasury (coins, partly notes), central bank (notes, reserves, CBDC), banks (bank money), money market funds (MMF shares), e-money institutes (various e-monies), local or special-purpose communities (complementary currencies) and issuers or "mining" systems of cryptocurrencies.[1]

2.2 Base Level: Central-Bank Money

At the base level, money exists in the form of coins, notes and reserves, circulated by the central bank. Soon to be added is Central Bank Digital Currency (CBDC). Coins and notes are cash proper, traditional solid cash. Liquid bank deposits are often also referred to as cash, which is misleading. Coins are the oldest form of money still in use. In most countries, coins are customarily produced by the national mint and sold

[1] For a taxonomy of cryptocurrencies, cf. Bech and Garratt (2017, pp. 57–62) and Adrian and Mancini-Griffoli (2019a, pp. 2–5; 2019b). For a taxonomy of 100% e-money and stablecoins, see Hess (2019).

J. Huber, *The Monetary Turning Point*,
https://doi.org/10.1007/978-3-031-23957-1_2

Table 2.1 Three-tier taxonomy of money

Base level • Coins • Central-bank notes • Central-bank reserves (on central-bank account) • Central Bank Digital Currency (CBDC)	– Central-bank money/Treasury money – Money by sovereign fiat (sovereign money) – Legal tender – Base money. Need not be backed by other types of money and is not redeemable for such money
Second tier based on central-bank money • Liquid bank money (demand or sight deposits) • Deactivated bank money, aka near-money (savings and time deposits)	Based on central-bank reserves, albeit only to a small fraction
Third tier based on bank money • MMF shares • E-money • Stablecoins • Complementary Currencies	New money surrogates based ~1:1 on bank money and cash equivalents (near-money, sovereign bills, certificates of deposit, commercial paper, bank acceptances, short-term repos)
Base-level challengers • Uncovered and unwarranted cryptocurrencies, e.g. Bitcoin • Unbacked complementary currencies	Directly challenging base money, thus monetary sovereignty

at face value by the treasury to the central bank. The treasury receives the amount as a credit entry into its central-bank transaction account. The proceeds result in genuine seigniorage, that is, the gain from money creation as the difference between the coins' face value and their production costs. However, coins today account for only 2% of cash, or about 0.2% of the official stock of money in public circulation.[2]

98% of cash consists of central-bank notes. They are commissioned by the currency area's central bank from the state's printing office for banknotes. As monetary authorities, central banks today have the sovereign monopoly on banknotes, as they are still called after their private origins.

Central banks issue all cash—notes as well as coins—according to the banks' demand. A central bank does so in disbursement of credit to a bank against collateral, mainly sovereign bonds. Cash is thus loaned into circulation by the central bank to the banking sector. The banks in

[2] In the euro area, coins are 2.16% of cash.

turn circulate solid cash according to customer demand, that is, when customers withdraw cash from their current bank account, or when customers exchange foreign currency into domestic cash.

In more developed countries, the use of cash has been declining for decades. During the 1960s, payment of wages in cash-pay envelops largely disappeared. Where people are more cash-conservative, they still pay with cash at the shop checkout or a restaurant in 60% of the cases, but only smaller amounts. In Scandinavia or Britain, it is only 20% of payments or less. All other payments, in higher amounts throughout, are made cashless. The overall trend is undoubted and has intensified once more during the COVID-19 pandemic: ever less cash in counterpart to increasing cashless payments by bank transfer, direct debit, online banking, use of a debit or credit card, now also contactless via a card wallet app on mobile phone.[3]

Statistically, cash in more advanced countries is now down to about 15% or less of the public money supply M1. M1 includes cash and liquid bank deposits.[4] In Sweden and Norway, cash amounts to only 2–3% of M1. Less than 10% of payments are made in cash. Where there are still noteworthy amounts of cash, only about one-fifth of that cash is in active circulation. The rest is hoarded as a safety cushion in strongboxes or under the proverbial mattress. Moreover, the cash of major reserve currencies—most often US dollars, to lesser extent euros—serves as a parallel currency in countries with a weak home currency.[5]

Loaning cash to banks is usually not the first step in putting central-bank money into circulation. First come central-bank loans to banks, provided in the form of reserves. Reserves are account balances in the central-bank account of banks. Central-bank credit to banks is collateralised with pledging government bonds. This means collateralising the *credit (loan)*, not the *money*. Monetary coverage for central-bank money, as in the past by means of silver and gold, is no longer necessary as central-bank money has become base money by sovereign fiat.

[3] ECB (2020, chs. 2–3), Benson et al. (2017), Lalouette and Esselink (2018), and Dt. Bundesbank (2022).

[4] federalreserve.gov/releases/h6/current/default.htm. ECB, *Statistical Data Warehouse*, Monetary Statistics, Tab. 1.1, 1.4. Dt. Bundesbank, *Monthly Reports*, Tab. II.2.

[5] Rogoff (1998, 2014, 2016), Keohane (2017), Esselink and Hernández (2017), Dt. Bank (2020, Part I), Dt. Bundesbank (2022), and ECB (2020).

Since the late nineteenth century and particularly over the twentieth century, credit entries on account have become the original form of money, money-on-account, still called deposit or deposit money, even though neither cash nor anything else is being deposited here in the first place. It is the other way round. Cash is an exchange form of account balances since long, being withdrawn from a pre-existing account balance, and at some point paid back into one, then in a certain sense deposited indeed. At source, however, in its form of origin in modern banking, money is non-cash, be it bank money or central-bank reserves. Unlike cash—which is central-bank base money and which banks have to finance in full—banks only need a small base of central-bank reserves to create account-based bank money on their own balance sheet.

Reserves are for interbank use only. They are used for payment transactions between banks, including central banks, and partly also certain state bodies, such as for example higher levels of the tax office and the treasury. Most state bodies, however, as well as non-bank financial institutions, real-economic firms of all kinds and private households cannot obtain reserves, as they are not granted access to a central-bank account. There are a few exceptions depending on the country, but generally there are no direct payment transactions between central banks and non-banks. The latter have to settle for current bank accounts, since central-bank reserves can never be transferred directly into the current bank account of a non-bank, and no non-bank sight deposit is ever transferred directly into a bank's central-bank account. This is a special, and highly problematic, property of the two-tier money and banking system hitherto—the split-circuit structure of book-money circulation, consisting of the interbank circuit between central bank and banks, based on using central-bank reserves, and the public circuit between banks and non-banks, based on using bank money.[6]

It is almost certain by now that in the coming years, CBDC will be introduced as another type of central-bank money. Initially, the idea included to make central-bank reserves available to the non-bank public as well.[7] It is more likely, however, that it will be a new type of money: digital currency proper, that is, digital tokens, kept and managed in

[6] On the split-circuit structure and the interaction of bank money and central bank money, cf. Huber (2017a, pp. 57; 2017b, pp. 63–84).

[7] See Niepelt (2015, 2021).

an e-wallet, with the transactions between wallets being verified by the computer nodes in a central-bank payment system. Whatever the final design, and according to current plans, CBDC is to be loaned into circulation like reserves and cash so far, or issued 1:1 in exchange for these. The possible varieties of CBDC and its desirable as well as less desirable properties will be discussed separately in a later chapter.

Money issued by central banks under public law—coins, notes, reserves and CBDC—is chartal money, money by sovereign fiat, base money, high-powered money, unrestricted legal tender. These are different terms denoting the same thing under different aspects, or in different contexts, respectively. The same applies to the notion of sovereign money which, moreover, can vary in scope:

- It is issued by a state body, formerly treasuries, then, in more modern times, national central banks, the more so as these have been nationalised and otherwise subjected to state law.
- It is base money by sovereign fiat, non-redeemable in other types of money (no monetary reserves are needed), notwithstanding the exchange of its different forms into each other.
- It is issued debt-free (no interest and redemption).
- It is spent, not loaned, into circulation.

The first two characteristics are the minimum requirements for sovereign money. The third and the fourth were traditionally linked, in that new coins and treasury-issued paper money were issued by way of government spending. With today's total dominance of credit-and-debt money, issued by central banks as much as private banks, debt-free money issuance has been abolished. Credit-and-debt money has rendered the monetary system highly vulnerable to troubles in the financial system, in that bank money is exposed to the risks of banking. The latter are generally much higher than the risks of central banking. The recomposition of the money supply as a result of introducing CBDC makes debt-free money of safe stock, side by side with credit-and-debt money, possible again. Whether and to what extent this possibility will be realised sooner or later is not yet foreseeable.

Central-bank issued sovereign money (or maybe Treasury issued sovereign money in the U.S.) is the only type of money having the status of legal tender. This does not mean that using legal tender is compulsory; rather that tendering payment in such money settles a payer's debt, regardless of the payee's acceptance of the respective form of legal tender; at least in principle. In actual fact, however, most payees today no longer accept being paid in cash, insisting on being paid in bank money which is neither base money nor legal tender, but a second-tier surrogate for central-bank money.

The fact that central-bank money is base money means that second-tier bank money is built on it, just as new third-tier money surrogates are built on bank money. Banks are obliged to exchange their bank money into central-bank money at the request of customers, just as issuers of new third-level money surrogates are obliged to redeem them into bank money at the request of the holders. How far this is actually the case in practice remains to be discussed.

Non-redeemability of fiat base money was a matter of fact already at the time of the nineteenth-century gold standard. Although central-bank notes and balances had to be backed by silver and gold bullion, that underlying was not paid out. Furthermore, silver and gold coins were increasingly replaced with metal-alloy token coins from the later nineteenth century onwards. Coins generally lost importance compared to central-bank notes and reserves (for banks) and bank money (for non-banks). Since the end of the gold standard around 1930 until 1971, all money is pure token money. From a *technical* point of view, money issuers can produce respective tokens hypothetically in any quantity. Central-bank money, however, is the only type of money to be base money and legal tender by sovereign fiat, not being backed by and not redeemable in other types of money.[8]

Obviously, modern money is created *ex nihilo* by those who are je jure authorised or de facto able to do so, "out of thin air", "at the press of a button". One will ask why money created *ex nihilo* is worth something. The value of money is its purchasing power, covered by what money can actually buy, first and foremost on the basis of real-economic productivity and the prices of the items entered into real-economic output, such as recorded by GDP. This also serves as an anchor for asset prices, even if

[8] In this sense, G. Fr. Knapp (1924, pp. 88–96), the founder of monetary chartalism, already distinguished between "definite or obligatory" money (base money) and "facultative" or redeemable money (second- and third-tier means of payment, i.e. bank money and new money surrogates).

the dependence of asset prices on current economic output is of a more indirect, longer-term and complex nature. In connection with this, the value of money also depends on the trust placed in a national currency at home and abroad, which is rooted in the political stability and economic strength of a given state or community of states.

To be distinguished from the *value* of money is its *validity*. The validity of a means of payment denominated in a national currency unit is partly established by law, partly by everyday practice. A main criterion is whether important state bodies such as the tax office or the courts accept and use a particular means of payment. From this angle, bank money is just as valid today as central-bank money (legal tender). New third-tier money surrogates and uncovered base-money challengers are not generally accepted by government bodies, but they are accepted in special areas of private finance. From this point of view, one can generally say that any means of payment accepted in more general circulation is valid money, even if it is not necessarily about a *universal* means of payment.

2.3 Second Tier: Active and Deactivated Bank Money

2.3.1 Second Tier Active: Liquid Bank Money

The means of payment at the second level of moneyness, actually the only type of money at this level, is bank money. Quite a few names have been given to that creature of the banking sector: deposit money, sight deposits, demand deposits, overnight deposits, checkable deposits. Let's leave it at bank money.

As with central-bank reserves, nothing is deposited here in the first place, neither gold nor silver nor paper money. And although bank money is a substitute for central-bank money, it has nevertheless become a universal means of payment. The bank booking entry as such creates and *is* that type of money. And much like central-bank reserves, bank money too is issued in connection with the extension of credit, as a provision of the loan principal to a non-bank borrower. The credit may also take the form of a purchase of securities, or anything else that is bought by a bank from non-banks, and can be paid for with bank money and booked as an asset on a bank's balance sheet.

Such being the case, and again just like central-bank money, bank money is often referred to as credit money or debt money. As metaphorical shorthand, this may do. Taken literally, it is misleading. The credit-and-debt contract, the creditor-debtor relationship for one thing, and the money for another, are two different things. The money is the means of payment to disburse a credit or discharge a debt. The credit contract, including conditions such as interest and repayment, concerns only the respective creditor and debtor, binds only them and basically remains bound to them. The bank money, by contrast, starts to circulate from the debtor to whomever, keeping to circulate further on. The alleged identity of money and credit is a false identity, and a serious impediment to modernising and stabilising the monetary system and banking.

In the euro area, liquid bank money statistically represents 87%, in real terms (minus dormant cash) 92% of the public money supply M1. Measured against the official total money supply, bank money amounts to 97%. This also includes normal savings and time deposits as well as longer-term deposits with banks.[9] Figures for other currency areas are structurally similar.

Basically, banks are free to create or not to create as much bank money as they see fit for their purposes. Certainly, there are legal requirements and practical restrictions (increasing with each crisis), at least in the short run. One of the most important variables here, if not the most important at all, is subject to the least constraints: holdings of central-bank money in the form of cash and liquid reserves. Banks usually have them available only at a small fraction of the bank money. The fractional reserve underlies bank money, in that it represents the liquidity of banks in payment transactions. For managing the customers' bank money, banks always need to have enough central-bank money available. This continues to apply to cash, when customers withdraw some of their bank money in cash. Banks need to make sure there is enough cash in vault or for replenishing the ATMs.

With transferring account balances, it's similar. Banks have to make sure they always have enough liquid reserves (excess reserves) on their central-bank account. This does not yet matter if bank money is transferred from customer A to customer B of the same bank X. To do this, bank X does not need central-bank reserves, a simple booking swap is

[9] ECB, *Statistical Data Warehouse*, Monetary Statistics, Tab. 1.1, 1.4. Dt. Bundesbank, *Monthly Reports*, Tab. II.2.

enough: the amount of bank money is deleted in A's current account and added to B's current account. If, however, customer A of bank X makes a cashless payment to customer B at bank Y, bank X transfers the amount in reserves to bank Y, while the same amount of bank money is deleted by bank X in the current account of A, and re-created by bank Y as a booking entry into the current account of B.[10]

In this way, reserves always remain in interbank circulation, while customers only ever receive bank money. The two-tier money and banking system (banks and central bank) has developed increasingly cashless in just that way. The banks provide bank money for non-banks (the money using public), while the central bank provides reserves for the banks. The two-tier structure thus involves a split circuit, consisting of the public circuit of bank money among non-banks, tied back to, but different from, the interbank circuit of central-bank reserves.

Prior to the introduction of central banks' Real-Time Gross Settlement payment systems (RTGS), interbank transfers were not executed immediately, but mutually cleared. Settlement in reserves was made only once in a given period of time, or upon reaching an agreed limit. In today's RTGS systems reserves are transferred immediately, or cleared immediately and transferred at the end of day. Should there not be enough reserves in a bank's central-bank account, the system grants intraday overdraft.

Despite immediate or daily settlement—and to the incredulous astonishment of many, including many bankers—to carry out all these payments, banks need to have available reserves of only a fraction of the bank money. Hence, the term "fractional reserve banking". Until the 2008 crisis, the interbank money market, in fact a reserves market, still worked properly. This enabled banks to minimise the stock of liquid reserves operationally necessary to carry out all payments due. The banks managed with reserves in the amount of about 2–6% of their customers' current account balances, depending on a bank's size. The bigger the banks and the higher the market concentration, the fewer reserves the banking sector needs.

What more precisely enables the minimisation of the reserve base? There are four mechanisms or conditions making this possible. First, within the banking sector, outgoing reserves are incoming reserves. As

[10] For further explanations of how the present bank money regime works, cf. Ryan-Collins et al. (2012, pp. 28–88), Huber (2017a, pp. 97–97), McLeay et al. (2014), and Dt. Bundesbank (2017).

payments take place continuously from anywhere to anywhere, outgoing and incoming payments in a bank largely balance out.

Second, customer payments are unevenly distributed over individual customers regarding point in time and payment amount. Not all customers pay at the same time and they do not transfer their entire account balance all at once, but usually only a smaller part of it. Thus, only a rather small share of bank money is needed in reserves at any one point in time. The effect of these mechanisms became all the more pronounced, the more cashless payment became widespread and technically efficient, and the more market concentration in the banking sector increased (ever fewer but larger banks, which, in addition, settle internal customer payments by mere rebooking).

A third condition is the non-segregation of customers' bank money from the banks' central-bank reserves. The customers' money and the bank's money do not exist independently of one another and cannot be separated from each other. All external payment transactions of a bank run through one and the same central-bank account. Within the framework of the existing system, a bank's means of payment (cash and reserves) cannot be attributed to the account balances of its customers. As a liability of a bank to its customers, bank money is largely uncovered.

Finally, fourth, and as far as a growing money supply is concerned, the above mechanisms work all the better the more the banks expand credit and thus their balance sheets and the bank money supply roughly in step with each other. Thus—even with strong growth of money, credit and debt—payment deficits and surpluses within the banking sector remain within certain limits, and thus manageable by means of interbank credit in reserves and ultimately additional central-bank credit.

2.3.2 Second Tier Inactive: Deactivated Bank Money

The entire stock of bank money is bigger than just demand deposits, which is the liquid part of bank money. A considerable part of bank money consists of various sorts of savings and time deposits. In the euro area, that other part of bank money adds up to 20 trillion euros, well twice the amount of liquid bank money of 9.5 trillion.[11] That part of bank money is: largely deactivated, out of circulation, formally until further

[11] ECB, *Statistical Data Warehouse*, Monetary aggregates.

notice or up to maturity, in practice very long term. The share of savings and time deposits in the monetary aggregate fluctuates somewhat cyclically, but overall the stocks remain stable on trend. A technical term for temporarily deactivated bank money is near-money. To the extent that such deposits are available at any time, they are not adequately recorded but are in fact liquid deposits.

The *liquid* part of bank money can only be used by the respective customers, that is, non-banks, while a bank carries out customer transfers of bank money but cannot make use of customer balances for proprietary transactions. The *deactivated* part of bank money can be used *neither* by the customers *nor* the banks, contrary to what is widely believed. Such deposits are *not* available as loanable funds for a respective bank. Banks create bank money for non-banks. Banks do not and cannot use the customers' bank money for their interbank business. For funding interbank payments, banks need central-bank reserves. At best, banks obtain reserves via customer deposits if they succeed in attracting new customers and their credit balances from outside, as a result of which they receive additional reserves from the previous bank of the newly won customers. Deactivated bank money is useful nevertheless; for the customers as savings and own capital, as an asset buffer, and for the banks, in that deactivated bank money reduces their need for central-bank reserves, which in turn facilitates the extension of additional bank credit, thereby creating additional bank money.

2.4 Third Tier: New Money Surrogates (Money Market Fund Shares, E-money, Stablecoins, Complementary Currencies)

So far, the money system has been described as a two-tier system, comprising the central bank and the banking sector, or central-bank money and bank money, respectively. Since around 1980, however, additional means of payment emerged; in particular money market fund shares (MMFs), e-monies, complementary currencies and more recently stablecoins. They have turned the two-tier system into a three-tier system, in that the new money surrogates are largely based on bank money. The new surrogates are issued in various ways on a 1:1 basis against bank money and partly other of the new types of money. To the extent the exchanged money does not have to be held as cover for the new money surrogates, but remains available for investments and other transactions; this means doubling the money supply.

The issuers of new means of payment are fintechs, bigtechs, IT firms, web companies, payment services and financial brokers. They are not conventional banks, even if, like MMFs, they may belong to a banking corporation as a separate unit. However, the issuers of new means of payment are in fact monetary financial institutions of a new kind and, like banks, thus differ from non-monetary or non-bank financial institutions. Including the issuers of new money surrogates in the group of shadow banks is, say, inaccurately true; true because they are in a way deposit-taking and rendering a money service, but inappropriate, since most shadow banks are financial intermediaries (lenders, credit and investment brokers, institutional investors) usually working with bank money, *not* issuing their own means of payment. The US Office of the Comptroller of the Currency considers the issuers of the new types of money, unless otherwise defined by law, provisionally as special-purpose banks.[12]

Among the pivotal questions concerning all money surrogates is the institutional status of the issuers as well as the coverage of the money units they issue. MMFs and e-money are already regulated in this respect; stablecoins not yet, or still insufficiently. The coverage of third-tier monies replicates the problem of second-tier reserve banking. The quantity of such monies must be backed by pre-tier or same-tier funds, if only because they have to be convertible or redeemable on demand, but equally for reasons of effectual monetary policy and governability of the money system.

A contentious point here is whether the coverage must be 100% or can be less, and whether the coverage at the third tier must be held as bank money or rather central-bank money, or near-money, or cash equivalents, or even longer-term debentures, bonds and other capital assets.

The larger and more liquid the cover, the stronger the transmission of monetary policy impulses, the higher the monetary safety of the respective surrogate, but also the smaller the gain that can be drawn from issuing the respective money surrogate. Put the other way round, the smaller and less liquid the cover, the weaker monetary control, the lower the monetary safety of the respective money surrogate, but the bigger the potential profit that can be drawn from issuing that money surrogate.

[12] Gorton and Zhang (2021, pp. 18–19).

2.4.1 Money Market Fund Shares (MMFs)

MMFs are investment trusts that put the investors' bank money into short-term treasury bills and other highly rated securities. Investment bankers and non-monetary financial institutions use the shares of MMFs as an alternative deposit-like means of payment.[13] MMFs appeared in the U.S. in the 1970s. The reason was an official cap on deposit interest at a low level under the then conditions of high inflation. MMFs were not subject to the cap and thus able to pay higher interest. In Europe, MMFs only spread in the 1990s.

The total stock of MMFs is considerable. In the U.S., it amounted to 3.8 trillion dollars at the time of the 2008 crisis. This was 120% of M1, thus more than cash and liquid bank money combined.[14] Thereafter, the size of MMFs declined somewhat to expand since 2007 to the current peak of 4.5 trillion dollars. This is almost as much as the amount of available bank money (checkable deposits) of 4.8 trillion dollars.[15] In the EU, the value of MMFs was one-third of M1 in 2008 and is currently around 1 trillion euros.[16] Official statistics do not show how many MMF shares are regularly or occasionally used as a means of payment. But even if it were only half or less, this would still be a monetary quantity of systemic importance.

The funds are managed such that their investment value does not fall below 99.5% of the money invested in the fund. Basically, 1 fund unit should be 1 currency unit. In a crisis, this does not always work. Unlike bank money, MMFs are almost fully covered, but the value of the cover funds and securities fluctuates and can even collapse in a crisis. Runs on MMFs occurred in both 2008 and 2020. One fund, the Reserve Primary Fund, collapsed in the wake of the Lehman bankruptcy. On the part of

[13] On MMFs cf. Baba et al. (2009), Hilton (2004), and Mai (2015).

[14] FRED Economic Data Time Series: MMF total, retail MMF, M1, demand deposits. In the U.S., the share of cash in M1 is very high, the share of demand deposits correspondingly lower than elsewhere, since most of the US cash circulates abroad and is hoarded in safes worldwide.

[15] FRED Economic Data Time Series: MMF total, retail MMF, M1, demand deposits, total checkable deposits. Bank money and M1 have expanded even more since then, so that MMFs are currently only a quarter of M1. This is due to the expansionary monetary policy of Quantitative Easing and therefore defies normal interpretation.

[16] www.consilium.europa.eu/en/infographics/money-market-funds, as of September 28, 2022. Baba et al. (2009), Hilton (2004), and Mai (2015).

the Federal Reserve and the US Treasury, the opinion is that in the event of a crisis MMFs should be supported like banks.[17] This would replicate the instability problem of second-tier bank money with the new third-tier money surrogates on an extended basis.

MMF shares were not designed as money, but as securities. However, due to the deposit-like easy transferability of MMF shares, the shares are used as money as well. Nevertheless, it is still a security that yields a return. In this sense, MMF shares are an interest-bearing means of payment, which is not the case for e-money, stablecoins, other cryptocurrencies and complementary currencies.

MMF shares have also been dubbed shadow money.[18] Some authors consider not only MMF shares to be shadow money, but also asset-backed securities and overnight repos.[19] These financial instruments, however, are not used as a means of payment. They serve as pledge or collateral. This helps to provide liquidity by mobilising capital prior to final maturity, thus accelerating the circulation of money rather than creating additional money.

2.4.2 *E-money*

E-money emerged in the 1990s and was legally regulated around 2000. It is issued partly by banks, partly by licensed e-money institutes and accepted as a means of payment by other actors. The first carriers of e-money units were bank debit cards with the additional function of top-up e-money units. Prepaid credit card balances and mobile e-money apps have been added. Apart from banks, e-money institutes are now mainly PSP and web companies such as PayPal or Amazon Payments. The annual increase of e-money transactions in the EU since 2000 is exponential and has exceeded six trillion euros in 2021.[20]

[17] Gorton and Zhang (2021, pp. 22–25).

[18] Cf. Murau (2017).

[19] McMillan (2014, pp. 65–80).

[20] Statista.com/statistics/443399/electronic-money-payment-in-european-union, as of October 3, 2022. The definition of e-money and electronic payment methods varies from one currency area to another, or is not defined at all. Since it refers in part only to non-bank payment services and in part also to bank-mediated payments, it has so far been difficult to make meaningful international comparisons. Cf. Ehrentraud et al. (2021).

As far as non-bank e-money institutes are concerned, the e-money must be issued on a 1:1 basis against bank money, which is then to be held in escrow accounts by a third party.[21] A small part can be invested in near-money or cash equivalents. Another option is to take out insurance in the amount of the e-money in question. Banks, when issuing e-money, create a corresponding customer deposit pool 1:1, for example on prepaid cards. Since e-money regulation requires 100% coverage, especially in bank money, the expansion of the total money supply through e-money remains limited.

In developing countries, the proportion of the population with a bank account varies between 15 and 70%. Most account holders live in East Asia, the fewest in Africa. On average, hardly more than half of households in developing countries have a bank account.[22] But most people in these countries have cash and now also a mobile phone. This has enabled the spread of e-money there.

The pioneering example is M-Pesa, set up in Kenya in 2007 and thereafter in other countries more. M-Pesa means "Mobile cash", and in fact the mobile e-money units are largely based on swapping cash. Thousands of M-Pesa agents, mostly small retailers, convert cash paid in by customers into accounting units of the operating mobile phone company. The paid-in money is held by the involved telecoms in a commercial bank account (thus in bank money). The accounting units are airtime units worth the respective amount of money. Available airtime balances are transferable real time and directly from payer to payee (P2P) using a special e-wallet app. The service is not cheap, but less expensive than comparable banking services.[23] Meanwhile, M-Pesa circulation is firmly established. Cash continues to be exchanged for M-Pesa, but ever less M-Pesa is re-exchanged for cash.

E-money is particularly widespread in Zimbabwe, Uganda, Kenya, Zambia and Rwanda, as well as in Cambodia.[24] A similar system offered in a number of Latin American and African countries is Tigo Cash which

[21] I would like to thank Simon Hess for relevant information.

[22] Oliveros and Pacheco (2016).

[23] Groppa and Curi (2019, pp. 5–6, 16).

[24] Garrido and Nolte (2021).

transfers currency units rather than airtime.[25] E-money in developing and newly industrialising countries facilitates financial inclusion and is an example of innovative leapfrogging. Hence also the particular interest of such countries in the soon introduction of retail CBDC for everyone's use.

2.4.3 *Stablecoins*

Stablecoins are a special type of cryptocurrency. They, too, are issued in exchange for bank money, and also in exchange for other digital tokens, mostly Bitcoins. Stablecoins are issued by way of ICO, Initial Coin Offering, following the expression IPO, the Initial Public Offering of equity shares. One unit of a stablecoin is sold for bank money or Bitcoins worth one US dollar, and managed by the issuer in such a way that the 1:1 parity is maintained with only minor deviations. Just as with MMFs, this cannot always be guaranteed.

The dollar exchange rate is variable, but the peg of a stablecoin to the US dollar is not. Stablecoins do not promise constant value (purchasing power). What they do promise is a stable peg to a national anchor currency, in contrast to the volatility of uncovered cryptocurrencies like Bitcoin and Ether.

In the EU, euro-denominated stablecoins are considered e-money tokens subject to e-money regulation. However, most stablecoins, like most cryptocurrencies, are denominated in US dollars, only a few in euro, pound and yen. In the U.S., crypto tokens are not yet specifically regulated. Stablecoins are redeemable by issuer self-obligation.[26]

Stablecoins are thus partly similar to e-money, partly to MMF shares.[27] Technically though, they have the form of digital tokens. Payment is made by transferring the tokens directly from one e-wallet into another, verifying the transfer in the distributed ledger of a computer network, and finally documenting the transaction in a blockchain.

Currently, the stablecoins with the highest market capitalisation include Tether, USD Coin and Binance USD. In May 2022, the total stock of

[25] tigomoney.com/py/home-py, as of May 11, 2022. https://ayuda.tigo.com.py/hc/es/articles/360047861053-Funcionalidades-de-la-billetera-Tigo-Money, as of May 11, 2022.

[26] Gorton and Zhang (2021, pp. 10–24).

[27] Cf. Hess (2019) and Gorton and Zhang (2021, pp. 10–24).

stablecoins amounted to 180 billion dollars.[28] Measured against the total market capitalisation of cryptocurrencies at 2,400 billion dollars at that point in time, this still seems low.[29] However, the stablecoin take-off in 2020/2021 was spectacular. Moreover, it is no longer IT nerds who determine the market, but large institutional investors and other professional traders. They account for 95% of the trading volume.[30] A growing number of large companies are announcing their intention to use cryptos, especially stablecoins.[31] At the same time, the broadening user base of cryptos is also reflected in the fact that in 2021, 22% of adult Americans are reported to have owned cryptos and 51% to have traded cryptos at some point in time.[32]

So far, stablecoins have for the most part been used to make transfers between crypto exchanges, because stablecoins serve as a safe haven that is sought when the prices of unbacked volatile cryptocurrencies threaten to plummet. Increasingly, however, other financial and commercial transactions dock on to this. Most Bitcoins are traded evenly against the stablecoin Tether and against US dollar bank money.[33] Stablecoin trading against unbacked cryptocurrencies is a risky business connection, from which stablecoins have yet to break free.

The Libra, initiated by Facebook in 2020, was planned to be a stablecoin, 1:1 backed by bank money and cash equivalents, and representing an international basket of currencies. It was announced that 50% of the Libra currency basket would be denominated in US dollars, the rest split between euro, pound, yen, Singapore dollar and Swiss francs. A syndicate consisting of a larger number of globally active financial and commercial corporations was to implement the plan, potentially reaching a clientele of hundreds of millions.[34]

[28] Coinmarketcap.com/en/view/stablecoin, as of June 6, 2022.

[29] Coinmarketcap.com/en/charts, as of June 6, 2022. coingecko.com/en, as of June 6, 2022.

[30] Chainanalysis, repr. *The Economist* (August 7, 2021, p. 53, February 5, 2022, p. 36).

[31] Birch (2022).

[32] Howarth (2022).

[33] *The Economist* (October 12, 2019, p. 68).

[34] Libra Whitepaper (2019).

Such a stablecoin based on a supranational basket of currencies would soon become systemically relevant and potentially even superior to individual national currencies, exactly due to its being supranational and involving a worldwide clientele. Because of that, the Libra concept met with strong political opposition worldwide. The bone of contention was not that Libra would have been a stablecoin, but its being based on a supranational currency basket.

The strong political opposition to the project prompted Facebook to relaunch the project under the name Diem in 2020. The modified concept was to back the Diem exclusively by US dollar-denominated money and cash equivalents.[35] The Diem headquarter was to be moved from Switzerland to the U.S. This then found favour with US politics and authorities. In the meantime, however, the syndicate members were dropping out in droves. Some of them had apparently recognised the conflict of interest between stablecoins and bank money. On the other hand, the strict coverage requirements that were to be expected made the project no longer lucrative enough for some. The plan was abandoned at the beginning of 2022.[36] Facebook (now Meta) is working on a new cryptocoin. Whatever the outcome of this story, the development of stablecoins has only just begun.

The moneyness of private cryptocurrencies is not settled yet. The question is whether cryptocoins, including stablecoins, classify as money or as a new type of security.[37] For MMFs, this isn't clear either. They are a security widely and regularly used as a means of payment, thus money. In the euro area, MMFs and e-money are subject to specific regulation. Stablecoins are treated as e-money. Stablecoin issuers need an e-money licence and are required to maintain coverage close to 100% in other types of money and cash equivalents. In the U.S., stablecoins are rather seen as a security, but things are partly similar to Europe. American e-money institutes need a licence as Money Transmitter. This does not imply a commitment to any kind of 100% coverage. Some stablecoin issuers promise high coverage without having to. Others, like Tether, don't, but they are nevertheless subject to financial oversight since they promise to

[35] Diem Association (2020), Dalton (2020), and De (2020).

[36] cnbctv18.com/cryptocurrency/adieu-diem-how-metas-short-lived-stablecoin-dream-ended-12351742.htm, as of February 4, 2022.

[37] Gorton and Zhang (2021, pp. 6–17).

maintain a 1:1 peg to the dollar. This in turn involves a credibly high backing with other types of money and cash equivalents.[38]

In the case of Tether, the promise was not kept in 2021. On the day of an audit, the liquid coverage was only at 5% of the digital tokens issued and consisted of dollar bank money and US Treasury bills. The dollars were only deposited in the morning and a portion of them were transferred elsewhere soon after. The whereabouts of several hundred million dollars remained undisclosed. A significant part of the reserves consisted of riskier commercial bills and corporate bonds, another part of Bitcoins. Even with only a small loss in value, Tether would not have been able to redeem its tokens. Tether's coverage practices were classified as fraudulent and it was imposed a fine of 18.5 million dollars, followed by another fine of 41 million for providing incorrect information on its cover funds.[39]

Even if MMFs and stablecoins are seen as new types of securities, they cannot be denied to be new types of money to the degree they achieve wide circulation as a means of payment, the more so as they represent money surrogates almost 100% backed by other money and cash equivalents denominated in the official home currency. Bitcoin, by contrast—although a number of companies advertise accepting it as a payment method—is primarily traded as a speculative financial investment and is correctly classified as such. Bitcoin is not considered a regular means of payment, not even a reasonably predictable security, the more so as it is not backed by money or near-money assets and not tied to a national currency. This basically applies to all uncovered and unwarranted cryptocurrencies.

2.4.4 Complementary Currencies (CCs)

CCs occur in many places across the globe, be it as emergency money in the context of severe economic crises, or for the joy of social experimentation, or as a social-work approach to neighbourhood revitalisation or an approach to municipal development.[40] CCs are most often issued by

[38] Clifford Chance & R3 (2019).

[39] Dilmegani (2021). *The Economist* (February 27, 2021, p. 11, 58).

[40] Overviews on CC in Greco (2001), Belgin and Lietaer (2011), Hallsmith and Lietaer (2011), Kennedy et al. (2012), and Lietaer et al. (2012).

some community or municipality not-for-profit as local money or special-purpose money in the form of simple paper scrip. If CCs are issued 1:1 against bank money, they represent a third-tier surrogate. CCs are unregulated and thus free to proceed with the coverage as they wish. Most often, the coverage is deposited at a local savings bank or cooperative bank.

Many initiators of CCs believe in S. Gesell's concept of shrinking money, dating from 1916, nowadays referred to as demurrage.[41] This involves a periodically administrated loss of money by imposing a shrinkage rate, similar to the negative interest that has been imposed by the ECB, the Swedish Riksbank and other central banks as well as by many commercial banks in the zero-interest environment of the 2010s. The measure is expected to accelerate expenditure and thus economic activity. Gesell advocated the under-consumption theory of the business cycle. The practice of negative interest rates in the euro area has pointed to results different from those expected, such as evasive behaviour, unsteady spending behaviour and compensatorily increased saving instead of spending. The concept apparently starts from unrealistic assumptions about people's behaviour, partly also from an overstatement of Keynes' concept of liquidity preference.

2.5 Base-Level Challengers: Uncovered and Unwarranted Cryptocurrencies and Complementary Currencies

Uncovered and unwarranted cryptocurrencies as well as unbacked CCs represent another class of money, not a fourth tier in the sense of the monetary taxonomy thus far, rather a kind of private base money. They rely on no other money as if they were fiat money in their own right. Hence, unbacked cryptocurrencies and CCs are base-level challengers strictly speaking, private role competitors to the sovereign base money of central banks and treasuries.

In the crisis years around 1930, this was the reason why central banks and governments banned CCs, thereby worsening the crisis. Today, things are different. CCs, whether backed or unbacked, have remained confined to their milieu and found no wider dissemination. The quantities of CCs

[41] Gesell (1958 [1916]).

in circulation are too small by volume and range to be considered a challenge. In the Argentine crisis 1998–2002, and temporarily in other places in Latin America, unbacked CCs were welcome to alleviate economic deadlock and hardship at the local level.

As for unbacked cryptocurrencies, the now classical and most important case in point is Bitcoin. A “mining” algorithm produces the Bitcoin supply. The algorithm is built into the verification process of a Bitcoin transaction to reward the “miners”. Over time, Bitcoin mining is approximating a maximum built into the algorithm, similar to a gold standard at the geological boundary of profitably mineable gold. Bitcoin’s artificial scarcity is supposed to act as a value-enhancing anchor against all other, free-to-create types of money. The overall rise in the price level since Bitcoin’s launch in 2008 seems to confirm that expectation, while the extreme price volatility accompanying Bitcoin’s development disproves it.

Most of the many follow-up cryptocurrencies to Bitcoin have scrapped its quantity limit. They issue as many coins via ICO as market demand buys. With or without limited quantity, there is no monetary or financial reserve to cover respective cryptocurrencies. The coins are certainly convertible into bank money or other cryptocoins on specialised platforms such as Coinbase or Binance, but only as long as the operators of the platforms broker such deals. Bitcoins are irredeemable by design. The issuers of other unbacked tokens are also not generally required to take back the coins on demand. It depends on the individual terms and conditions of respective ICOs.

Although unbacked cryptocurrencies enter into base-level competition with the official national currencies, central banks and governments have so far perceived cryptocurrencies rather hesitantly and incredulously as a threat to their official currencies. Until 2021, one apparently believed that the multitude of small cryptocurrencies were not to be taken any more seriously than CCs, even though there were over eight thousand cryptocurrencies at the beginning of 2022, and their total stock at market value amounted to 2.3 trillion dollars. Bitcoin alone accounted for over one trillion dollars.[42] Although that was the high point of a temporary bull market, such magnitudes can no longer be dismissed as a negligible quantity. Most of the current cryptocurrencies are bound to disappear in a coming concentration process to make way for a small number of remaining cryptocurrencies which grow in the process into much higher magnitudes.

[42] coingecko.com, as of December 9, 2021. coinmarketcap.com/all/views/all, as of December 9, 2021.

References

Adrian, Tobias, and Tommaso Mancini-Griffoli. 2019a. The Rise of Digital Money, IMF Fintech Note 19/01.

Adrian, Tobias, and Tomaso Mancini-Griffoli. 2019b. Digital Currencies: The Rise of Stablecoins. IMF Blog, September 19.

Baba, Naohiko, Robert N. McCauley, and Srichander Ramaswamy. 2009. US Dollar Money Market Funds and Non-US Banks. *BIS Quarterly Review* (March): 65–81.

Bech, Morten, and Rodney Garratt. 2017. Central Bank Cryprocurrencies, Basel Bank for International Settlements. *BIS Quarterly Review* (September): 55–70.

Belgin, Stephen, and Bernard A. Lietaer. 2011. *New Money for a New World.* Coulder, CO: Qiterra Press.

Benson, Carol C., Scott Loftesness, and Russ Jones. 2017. *Payments Systems in the U.S. A Guide for the Payments Professional.* San Francisco, CA: Glenbrook.

Birch, Kate. 2022. How Large Enterprises Are Driving Digital Currency Adoption. *Business Chief*, January 6.

Clifford Chance & R3. 2019. *A Global Overview of Regulatory Requirements in Asia Pacific, Europe, the UAE and the US*, September.

Dalton, Mike. 2020. What Is Diem? Introduction to the Facebook-Backed Stablecoin. Crypto.com, December 17.

De, Nikhilesh. 2020. Libra Rebrands to 'Diem' in Anticipation of 2021 Launch. Coindesk, December 1.

Diem Association. 2020. White Paper. https://wp.diem.com/en-US/wp-content/uploads/sites/23/2020/04/Libra_WhitePaperV2_April2020.pdf, as of October 28. Also cf. https://www.diem.com/en-us, as of October 28.

Dilmegani, Cem. 2021. Tether USDT Is Probably a Scam But It Can Remain Valuable. AI Multiple, November 6.

Dt. Bank. 2020. *The Future of Payments.* Corporate Bank Research, January.
Part I—Cash: the Dinosaur Will Survive … For Now.
Part II—Moving to Digital Wallets and the Extinction of Plastic Cards.
Part III—Digital Currencies: the Ultimate Hard Power Tool.

Dt. Bundesbank. 2017. The Role of Banks, Non-Banks and the Central Bank in the Money Creation Process. *Monthly Report* (April): 13–33.

Dt. Bundesbank. 2022. *Payment Behaviour in Germany 2021.* Frankfurt: Bundesbank.

ECB. 2020. *Study on the Payment Attitudes of Consumers in the Euro Area (SPACE).* Frankfurt, December.

Ehrentraud, Johannes, Jermy Prenio, Codruta Boar, Mathilde Janfils, and Aidan Lawson. 2021. Fintech and Payments: Regulating Digital Payment Services and E-money. Bank for International Settlements, Financial Stability Institute, Insights on Policy Implementation, No. 33, July.

Esselink, Henk, and Lola Hernández. 2017. The Use of Cash by Households in the Euro Area. European Central Bank Occasional Paper Series, No. 201, Frankfurt, November.

Garrido, José, and Jan Nolte. 2021. Making Electronic Money Safer in the Digital Age. IMF Blog, December 14.

Gesell, Silvio. 1958 [1916]. *The Natural Economic Order*. London: Peter Owen.

Gorton, Gary B., and Jeffery Y. Zhang. 2021. Taming Wildcat Stablecoins. SSRN Working Paper, September 30. Available at https://doi.org/10.2139/ssrn.3888752.

Greco, Thomas H., Jr. 2001. *Understanding and Creating Alternatives to Legal Tender*. White River Junction, VT: Chelsea Green Publishing Company.

Groppa, Octavio, and Fernando Curi. 2019. Mobile Money Regulation: Kenya, Ecuador and Brazil Compared. Working Paper. Universidad Católica Argentina, Buenos Aires.

Hallsmith, Gwendolyn, and Bernard A. Lietaer. 2011. *Creating Wealth: Growing Local Economies with Local Currencies*. Gabriola Island, BC: New Society Publishers.

Hess, Simon. 2019. 100% E-Money and Its Implications for Central Bank Digital Currency. SSRN Working Paper. June 26. Available at https://doi.org/10.2139/ssrn.3410242.

Hilton, Adrian. 2004. Sterling Money Market Funds, Bank of England. *Quarterly Bulletin* (Summer): 176–182.

Howarth, Josh. 2022. How Many People Own Bitcoin? 95 Blockchain Statistics. Exploding Topics, January 10.

Huber, Joseph. 2017a. *Sovereign Money. Beyond Reserve Banking*. London: Palgrave Macmillan.

Huber, Joseph. 2017b. Split-Circuit Reserve Banking—Functioning, Dysfunctions and Future Perspectives. Real-World Economics Review, No. 80, 63–84, June.

Kennedy, Margit, Bernard A. Lietaer, and John Rogers. 2012. *People Money: The Promise of Regional Currencies*. Bridport, UK: Triarchy Press.

Keohane, David. 2017. Goldman Calls Peak Cash. *Financial Times Alphaville*, March 24. ftalphaville.ft.com/2017/03/24/2186391/snap-av-goldman-calls-peak-cash, as of April 29, 2018.

Knapp, Georg Friedrich. 1924 [1905]. *The State Theory of Money*. London: Macmillan.

Lalouette, Laure, and Henk Esselink. 2018. Trends and Developments in the Use of Euro Cash Over the Past Ten Years, *ECB Economic Bulletin* (6).

Libra Whitepaper. 2019. https://de.slideshare.net/HermannDjoumessi/libra-whitepaper-english.

Lietaer, Bernard A., Christian Arnsperger, Sally Goerner, and Stefan Brunnhuber. 2012. *Money and Sustainability. The Missing Link*. Axminster, UK: Triarchy Press.

Mai, Heike. 2015. Money Market Funds, an Economic Perspective. In *EU Monitor Global Financial Markets*, ed. DB Research. February 26.

McLeay, Michael, Amar Radia, and Ryland Thomas. 2014. Money Creation in the Modern Economy. *Bank of England Quarterly Bulletin* 2014 (Q1): 14–27.

McMillan, Jonathan. 2014. *The End of Banking. Money, Credit, and the Digital Revolution*. Zurich: Zero/One Economics.

Murau, Steffen. 2017. Shadow Money and the Public Money Supply: The Impact of the 2007–2009 Financial Crisis on the Monetary System. *Review of International Political Economy* 24 (5, September): 802–838.

Niepelt, Dirk. 2015. Reserves for Everyone—Towards a New Monetary Regime? VOX CEPR's Policy Portal, January 21.

Niepelt, Dirk, ed. 2021. *Central Bank Digital Currency. Considerations, Project, Outlook,* London: CEPR Press.

Niepelt, Dirk. 2021. 'Reserves for All': Political Rather Than Macroeconomic Risks. In Niepelt, ed., 39–44.

Oliveros, Rosa M., and Lucia Pacheco. 2016. Protection of Customers' Funds in Electronic Money: A Myriad of Regulatory Approaches, BBVA Research. Financial Inclusion Watch, October 28.

Rogoff, Kenneth S. 1998. Blessing or Curse? Foreign and Underground Demand for Euro Notes. *Economic Policy* 13 (26, April): 261–303.

Rogoff, Kenneth S. 2014. Costs and Benefits to Phasing Out Paper Currency. NBER Working Papers, May.

Rogoff, Kenneth S. 2016. *The curse of cash*. Princeton University Press.

Ryan-Collins, Josh, Tony Greenham, Richard Werner, and Andrew Jackson. 2012. *Where Does Money Come From? A Guide to the UK Monetary and Banking System*, 2nd ed. London: New Economics Foundation.

CHAPTER 3

Dominant Money. The Bank Money Regime

3.1 Dominant Currency and Dominant Money

The *Dominant Currency Paradigm* is a theory about the international dominance of a national currency. It deals with the dominant position of the US dollar in today's international fabric of national currencies.[1] A theory of dominant money, by contrast, deals with the rise and decline of means of payment.

The use of the terms currency and money partly overlaps. In particular, currency and cash are often used interchangeably. In this place, currency refers to a national monetary unit of account, while money refers to the means of payment denominated in a particular currency. An occasional overlap in word usage cannot entirely be avoided.

In Gopinath et al., the dominant currency paradigm says that export–import prices are set in the dominant currency and tend to be unvaried regardless of bilateral exchange rates.[2] In this respect, the dominant currency paradigm is about international pricing in the dominant currency.[3] More generally speaking, the dominant currency is that in which international prices are quoted and transactions invoiced (85% in

[1] Cf. Gopinath et al. (2016). Gopinath and Stein (2018), as well as Eichengreen (2011, pp. 39–68) and prior to them Hudson (2003 [1972], 2012, pp. 367–383).

[2] Gopinath Casas et al. (2016). Gopinath and Stein (2018).

[3] Carney (2019).

J. Huber, *The Monetary Turning Point*,
https://doi.org/10.1007/978-3-031-23957-1_3

US dollars, even though the U.S. accounts for just 15% of international trade). Equally, most international finance contracts are concluded in the dominant currency. Presently, two-thirds of the international debt of non-banks are denominated in US dollars (in euros one-fifth).[4] Furthermore, the US Federal Reserve and the American banking sector control the dollar-based international payment channels.

The dominant currency also serves as the preferred reserve currency. Presently, the US dollar accounts for 64% of international currency reserves. The euro accounts for 20%, yen and pound 4% each. The Chinese yuan presently accounts for 1.2%, although it looks poised to become more important in the decades to come.[5] Individual countries may peg their currency to the dominant one as this helps them avoid foreign exchange risk. They thus suspend monetary sovereignty, which from the perspective of a small or weak currency is relative anyway.

Dominant *money* cannot be defined by simple analogy. For example, the oft-quoted store-of-value function of money seems to be an analogy with the reserve function of lead currencies. In actual fact, however, the store-of-value function of *money* has shrunk today to holding enough liquidity for expenditure in the near term. Holding liquid money long term would be hoarding money. This might still cause problems even under modern conditions of freely creatable fiat money, but in actual fact the medieval and early modern problem of hoarding hardly exists anymore, certainly not under conditions of business-as-usual. Keynes' successor approach to hoarding—liquidity preference—is not about a general shortage of money, but about the fluctuating willingness of actors to spend, lend and invest. Store-of-value assets today normally take the form of *capital* invested in the short and long term.

The dominant money within a currency area is that which is system-defining during a certain historical period, in that it determines how the monetary system and monetary policy work, and which has the lead in creating money and readjusting its stock. Since money needs a quantity lever to exert dominance, the dominant type of money will usually account for the largest single stock of money among the types and forms of money available at the time. Today, bank money is in that dominant position.

[4] According to data by the Basel Bank for International Settlements. In 2008, the share of US dollar-denominated international debt was 50%. Cf. Eichengreen (2011, p. 2, 68, 123).

[5] IMF Data, Currency Composition of Official Foreign Exchange Reserves, http://data.imf.org.

3.2 Bank Money as Dominant Money. Substantial Loss of Monetary Control

3.2.1 *Dominant Bank Money. Central-bank Money as Subordinate Reserve*

Bank money accounts for 85–98% of the public money supply, depending on the currency area and statistical aggregation. If one goes beyond the two-tier money and banking system and now also includes new third-tier money surrogates, the overall share of bank money decreases somewhat. Nonetheless, central-bank supported bank money is systemically still by far dominant. Moreover, MMFs and e-money are based on bank money as an underlying second-tier reserve, as are stablecoins to a certain extent.

Monetary dominance can also be seen empirically in the biggest share of payments in number and volume of transactions. From this angle, the picture is more varied, but still much the same. For example, many everyday household transactions may still be carried out in small amounts of change, while bigger transactions and generally almost all payments made by firms and public households have been cashless for long, and thus for the most part carried out in bank money. In financial transactions, MMF shares have gained significantly in importance since the 1980/90 s, while their role in payments for real-economic goods and services has remained marginal.

In view of the tiered structure of the money system, one might think that central-bank money is more important and determining in relation to bank money. Terms for central-bank money such as base money, legal tender, high-powered money—all of which bank money isn't—suggest the primacy of central-bank money over bank money. This is still true in some ways, but at the same time it has become misleading. It is still right because reserves are the money of first order, and in the case of strong national currencies also the safest type of money by which inherently insecure bank money balances are hedged or even rescued from collapse. This points to the instability and crisis-proneness of bank money, but nevertheless remains misleading in that it obscures the actual dominance of bank money today.

Within the present frame of split-circuit reserve banking, bank credit extension means bank money creation, being the initial and by far most predominant way of money creation. This is tantamount to saying that the entire money system and its dynamics are bank-led. The initiative of money creation is with the banks, not with the central banks, as is often assumed. It must be taken literally that central banks *re*finance the banks, re-actively, upon or after the facts the banks have created beforehand. Central banks do not pre-finance the system by setting reserve positions first. The causation runs in the opposite direction. Central banks accommodate the banks' defining demand for central-bank money (reserves and cash). This element was introduced into monetary economics by the accommodationist strand of post-Keynesianism.[6] As a result of the central banks' refinancing the banking sector at any time according to the banks' demand, the central banks have unilaterally become *bank of the banks*, fulfilling that function less in the exercise of monetary sovereignty, but rather as an auxiliary body of the banking sector.

3.2.2 Decline in Cash and Operationally Necessitated Reserves

Through its pro-active lead in primary credit extension and bank money creation, the banking sector determines the entire official money supply, including the accommodating provision of reserves and cash by the central bank. Bank money is not the result of some sort of multiplication of central-bank money. Quite to the contrary, the stock of central-bank money is a follow-up quantity, a kind of subset of the stock of bank money. Accordingly, it is not central-bank reserves, neither excess nor minimum reserves that control bank money creation. Central banks react to the banks' advance credit extension and bank money creation. This not only holds true under conditions of business-as-usual, but the more so under conditions of heightened uncertainty and crisis. Control of the money supply through predefined *reserve positions* has failed for decades, even more obviously than controlling the money supply through the *central-bank interest rate* (also called *bank rate* for short, or *rediscount rate*, and not to be confounded, for example, with the Federal Funds Rate

[6] Moore (1988a, pp. 162–63, 1988b). The horizontal or accommodationist approach of post-Keynesianism became revised as the structuralist approach. Cf. Palley (2013). The position contrasts with the verticalist view, which has it that central-bank credit comes first. Also cf. Bindseil and König (2013). Rochon (1999a, pp. 155–201, 1999b). Keen (2011, p. 309) as well as Kydland/Prescott (1990) have shown that the initiative for money creation is with the banks, not the central bank, and that the multiplier model is a myth.

in the U.S., which is the central bank's policy target rate for interbank overnight loans in reserves).[7]

As long as the levels of cash and reserves necessitated by the banking sector were high enough, conventional approaches of monetary quantity policy and interest-rate policy had more going for them, because the transmission lever of conventional monetary policy instruments depends on the ratio of central-bank money to bank money. The more central-bank money there is on which central-bank interest rates are payable, the more effective the transmission of monetary policy impulses. Thus, as long as the amounts of cash and non-cash reserves needed by the banks were comparatively high, one could assume that the base rate on central-bank money had an effective influence on the banks' credit expansion and bank money creation, without entirely determining it.[8] Of course, the quantity lever also works in reverse. The more cash and operationally necessitated reserves have been going down, the weaker conventional monetary policy has become.

Today, in the public money supply M1—composed of cash and liquid bank money (checkable deposits)—the share of cash is down to 15–2%, depending on the country. The decline in cash is even more pronounced than the figures would suggest, because the greater part of cash is not actively used.[9]

The declining share of cash in circulation has its parallel in the decline of banks' vault cash and central-bank reserves necessitated by the banks to create bank money and maintain its circulation. Until the 2008 crisis, the banking sector in the euro area got by with a base of central-bank money of just 2.5–3% of the stock of bank money. That reserve base consisted of 1.4% vault cash, a 1% largely idle minimum reserve requirement, and 0.1–0.6% excess reserves, that is, active interbank payment reserves, depending

[7] Bindseil (2004).

[8] In this sense already F. Lutz (1936, p. 92). Like his ordoliberal colleagues, he was of the opinion that central bank control over bank money creation was indispensable, but that the instrument of choice for achieving this was not a 100% reserve, as was discussed at the time. The central bank's interest rate and open-market policy would do the job satisfactorily. At that time, the idea was plausible to the extent that the share of bank money was only a little more than half of M1 and thus the cash to be refinanced 100% still played a considerable role. Also the fractionality of the non-cash reserve was not yet as extremely low as it has been since around 1980.

[9] Esselink and Hernández (2017), Krüger and Seitz (2014).

on a bank's size.[10] In the U.S., a hundred years ago, the amount of fractional excess reserves was 10–15% of the stock of bank money.[11] Today, that fractional percentage is down to between 0.1% (large banks) and 2–3% (smaller banks). These numbers are based on data up to 2008. As a result of the central banks' QE policy since then, statistics on bank reserve holdings are no longer meaningful in terms of actual operational necessity.

In addition to liquid reserves (excess reserves), banks in most countries are required to hold largely unavailable minimum reserves. Such minimum reserves are not a safety cushion, as is often assumed, but are meant to work as an instrument for controlling the bank money supply. The more minimum reserves and the higher the central-bank rates on them, the less banks would be inclined to extend credit and thus their bank money supply. But with the decline of operationally necessitated central-bank money, minimum reserves have become largely ineffectual. After all, the reserves on which the banks pay central-bank interest as well as the interbank loans on which banks pay overnight interest, represent only a fraction of the loans and investments made out in bank money on which the banks earn much higher banking rates and capital-market rates.

Against this background, minimum reserve requirements have been abolished in the countries of the British Commonwealth and a few more. In the U.S. and the euro area, there is still a formal reserve requirement; in the euro area 1%, in the U.S. 10% minus vault cash. However, many banks in the U.S. are unbound by reserve requirements. Certain positions such as wholesale time deposits are generally exempt from the requirement. Banks are allowed to temporarily "sweep" deposits to accounts that are not subject to reserve requirements. As a result, actual US reserve requirements have "rapidly been losing relevance" (Bennett/Perestiani) and are now near the vault cash.[12]

The sharp decline in the operational reserve base enabled the rise of bank money from around 20% still in the mid-nineteenth century to its current level of 85–98%.[13] This raises the question of how the

[10] Macfarlane et al. (2017), Huber (2017, pp. 72–74).

[11] Fisher (1935, p. 52).

[12] Bennett and Perestiani (2002, p. 53, 65).

[13] Compiled according to data in Schularick and Taylor (2009). Friedman and Schwartz (1963). Stevens (1971). Swiss National Bank, *Historical Time Series*, No.1, Feb 2007, Tab. 1.3, 2.3. Dt. Bundesbank, *Monthly Reports*, Tables on bank statistics total accounts 1954–2017.

continued generation of bank money on such a small fractional reserve base is possible at all, particularly as in today's RTGS payment systems, a bank must execute every customer transfer and own transfer fully in reserves. The reasons are to be found in the mechanisms of the two-tier banking system and its split money circuit as outlined above (much faster circulation of reserves than of bank money due to the non-simultaneity and partiality of customer payments and the non-separability of customer money and the banks' proprietary funds).

In seeming contradiction to the decline in required and necessitated reserves, an exceptionally high level of reserves has been built up from 2008 to recently, along with a persistently low level of interest until 2021/22. This flood of reserves is an anomaly rather than the new normal, the result of the central banks' QE crisis policies. The purpose of QE was stabilising sovereign bonds and financial markets. Providing liquidity to the banks was another reason, but only at the beginning of the crisis when the interbank money market temporarily stopped functioning. Thereafter, the reserves flowed to the banks unsolicited, as many of the sovereign bonds were purchased by the central banks from shadow banks and other non-bank financial institutions. This accumulated the reserves, which the central banks paid for the bonds, in the banks, while the bond-selling non-banks obtained bank money. The vast amount of reserves was then reinterpreted to be an economic stimulus. This is misleading, because reserves cannot leave the interbank circuit. QE for the most part thus remained QE for finance only. If the banks really wanted to extend more bank-money credit according to demand, they can do so without needing vast amounts of reserves.

With the continued decline in required quantities of central-bank money and the maximum expansion of bank money, the quantity lever of conventional monetary policy was shortened. The transmission of central-bank interest rates onto the extension of bank credit, bank money creation and general levels of interest decreased accordingly. Conventional monetary policy has been losing effectiveness. To that extent, a loss of monetary control has taken place. The new money surrogates and the spread of unbacked cryptocurrencies are added to this. Even if central bankers cannot be expected to say so publicly, and may often not even think so internally, in view of the state of affairs that has been reached the question arises as to the governability of the monetary system.

3.3 Monetary Credit and Intermediary Credit. Payment Processing and Financial Intermediation

The development of the bank money regime and today's three-tier hierarchy of monies has led to macro-sectoral differentiations that did not exist in the same way or to the same extent in the past. The macro-sectoral difference between the private and public sectors, between private and public finances, has existed since ancient times. Of more recent origin is the difference between GDP-contributing finance and non-GDP-contributing finance as discussed further below.

Similarly, with the development of fiat money and the bank money regime, the differentiation into monetary and non-monetary financial institutions, banks and shadow banks, has unfolded, and with them the difference between what is referred to here as monetary credit and intermediary credit. Generally speaking, monetary credit is extended by all issuers of means of payment that are not based 100% on an equal stock of pre-existing money. Intermediary credit, by contrast, does not involve money creation and is based on the full disbursement of an already existing means of payment.

In the first step, credit is expanded by the banking sector, which creates bank money as explained. In recent decades, the major part of bank credit went into non-GDP finance. This led to an upswing in investment banking. Furthermore, the new third-level money surrogates emerged, monetarily based on bank money, even though in many cases not fully covered by bank money and base money. The bank money and the new money surrogates in turn spurred financial intermediation.[14]

Financial intermediaries are not banks, but non-monetary financial institutions. Unlike the disbursement of credit by a bank, which generates bank money, financial intermediaries do not generate their own means of payment. They grant or broker loans, investments and other financing on the basis of bank money and other money surrogates. An exception is MMFs, whose shares are used as a new money surrogate. However, what MMFs operate with, as do all shadow banks, are savings, set-asides and surplus funds of non-banks, all in bank money. Non-monetary credit and investment institutions—shadow banks—are, for example, investment funds of all kinds (equity, bonds, real estate, foreign exchange), intermediaries of private equity, building societies that are not also banks, financial

[14] Cf. Turner (2012, pp. 35–65).

special-purpose vehicles, issuers of derivatives (options, futures, swaps), also insurance companies to the extent they invest money and grant loans or operate their own investment funds.

Commercial banks are *not* themselves *financial* intermediaries that would borrow bank money from their customers upstream in order to lend it to other customers downstream. Banks cannot do that. They are not intermediaries of bank money, but the creators of bank money whenever they grant loans to non-banks or buy securities or other valuables from non-banks.[15] Banks, however, manage the current accounts and bank money transfers for their customers, and in this sense, banks can be regarded as *payment* intermediaries, as payment service providers for payments in bank money. So this is about payment processing rather than financial intermediation.[16]

Credit-created bank money serves in the second step as a secondary base for the financial intermediation by non-monetary shadow banks. Financial intermediation now takes place to a greater extent than financing by bank credit. Between 2013 and 2017, shadow banks raised twice as much bank money for financial investment in bonds, shares and mutual funds than real-economic companies have borrowed. The shadow banking sector today has a larger volume of lending and financial investment than the deposit-creating banking sector. Globally, the shadow banking sector in 2020 already had 227 trillion dollar in financial assets, larger than the banking sector's 180 trillion. The average growth of shadow banks has been significantly higher than that of banks.[17] With the introduction and spread of Central Bank Digital Currency (CBDC), the trend towards financial intermediation is likely to amplify.

The question arises of whether shadow banking may have become more important than conventional banking, not only in terms of total balance sheet volume, but also in terms of systemic dominance. So far, the dominance of bank money has still increased due to shadow banking, because the shadow banks mainly operate on bank money. To change that, shadow banks would have to switch to other means of payment, especially CBDC, but maybe also stablecoins and other cryptocurrencies.

[15] Cf. Jakab and Kumhof (2015). Werner (2014a, b). Keen (2014). Lavoie (2014). Huber (2017, p. 59).

[16] On money and payments, see Rossi (2003, 2007).

[17] Financial Stability Board (2020).

In any case, it can be observed that there are growing numbers of financial institutions that are non-banks, but nevertheless fulfil one or even several banking functions. For example, the issuers of new types of money are a new kind of *monetary* financial institutions. Non-bank PSP are increasingly fulfilling money service functions of banks such as currency exchange and carrying out payments. Above all, shadow banks as lenders and investors are part of the traditional credit business. In the U.S. and UK, some shadow banks can now maintain an account with the central bank and thus make payments in central-bank reserves without needing a bank. The previous boundaries between monetary and non-monetary financial institutions, banks and shadow banks, are in flux. Banks and non-bank financial institutions are becoming more similar.

The distinction between monetary and non-monetary *financial institutions* corresponds to that between monetary and intermediary *credit* made here.[18] *Monetary* credit is granted by banks, central banks and, depending on the mode of issuance, increasingly also by the issuers of new types of money. In contrast, non-monetary financial institutions or shadow banks grant *intermediary* credit. With regard to the respective creditor, *monetary* credit results in a balance sheet extension. An additional credit claim (asset) is entered in pairs with the additional liability to pay out or redeem the credit amount. *Intermediary* credit, in contrast, involves an asset switch. The money is disbursed in exchange for the credit claim on the debtor to pay interest and repay the principal.

With regard to the *monetary* credit of banks and central banks, the older textbook models of a credit multiplier are misleading. Banks don't multiply pre-existing positions of cash and reserves, but create bank money in the first place and, as far as necessary at all, look for fractional refinancing in central-bank base money thereafter. However, multiplier models are correct with regard to *intermediary* credit, that is, non-monetary financial intermediation by shadow banks. Intermediary credit can only multiply within the limits given by the velocity of circulation (the turnover or use frequency of money). That nexus enables effectual monetary policy—provided that *monetary* credit is under monetary-policy control, rather than being largely out of control as is the case in today's bank money regime.

[18] Sometimes, the terms "credit" and "loan" are used in the sense of monetary versus intermediary credit. In common usage, however, the terms "credit" and "loan" tend to be used ad libitum and quasi synonymously.

3.4 The Hemispheres of Finance: GDP Finance and Non-GDP Finance. Consumer Price Inflation and Asset Inflation

The period from around 1980 to the late 2010s was characterised by GDP-disproportionate increases in bank credit extension and thus the money supply, fostered by falling interest rates. In industrial countries until around 1980, bank credit, and thus the money supply, grew at about the same rate as nominal GDP. Thereafter, however, money and credit growth sharply diverged from GDP growth. In general, money supply growth exceeded GDP growth by a factor of 3.5 to 4.5.[19] The M1/GDP ratio (the Marshallian *k*) has risen accordingly. For decades, it had been stable below 0.2, but since around 1980 it has multiplied, to 0.86 in America and 1.1 in the EU.[20]

The result was a feedback process in which savers and non-bank financial institutions had ever more money to lend while deposit and lending interest continued to fall. This triggered a shift in investor preferences. It was becoming increasingly unattractive for savers to deactivate their bank money in savings and term accounts, or to lend the money as borrowed capital, for example by buying bonds, MMFs, pension funds or the like. In turn, it was becoming increasingly interesting to acquire proprietary capital, or to finance the acquisition of such proprietary capital with ever cheaper credit, particularly for the purchase of stocks and property. The market value of stocks and real estate increased accordingly. On top, proprietary capital may also yield a return in the form of dividends, rents and leases.[21] In the process, only some part of new credit went into the real economy, while the major part was spent on such financial market transactions that do not contribute to financing real-economic output, that is, the money went into non-GDP finances (see Box 3.1).

[19] Calculated according to the periodically published statistics of the European Central Bank, Deutsche Bundesbank, Swiss National Bank, Bank of England, UK Office for National Statistics, and FRED Data by the Federal Reserve Bank of St. Louis. More figures on monetary quantities and disproportionate credit extension in Huber (2017, pp. 109–124).

[20] fred.stlouisfed.org/series/GNP, .../WM1NS, Bundesbank Monthly Bulletins, Tab. II.2, XI.1.

[21] Cf. McKinsey Global Institute (2021).

Box 3.1—The hemispheres of finance: GDP finance and non-GDP finance

One tenet of today's criticism of financial markets is that money should serve the real economy, not financial market transactions. Opposites of this kind are not appropriate. The real economy cannot be separated from its financing. Modern economies are based on credit and finance. Real-economic investment and other capital expenditure are only partly funded out of current revenues and reserves, and partly *pre*-financed by credit in various forms as well as by equity investment. The real economy and the related financial economy certainly fulfil two different functions, but nevertheless form a coherent whole.

However, the rough juxtaposition of the real and the financial economy also involves a fact that is often overlooked, namely that large areas of the financial economy no longer have much or even nothing at all to do with financing the real economy. The actually relevant dividing line thus runs between the hemispheres of the financial economy: for one thing, those subsectors that contribute to financing the output of the real economy, and for another thing, those subsectors that do not. In short, the dividing line is between GDP finance and non-GDP finance.[22]

There are occasional overlaps between the two, but the functional difference is clear. Financial transactions that contribute to financing real-economic output are, for example,

- Extending credit for real-economic investment and expenditure of all kinds (e.g. on labour, goods, services, infrastructure, use rights and other intangibles) by firms, private and public households.
- Funding of government expenditure through taxes and levies, or optional money transfers through sponsoring, donations or the like.
- The initial issue of shares and bonds as well as repo-transactions to finance real-economic activities and government spending.
- Venture capital in research, development and marketing in the real economy.
- Private equity transactions as a "white knight" recapitalisation of a company with viable substance but in need of overhaul.

By contrast, non-GDP finance includes, for example,

- Trading in shares, bonds and other securities after their issue (secondary trading).
- Repo transactions to finance non-GDP business.
- Forex trading without a background of real-economic use of the currencies.

- Derivatives trading beyond the hedging of real-economic risk positions held.
- Trading in shares of investment funds of any kind as far as these invest in non-GDP assets.
- Asset management is generally part of non-GDP finance.
- This also applies to de-activated but interest-bearing bank deposits (savings and time deposits). Leveraged buy-outs, financing of mergers and acquisitions, consensual and hostile (even if these change the market position of a company with longer-term real-economic effects).
- Private equity transactions as a "locust" activity of breaking up companies with immediate sale of profitable residual segments.
- Insurance companies to the extent they practice capital building through non-GDP investments. Trading in real estate as a mere capital investment without significant contribution to the use value of the real estate involved.
- Similarly, trading in commodities as a purely financial investment.
- Last but not least: Leverage for non-GDP financial transactions.

Especially in transactions with real estate and commodities, the dual-use character as real-economic and financial assets can be pronounced.

Non-GDP finances serve to build up savings, reserves, equity and other capital. Basically, this is something useful and desirable. So the point is not to decry non-GDP finance across the board, but to restrain what actually causes problems, that is, the overshooting dynamics of non-GDP finance, or to prevent abusive practices such as artificial food, commodity and energy shortages, and to exclude pure gambling (such as derivatives trading without real underlying) from the regulated business of banks, shadow banks and other financial institutions.

Money that does not flow into the real economy does not affect the real economy and has no immediate impact on CPI. Money flowing into the financial economy affects asset prices and the expansion of financial market supply (asset inflation, and inflationary finance). Some of the additions to the money supply from around 1980 to 2020/22 certainly fed into CPI. But to the extent, the money contributed to financing real-economic growth, this is already reflected in the growth of

[22] A similar distinction—between GDP-based transactions and non-GDP-based transactions—was made by Werner (2011, p. 29).

nominal GDP. The GDP-disproportionate growth of the money supply thus served primarily the expansion of self-referential non-GDP finances. These drive asset inflation and bubble building, not however CPI. This was the other side of globalisation—financialisation in the sense of a massive GDP-disproportionate expansion of non-GDP finance.

GDP-disproportionate credit expansion is a reliable indicator of overheating financial cycles, bubble building and thus banking and financial crises looming.[23] To the extent that financial crises are severe, they also entail severe crises of the real economy. However, the theory of financial cycles is still in its beginnings.[24] For representing aggregate asset inflation and financial cycles there is no analogon to the measurement of business cycles and GDP. Thus, one has to make do with a variety of individual indicators.

The share of GDP-contributing loans, for example in the UK, went down to only 15% of all loans, while 85% went into non-GDP finance.[25] The volume of financial market transactions increased from 15 times GDP in 1990 to 70 times in 2007.[26] The market capitalisation of shares in the 17 biggest industrial countries had developed roughly in parallel with GDP since 1870 (!) until around 1980. Since then, however, ratios of the market value of all shares to GDP have tripled, as a result of share price inflation that began around 1980.[27]

All US financial assets too, such as shares, bonds, other securities, but excluding real estate, developed roughly in line with GDP from 1870 until 1975/80, oscillating around 4.5 times GDP. From 1980 to 2007, they then rose to over 10 times GDP.[28] Financial assets held by US asset managers reached 50% of GDP in 1946, but 240% of GDP in

[23] Shiller (2015). Minsky (1982, 1982b, 1986). Jordà et al. (2010, 2014). Schularick and Taylor (2009). Aliber and Kindleberger (2015 [1978]). Kindleberger and Laffargue (Eds.) (1982). Kindleberger (1993).

[24] Borio (2012, 2017). Rogoff (2017).

[25] Van Lerven et al. (2015, p. 26).

[26] Dt. Bundestag (2020, pp. 7–8). Sigl-Glöckner (2018).

[27] Kuvshinov and Zimmermann (2021).

[28] Thomson Datastream. Federal Reserve. Trader's Narrative, Nov 7, 2009. Other delimitations produce a lower level but the same proportions, e.g. in Bhatia (2011, p. 8).

2014.[29] From 1980 to 2014, the average valuation of bonds, stocks and housing rose fourfold in 15 developed countries, while nominal GDP only doubled.[30] In the euro area, all sorts of financial assets or wealth have about doubled since 2008.[31]

In the short period from 2014 to 2019, CPI in Europe rose by a total of 5%, while the increase in asset prices was at 20% four times as high. This included land and real estate as a financial investment. Their use value is of course not dispensable, but has tended to be pushed into the background (which has long been true for real-economic equity). Real property prices in the U.S. rose by only 7% in the hundred years between 1890 and 1997, but by 85% in the ten years from 1997 to 2007.[32] In all developed countries, house prices have risen 14 times on average since the late 1970s, even up to 21 times in Australia.[33]

The QE crisis policies since 2008—reserves flood and entrenched low interest rates—have intensified financialisation and asset inflation, reminiscent of a strategy of firefighting with even more fire. It was not until the Covid-19 pandemic starting in 2020 that QE served not only to (re)finance the banking sector and the financial economy, but also, openly and near-time, to refinance extensive government spending programmes.

An early exception was the TLTRO programme launched by the ECB in 2014, which has since been increasingly expanded. The programme refinances longer-term bank loans to real-economic companies and businesses at favourable conditions.[34] In the first place, all of these funds serve real-economic spending which, in contrast to non-GDP finance, has a direct impact on inflation. From 2021 onwards, this was reflected for the first time again in a sharp rise in CPI, triggered by pandemic-related supply shortages and war-related hikes in energy prices. The question

[29] A. Haldane, chief economist of the Bank of England, in a speech on big institutional investors, reported in *FAZ* from April 8, 2014, p. 25. FRED Economic Data St. Louis Federal Reserve, Financial business total financial assets to GDP 1952–2018.

[30] Dt. Bank Markets Research (2017, pp. 8–33). OECD data https://data.oecd.org/gdp/gross-domestic-product-gdp.htm.

[31] www.flossbachvonstorch-researchinstitute.com/en/fvs-wealth-price-series-for-the-euro-area.

[32] Shiller (2015, p. 20).

[33] Jordà et al. (2014). Ryan-Collins et al. (2017). www.imf.org/external/research/housing/index.htm.

[34] TLTRO = Targeted Longer-Term Refinancing Operations.

arises as to what extent the funds will continue to circulate in the real economy, and how far they will gradually drain off into non-GDP finance.

The greatly expanded use of money for non-GDP finances does not have to be at the expense of the real economy, just as state borrowing does not have to be at the expense of the private sector (crowding-out hypothesis). Modern fiat money can be freely created by banks and central banks, under certain conditions and rules, but basically in any quantity. So the problem is not so much a lack of GDP finances as too much non-GDP finances.[35] Money that is once invested in non-GDP finance is for the most part likely to stay in this hemisphere. Even money that initially is used in GDP finances continues to circulate in the real economy only in part, while the other part drains off into the non-GDP hemisphere.

The consequences of overshooting monetary credit and the GDP-disproportionate expansion of non-GDP finance continue to be relevant: the transformation of central banks into accommodative auxiliary bodies of banking and finance, the far-reaching loss of effectiveness of monetary policy, increased financial and monetary instability, thus increased proneness to crisis, re-increased inequality in the distribution of income and wealth as a result of the surge in financial income at the expense of the share of earned income, and, as a result, new social discord and political polarisation.[36] Not least, the downsides of an ecologically maladjusted industrial metabolism have become a permanent challenge since the 1960/70s.

3.5 Recurrent Financial Market Failure

Why do financial markets not find a limiting equilibrium by themselves and tend to overshoot repeatedly? According to prevailing teachings, markets actually should. It is assumed that rising supply prices dampen demand until a point is reached where supply or its price stop rising and demand is stable. Supply and demand are then said to be in equilibrium, the price is the equilibrium price, and the market is cleared. But whether demand has really been met or supply has really exhausted its potential cannot actually be known. The supposed equilibrium is more

[35] Arcand et al. (2012).

[36] See McKinsey Global Institute (2010, 2021). Kuvshinow and Zimmermann (2021). Fullbrook and Morgan (2020). Atkinson (2015, pp. 16–44, 180). Atkinson et al. (2011). Chansel et al. (2022).

about language convention than empirical objectification. Nevertheless, a mechanism of the kind described undoubtedly exists. In cybernetic terms, it is a process of negative feedback, in this case between price increases and decreasing willingness to pay, or, respectively, price reductions and increasing willingness to buy.

However, this is only half the truth. For there is also a positive feedback loop in markets, such that high or rising prices go hand in hand with a stable or even increasing willingness to pay. This applies, for example, to prestigious club goods, conspicuous consumption, and especially financial markets. In the latter, too, price increases eventually reach a threshold of discomfort on the demand side. Prior to this, however, there is a positive feedback spiral of increasing supply, prices and demand, be it because demand for a given good is high from the outset, or because demanders expect a sustained price increase, meaning that buying at a later point in time would be even more expensive. Particularly in the case of financial assets, when an increase in yield or market value is expected, this initiates positive-feedback dynamics.

A positive feedback loop as such does not have a specific limit. One does not know where the willingness to pay or to take risks will end, less so in view of increasing asset values. Everyone knows that a financial market boom will end at some point. But when and at what price level that will be, no one reliably knows. It works until it doesn't. But one knows what happens then: a market slide or even a crash, destruction of financial capital, perhaps to a limited extent, or perhaps as the next major financial collapse and the economic crisis it will trigger. The main causes of this are always to be found in over-crediting, be it by hypertrophic monetary credit or equally hypertrophic intermediary securitisation procedures, leading to over-investment and over-indebtedness.

No doubt that limiting negative feedback loops are at work in financial markets. The actors are well aware of the appropriateness of prices and risk exposure. But if you are in a business and want to stay in business, you cannot pass up a seemingly good deal. Ch. Prince, former Citigroup CEO, put that nicely: *As long as the music is playing, you've got to get up and dance.* Thus, reason is repeatedly overridden by un-limiting positive feedback loops—until respective limits of financial carrying capacity are exceeded, triggering a financial crisis. Financial market failure as a dynamics of self-propelling overshoot has been described in Minsky's financial instability hypothesis, in particular the final Ponzi stage (exponential snowball effect).[37] Shiller, in his feedback theory of financial crises, coined the expression irrational exuberance.[38] These mechanisms have always existed in capitalism.[39]Real-world markets are certainly about crowd intelligence, but sometimes also about crowd foolishness. Nescience about the limits of an economy's monetary absorptive capacity and financial carrying capacity is a momentous knowledge gap, not least for monetary policy and financial market regulation.

References

Aliber, Robert Z., and Kindleberger, Charles P. 2015 [1978]. *Manias, Panics, and Crashes. A History of Financial Crises*, New York: Basic Books. 7th edition.

Arcand, Jean-Louis, Berkes, Enrico, and Panizza, Ugo. 2012. Too Much Finance? *IMF Working Paper*, WP/12/161.

Atkinson, Anthony B., Piketty, Thomas, and Saez, Emmanual. 2011. Top Incomes in the Long Run of History, *Journal of Economic Literature*, 49 (1): 3–71.

Atkinson, Anthony B. 2015. *Inequality. What can be done?* Cambridge, MA: Harvard University Press.

Bennett, Paul, and Peristiani, Stavros. 2002. Are U.S. Reserve Requirements still Binding? Federal Reserve Bank of New York, *Economic Policy Review*, 8 (1): 53–68.

Bhatia, Ashok Vir. 2011. Consolidated Regulation and Supervision in the United States, *IMF Working Paper*, No.23.

Bindseil, Ulrich, and König, Philipp J. 2013. Basil J. Moore's Horizontalists and Verticalists: An appraisal 25 years later, *Review of Keynesian Economics*, 1 (4) (Winter): 383–390.

Bindseil, Ulrich. 2004. The Operational Target of Monetary Policy and the Rise and Fall of Reserve Position Doctrine, *ECB Working Paper Series*, No. 372.

Borio, Claudio. 2012. The Financial Cycle and Macroeconomics: What have we Learnt? *BIS Working Papers*, No. 395, Basel: Bank for International Settlements.

Borio, Claudio. 2017. *Secular Stagnation or Financial Cycle Drag?* Basel: Bank for International Settlements.

[37] Minsky (1982a, 1986).

[38] Shiller (2015, p. 225).

[39] Laeven and Valencia (2008). Dt. Bank Markets Research (2014, 2017).

Carney, Mark. 2019. *The Growing Challenges for Monetary Policy in the Current International Monetary and Financial System*, Speech at the Jackson Hole Symposium 2019, publ. by the Bank of England, August 2019.

Chansel, Lucas, Piketty, Thomas, Saez, Emmanuel, and Zucman, Gabriel. 2022. *World Inequality Report 2022*, publ. by World Inequality Lab with support from UNDP.

Dt. Bank Markets Research. 2014. *Long-Term Asset Return Study*, London, September 2014.

Dt. Bank Markets Research. 2017. *Long-Term Asset Return Study*, London, July 2017.

Dt. Bundestag. 2020. *Dokumentation zu den Begriffen Finanz- und Realwirtschaft*, WD 5—3000—003/20.

Eichengreen, Barry. 2011. Exorbitant Privilege. The Rise and Fall of the Dollar and the Future of the International Monetary System, New York: Oxford University Press.

Esselink, Henk, and Hernández, Lola. 2017. The use of Cash by Households in the Euro Area, *European Central Bank Occasional Paper Series*, No. 201 Frankfurt.

Financial Stability Board. 2020. *Global Monitoring Report on Non-Bank Financial Intermediation 2020*, www.fsb.org/2021/12/global-monitoring-report-on-non-bank-financial-intermediation-2021.

Fisher, Irving. 1935. *100%-Money*. New Haven: Yale University.

Friedman, Milton, and Schwartz, Anna J. 1963. *A Monetary History of the United States and the United Kingdom 1867–1960*. Chicago: University of Chicago Press.

Fullbrook, Edward, and Morgan, Jamie, (Eds). 2020. *The Inequality Crisis*. Bristol: World Economics Association Books.

Gopinath, Gita, Boz, Emine, Casas, Camila, Díez, Federico J., Gourinchas, Pierre-Olivier, and Plagborg-Möller, Mikkel. 2016. Dominant Currency Paradigm, *NBER Working Paper*, No. 22943.

Gopinath, Gita, and Stein, Jeremy C. 2018. Banking, Trade, and the Making of a Dominant Currency, *NBER Working Paper,* No. 24485.

Huber, Joseph. 2017. *Sovereign Money*. Beyond Reserve Banking, London: Palgrave Macmillan.

Hudson, Michael. 2003 [1972]. *Super Imperialism. The Origin and Fundamentals of U.S. World Dominance*, New edition, London: Pluto Press.

Hudson, Michael. 2012. *The Bubble and Beyond*, Dresden: Islet Verlag [FIRE sector].

Jacab, Zoltan, and Kumhof, Michael. 2015. Banks Are Not Intermediaries of Loanable Funds—and Why This Matters, *Bank of England Working Paper*, No. 529.

Jordà, Òscar, Schularick, Moritz, and Taylor, Alan M. 2010. Financial Crises, Credit Booms, and External Imbalances. 140 Years of Lessons, *NBER Working Papers*, No. 16567.

Jordà, Òscar, Schularick, Moritz, and Taylor, Alan M. 2014. The Great Mortgaging: Housing Finance, Crises, and Business Cycles, *NBER Working Papers*, No. 20501.

Keen, Steve. 2011. *Debunking Economics*. London/New York: Zed Books.

Keen, Steve. 2014. Endogenous Money and Effective Demand, *Review of Keynesian Economics*, 2 (3) (Autumn): 271–291.

Kindleberger, Charles P., and Laffargue, J.-P. (Eds). 1982. *Financial Crises. Theory, History, and Policy*, Cambridge University Press.

Kindleberger, Charles P. 1993. *A Financial History of Western Europe*. New York: Oxford University Press.

Krüger, Malte, and Seitz, Franz. 2014. *The Importance of Cash and Cashless Payments in Germany*, Proceedings of the International Cash Conference 2014: The Usage, Costs and Benefits of Cash. Frankfurt: Bundesbank.

Kuvshinov, Dmitry, and Zimmermann, Kaspar. 2021. The Big Bang: Stock Market Capitalization in the Long Run), *Journal of Financial Economics*, 145 (2) (Part B): 527–552.

Kydland, Finn, and Prescott, Edward. 1990. Business Cycles: Real Facts and a Monetary Myth. *Quarterly Review* 14: 3–18.

Laeven, Luc, and Valencia, Fabian. 2008. Systemic Banking Crises. A New Database, *IMF Working Paper*, WP 08/224.

Lavoie, Marc. 2014. A Comment on 'Endogenous Money and Effective Demand' by Steve Keen, *Review of Keynesian Economics*, 2 (3) (Autumn): 321–332.

Lutz, Friedrich. 1936. *Das Grundproblem der Geldverfassung*, Stuttgart/Berlin: Kohlhammer.

Macfarlane, Laurie, Ryan-Collins, Joshm, Bjerg, Ole, Nielsen, Rasmus, and McCann, Duncan. 2017. *Making Money from Making Money. Seigniorage in the Modern Economy*, publ. by New Economics Foundation, London, and Copenhagen Business School.

McKinsey Global Institute. 2010. *Debt and Deleveraging—The Global Credit Bubble and its Economic Consequences*, January 2010.

McKinsey Global Institute. 2021. *The Rise and Rise of the Global Balance Sheet*, November 2021.

Minsky, Hyman P. 1982a. The Financial Instability Hypothesis. Capitalist Processes and the Behavior of the Economy, In: C. P. Kindleberger, J.-P. Laffargue (Eds.), *Financial Crises. Theory, History, and Policy*, Cambridge University Press, 13–39.

Minsky, Hyman P. 1982b. *Can 'It' Happen Again? Essays on Instability and Finance*, Armonk, N.Y.: M.E. Sharpe.

Minsky, Hyman P. 1986. *Stabilizing an Unstable Economy*. New Haven: Yale University Press.

Moore, Basil J. 1988a. *Horizontalists and Verticalists: The Macroeconomics of Credit Money*. Cambridge University Press.

Moore, Basil J. 1988b. The Endogenous Money Supply, *Journal of Post Keynesian Economics*, 10 (3): 372–385.

Palley, Thomas I. 2013. Horizontalists, Verticalists, and Structuralists: The Theory of Endogenous Money Reassessed, *Review of Keynesian Economics*, 1 (4): 406–424.

Rochon, Louis-Philippe. 1999a. *Credit, Money and Production*. An Alternative Post-Keynesian Approach, Cheltenham: Edward Elgar.

Rochon, Louis-Philippe. 1999b. The Creation and Circulation of Endogenous Money, *Journal of Economic Issues*, 33 (1): 1–21.

Rogoff, Kenneth S. 2017. Dealing with Monetary Paralysis at the Zero Bound, *Journal of Economic Perspectives*, 31 (3) (Summer): 47–66.

Rossi, Sergio. 2003. Money and Banking in a Monetary Theory of Production, In L. P. Rochon, Rossi, Sergio (Eds.), *Modern Theories of Money*, Cheltenham: Edward Elgar, 339–359.

Rossi, Sergio. 2007. *Money and Payments in Theory and Practice*. London: Routledge.

Ryan-Collins, Josh, Lloyd, Toby, and Macfarlane, Laurie. 2017. *Rethinking the Economics of Land and Housing*. London: Zed Books Ltd.

Schularick, Moritz, and Taylor, Alan M. 2009. Credit Booms Gone Bust. 1870–2008, National Bureau of Economic Research, *Working Paper*, No. 15512. Reprinted In *American Economic Review*, 102 (2): 1029–61.

Shiller, Robert J. 2015. *Irrational Exuberance, revised and expanded*, 3rd ed. Princeton NJ: Princeton University Press.

Sigl-Glöckner, Philippa. 2018. Ein Blick ins Innere des europäischen Finanzgetriebes, *Makronom*, 7.

Stevens, Edward J. 1971. Composition of the Money Stock Prior to the Civil War, *Journal of Money, Credit and Banking*, 3 (1): 84–101.

Turner, Adair. 2012. *Economics After the Crisis. Objectives and Means*, Cambridge, Mass./London: The MIT Press.

van Lerven, Frank, Hodgson, Graham, and Dyson, Ben. 2015. *Would There be Enough Credit in a Sovereign Money System?* London: Positive Money.

Werner, Richard A. 2011. Economics as if Banks Mattered, *The Manchester School*, 79: 25–35.

Werner, Richard A. 2014a. Can Banks Individually Create Money out of Nothing? *The Theories and the Empirical Evidence, International Review of Financial Analysis* 36: 1–19.

Werner, Richard A. 2014b. How do Banks Create Money, and Why can Other Firms not do the Same? *International Review of Financial Analysis* 36: 71–77.

CHAPTER 4

Monetary Sovereignty. Bank Money as Para-Sovereign Fiat Money

The transition from scarce traditional commodity money of antiquity and early modern merchant capitalism to modern token money creatable at discretion was inevitable.[1] Otherwise, modern economies, productive industries, growing populations and overall improving living standards could not have developed. At the same time, however, money creation was rarely balanced over a longer period, neither that of the state (treasuries and central banks governed by state law) nor that of the banks (and central banks governed by private law). Furthermore, the development of modern money has given rise to an ongoing struggle between state money, which seeks to maintain its sovereign position, and banks as well as now also other issuers of private money, trying to dethrone the incumbent and seize the monetary power themselves.[2]

Already classical economics after 1800 was divided on this question. The Banking School defended the banks' practice of putting private banknotes into circulation at their own discretion. The free interplay of supply and demand, together with "real bills" as collateral, would ensure that there would never be more notes than were needed in "real" terms.

[1] Simmel (2004 [1900], p. 173) already saw it this way in his thesis of the progressive "dematerialisation" of money through the gradual superposition of material money by the symbolic form of money tokens.

[2] Also see Galbraith (1995 [1975]). Goodhart (1998). Goodhart and Jensen (2015). Graeber (2012, pp. 46–71).

J. Huber, *The Monetary Turning Point*,
https://doi.org/10.1007/978-3-031-23957-1_4

The Currency School contradicted this from the ground of real inflation phenomena, acceptance problems and banking crises. There had to be an institution, in that case the Bank of England, which would have a legal monopoly on banknotes which, in the context of the time, would itself be tied to a gold standard.[3]

Neoliberalism of the 1930–60s was similarly divided. The Hayekian strand of the neo-Austrian School, which decades later led to an unleashing of financial markets, preached radical free banking and unfettered currency and money competition without legal tender (denationalisation of money).[4] State bureaucracies, including central banks, were said to be subject to a presumption of knowledge. The crowd intelligence of markets was assumed to deliver superior search and learning processes. This, of course, is itself a kind of presumption of knowledge, especially in the face of the unmistakable realities of recurring crowd foolishness.

The opposite stance to the Hayekian ultra-wing of neoliberalism was ordoliberalism, and in terms of monetary policy also the early Chicago School and individual luminaries like I. Fisher. As far as monetary questions are concerned, ordoliberalism was in the tradition of the Currency School and of what is known since Knapp as monetary chartalism, also advocated by Keynes. According to that view, money is a general-purpose instrument pivotal to any market economy, although not a genuine creation of private law, but rather a creature of state law.[5] Control over the *creation* of money, *not the uses* of money, is seen as a prerogative of constitutional importance. Ordoliberalism thus opposed subjecting national currencies and the money denominated in these currencies to competition like any other goods and services.[6]

In this vein, after the Wall Street crash of 1929, the early Chicago School and I. Fisher advocated a 100% reserve on demand deposits so as to put an end to the recurrently overshooting creation of bank money.[7] A large number of American economists and politicians supported the plan.[8] But banking interests kept the upper hand. However, they had to

[3] Vgl. Lutz (1936, pp. 8–18). Goodhart and Jensen (2015). O'Brien (1994, 2007).

[4] Rothbard (1962). Hayek (1976). Huerta de Soto (2009, Chapter. 8).

[5] Knapp (1924 [1905]). Lutz (1936). Henry (2004). Hudson (2004). Graeber (2012).

[6] Lutz (1936, p. 14), Eucken (1959, p. 161).

[7] Soddy (1934). Hart (1935). Fisher (1935). Simons (1948). Friedman (1959).

[8] Cf. Douglas et al. (1939).

accept the introduction of a system of separate banking in 1933 (Glass-Steagall Act). The banks had to choose to be either commercial banks eligible for borrowing from the Federal Reserve and able to create bank money, or to be non-monetary investment banks. However, as there were no restrictions on commercial banks to finance the activities of investment banks, the measure was not particularly effectual. The separate banking system was gradually weakened and investment banks were again allowed to operate as commercial banks. In 1999, what was left from the law was repealed altogether.

Prior to modernity and in the ancient origins of money, private money was not an issue, although differentiation into public and private spheres of life already took place at the time. According to what is known, monetary units of account were developed by the administration of the rulers in remote antiquity in Mesopotamia and Egypt. Later on, almost 2,700 years ago, king Croesus of Lydia introduced money in the form of minted coinage. Since then, the coins bore the rulers' stamp, and money continued to exist as an element of what developed as public or state law, as distinct from private or civil law.

Money creation, or licensing and controlling private money issuance, became the prerogative of ancient and feudal rulers and subsequently modern nation-states. An exception was the time after the fall of the Western Roman Empire when private *monetarii* had seized the prerogative to mint coins, until Pippin III and his son Charlemagne restored monetary sovereignty in the second half of the eighth century. The reason behind was not only the striving of ruling dynasties for power and gain, but also the functional necessities of managing and financing state structures and public infrastructures.

The sovereign prerogatives comprise three components:

1. Determining the currency as the realm's monetary unit of account,
2. Creating and issuing the money or several types of money denominated in that currency, and
3. Benefitting from the seigniorage, the gain from money creation.

The monetary prerogatives are in line with other prerogatives of constitutional importance, such as lawmaking, jurisdiction, territorial administration, taxation and the use of force. No well-run state will deliberately leave these prerogatives to foreign or private powers. After all, no one would think any more of ceding the tax monopoly, even partially, to private entities, or sharing the monopoly on the use of force with self-appointed citizen militias and private armies, or allowing church law and the Sharia as competing parallel law and parallel justice alongside state law and state judiciary.

Many an interested party, however, wants to do away with money as a creature of state law, by re-declaring money as a creature of civil law and private contracts. The sovereign monetary prerogative is apparently too tempting in terms of profit, might and pride, not to try taking over as much of it as possible. In modern monetarised and financialised societies being in control of money—its creation, first uses and its ongoing allocation thereafter—means wielding superior power, second only to legal command power and the authority to issue directives.

As a result of bank money's rise to system dominance in the course of the twentieth century, of the three components of monetary sovereignty only one—defining the official currency unit—is still intact. But most of money creation and related seigniorage-like benefits (avoiding financing costs to a significant degree) has been ceded to the banking sector. Central banks, by origin *bank of the state*, have turned into *bank of the banks*. Systemically relevant banks today have a de facto support guarantee from the central banks in their considerably expanded role as *lender of last resort*, and meanwhile also as *market maker of last resort* in government bonds, partly also corporate bonds.

Governments for their part have assumed the role of *guarantor of last resort* for bank money and thus the existence of the banks. Since the 1930s, bank money has legal deposit insurance, provided by the banks themselves (on a rather small scale) and by the government (on a large scale). Governments stand ready to bail banks out if necessary, for example by temporarily nationalising large banks at risk of insolvency, or recapitalising them in some other way with state funds. In the meantime, even customer deposits are legally subject to bail-in (enforced conversion of customer deposits into bank equity) to save banks from bankruptcy.

Bank money would have perished as a private means of payment at the latest around 1930 and the Great Depression, had it not been supported to an ever greater extent by the national central banks, treasuries and government guarantees. To put it more accurately, bank money actually *did perish* as a purely private means of payment at that time, in that central banks and governments began to take responsibility for the existence of the banking sector in general and what is now called systemically relevant banks in particular. Bank money and central-bank reserves, thus commercial banks and central banks, have become intimately intertwined and interdependent. Referring to this as a mixed money system is not wrong, but trivialising and obscuring. In actual fact, we are dealing with a genuinely private bank money regime backed by national central banks and warranted by government, a system in which central banks and governments follow the corporate lead of the banking sector and shadow banks, and genuinely private bank money has accomplished para-sovereign status—a constitutional monstrosity.

Among the reasons behind that development was the recurrent experience of severe banking and financial crises, prompting concern about the national money supply, which in fact is the supply of bank money, and keeping the bank money in circulation to keep the economy going. Rather than thinking about the way of functioning of the present money and banking system, politicians and central bankers have opted time after time to strengthen the private bank money privilege, falling to the illusion of being able to make banks safe by ever more red tape. Among recent examples is the Dodd-Frank Act from 2010. It comprises almost a thousand pages, including, among many other things, ring fencing and living wills. Another example is the Basel rules on the liquidity and solvency of banks. Such measures remain inside the box and will help as little to prevent a next severe crisis as they did not help much in the past.

High liquidity risk is the inevitable characteristic of fractional reserve banking. The possibility of banking crises and insolvencies cannot be regulated away, because balance-sheet mismatches cannot be precluded, however diligent calculations may have been, but overthrown by unforeseen mishaps and engagements going awry. Trying to make banks risk-proof, and thus making bank money safe, is mission impossible. In the early to mid-1800s, banks in Europe had equity ratios of 30–40 per cent, in America 40–50 per cent.[9] Even this did not protect them from crises and, in not uncommon cases, insolvency. In 2008, the bank equity ratio was only 8 per cent, now it is 15 per cent due to new requirements (Basel rules). This too will not prevent future crises of fractional reserve banking. In a crisis, receivables default at an increased rate and other financial assets

[9] Benink and Bentson (2005). Benink (2016, p. 31). *The Economist,* December 20th, 2008, p. 58.

also lose value. In a severe crisis, no equity buffer will guarantee survival. It is not by chance that the term bankruptcy comes from banking.

There is something tragicomic about the widespread presumption that bank money is under central-bank lead and control, the system overall thus being supposed to represent a sovereign currency system rather than the bank-led para-sovereign bank money regime it actually is. If bank money is inherently unsafe and has to be rescued time after time by central-bank and government intervention, the question arises as to why this screwed-up situation is repeatedly accepted instead of leaving the banks to their private liabilities, and providing the non-bank public with central-bank sovereign money of safe stock—such as a dominant supply of sovereign cash once was, and as CBDC can become, if properly implemented. In constitutional terms as well as in the interest of effectual monetary policy, it is time to put the checks and balances in the monetary system right again.

References

Benink, Harald A., and George Bentson. 2005. The Future of Banking Regulation in Developed Countries: Lessons from and for Europe. *Financial Markets, Institutions & Instruments* 14 (5).

Benink, Harald A. 2016. Raising Bank Capital and the Implications for the Cost of Capital, In: Patricia Jackson (Ed.), *Banking Reform*, publ. by SUERF The European Money and Finance Forum, London.

Douglas, Paul H., Hamilton, Earl J., Fisher, Irving, King, Willford I., Graham, Frank D., and Whittlesey, Charles R. 1939. *A Program for Monetary Reform.* Unpublished, but widely circulated among economists at the time. Available from the Kettle Pond Institute for Debt-Free Money, www.economicstability.org/history/a-program-for-monetaryreform-the-1939-document.

Eucken, Walter. 1959. *Grundsätze der Wirtschaftspolitik.* Hamburg: Rowohlt.

Fisher, Irving. 1935. *100%-Money.* New Haven: Yale University.

Friedman, Milton. 1959. *A Program for Monetary Stability.* New York: Fordham University Press.

Galbraith, John Kenneth. 1995 [1975]. *Money. Whence it Came, Where it Went*, New York: Houghton Mifflin, 1st ed. 1975.

Goodhart, Charles A. E. 1998. The Two Concepts of Money—Implications for the Analysis of Optimal Currency Areas. *European Journal of Political Economy* 14 (1998): 407–432.

Goodhart, Charles A.E., and Meinhard Jensen. 2015. Currency School versus Banking School: An Ongoing Confrontation. *Economic Thought* 4 (2): 20–31.

Graeber, David. 2012. *Debt. The First 5,000 Years*, New York: Melville House Publishing.

Hart, Albert G. 1935. The Chicago Plan of Banking Reform, *The Review of Economic Studies*, 2: 104–116. Reprinted in Friedrich A. Lutz and Lloyd W. Mints (Eds.). 1951. Readings in Monetary Theory, Homewood, Ill.: Richard D. Irwin, 437-456.

Hayek, Friedrich A. von. 1976. *Denationalisation of Money*. London: Intitute of Economic Affairs.

Henry, John F. 2004. The Social Origins of Money: The Case of Egypt, In: Wray (Ed.), 79–98.

Hudson, Michael. 2004. The Archeology of Money. Debt versus Barter—Theories of Money's Origins, In: Wray (Ed.), 99–127.

Huerta de Soto, Jesús. 2009. *Money, Bank Credit, and Economic Cycles*, Auburn, Al.: Ludwig von Mises Institute, 2nd edition (1st 2006).

Knapp, Georg Friedrich. 1924 [1905]. *The State Theory of Money*, London: Macmillan & Co.

Lutz, Friedrich A. 1936. *Das Grundproblem der Geldverfassung*, Stuttgart/Berlin: Kohlhammer.

O'Brien, Denis Patrick. 1994. *Foundations of Monetary Economics*, Vol. IV—The Currency School, Vol. V—The Banking School, London: William Pickering.

O'Brien, Denis Patrick. 2007. *The Development of Monetary Economics*. Cheltenham: Edward Elgar.

Rothbard, Murray N. 1962. The Case for a 100-Percent Gold Dollar. In *Search of a Monetary Constitution*, (Ed.), B. Leland, Yeager, 94–136. Cambridge, Mass.: Harvard University Press.

Simmel, Georg. 2004 [1900]. *Philosophy of Money, edited by David Frisby*. London: Routledge.

Simons, Henry C. 1948. A Positive Programme for Laissez Faire. Some Proposals for a Liberal Economic Policy, and: Rules versus Authorities in Monetary Policy. Both articles In: H.C. Simons, *Economic Policy for a Free Society*, The University of Chicago Press, 1948. First published as 'Rules versus...', *The Journal of Political Economy*, 44 (1936): 1–30.

Soddy, Frederick. 1934. *The Role of Money. What it should be, contrasted with what it has become*, London: George Routledge and Sons Ltd.

Wray, L. Randall., (Ed.). 2004. *Credit and State Theories of Money. The Contributions of A.* Mitchell-Innes, Cheltenham: Edward Elgar Publishing.

CHAPTER 5

Historical Turning Points in the Composition of the Money Supply

5.1 Types of Money in Epochal Rise and Decline

The composition of the modern money supply has undergone structural changes throughout the last centuries.[1] The rise and later decline of a particular type of money can be likened to the rising and falling of tides. In the development of money in modern times, there have so far been three such tidal changes and the fourth is emergent right now:

1660s until 1840s:

↗ Rising tide of unregulated paper money
↘ Incipient decline in the systemic importance of sovereign coin.

1840s until around 1910:

↗ Rising tide of central-bank legal-tender notes in Europe.
↘ Falling tide for unregulated paper money in the form of private banknotes and various types of treasury bills (except for US Treasury notes).

[1] The sources on the history of money behind this chapter include Aliber and Kindleberger (2015 [1978]). Davies (2013). Ferguson (2008). Galbraith (1995 [1975]). Graeber (2012). Hixson (1993). Huerta de Soto (2009). Kindleberger and Laffargue (Eds.) (1982). O'Brien (1994, 2007). Siekmann (2016). Simmel (2004 [1900]). Skidelsky (2018). Zarlenga (2002).

J. Huber, *The Monetary Turning Point*,
https://doi.org/10.1007/978-3-031-23957-1_5

Late nineteenth century until around 2010:

↗ Rising tide of bank money.
↘ Falling tide for central-bank notes and reserves.

Upcoming from the 2020s:

↗ Rising tide of digital tokens, in particular CBDC.
↘ Incipient decline of book money, in particular bank money.

Of course, the real-world processes of structural recomposition of the money supply are never as straightforward as the abstracting idea of it suggests. Similarly, the tidal changes in the money supply do not mean there was always an absolute decline in the quantity of a particular type of money as was the case with medieval tally sticks as well as unregulated paper money. In terms of total quantity, stocks of treasury coins, treasury and central-bank notes, bank money and central-bank reserves in fact never stopped growing until very recently, reflecting the exponential growth in population and the economy over the last centuries. However, the *share* of a particular type of money in the composition of the money supply, as a percentage of the total, was increasing during a particular historical period from a low level upwards, and decreasing in a later period from the highest level achieved.

The rise and subsequent decline in the share of a means of payment is reminiscent of an aphorism attributed to Mark Twain: "History doesn't repeat itself, but it often rhymes". The characteristic turning points in the composition of the modern money supply occurred as problem- and crisis-induced changes showing certain structural similarities. The following discussion of monetary turning points allow*s* assuming that a significant shift in the composition of the money supply occurs

(1) when the respective monetary system, or the incumbent dominant money, respectively, pose problems that cannot be solved within the given framework, and
(2a) a new type of money emerges that offers some solution to the problems, and/or
(2b) efficiency advantages such as lower costs of production, provision and handling, improved ease of use and faster transferability of the money. So far, incumbent monies were less convenient, circulated at lower use frequency, and were more expensive to produce and handle than the competing new monies.

To put it simplified and pointedly, the pendulum-like restructurings of the money supply and the money system have so far represented alternating periods of too little and too much, of monetary scarcity and oversupply. As long as coinage was still dominant in early modernity, money remained very scarce, despite intermittent episodes of silver inflation. In the ensuing era of unregulated paper money, the creation of money was often too much of a good thing. The subsequent period of the central-bank note monopoly, based on the gold standard or a bimetallic monetary base, created artificial scarcity of money, which, however, was difficult to maintain and was undermined over time by the development of bank book money. The rise of the bank money regime, in turn, knew virtually no limits to money creation. To the extent that such limits were effective to some extent, the gradual demise of the short-lived Bretton Woods arrangement saw an unprecedented unleashing of the money supply.

In a similar sense, J.K. Galbraith already discussed changing periods of "tight vs loose money", with the pendulum of opinion and policies swinging back and forth between the two.[2] In a similar way, Skidelsky compares "hard and soft money theories" and discusses various historical shifts from one to the other.[3] Tightening or easing the money supply is certainly a fundamental concern of monetary policy. The monetary turning points discussed in this place, however, are not primarily about fluctuating opinions and attitudes, but about the actual rise of a particular means of payment to monetary dominance and its subsequent relative decline or outright demise.

5.2 1660s Until 1840s: Rising Tide of Unregulated Paper Money, Incipient Decline in the Systemic Importance of Sovereign Coin

Pre-modern currencies were coin currencies. The typical shortcoming of coin currencies was chronic shortage of silver and gold. The coin shortage was not really reduced by the influx of silver and gold from Latin America, known as the Spanish silver inflation. It started in the 1550s and made itself felt on and off for about hundred years. Prices rose in Spain and

[2] Galbraith (1995 [1975], chs. 7, 8, 19).

[3] Skidelsky (2018, p. 39).

other affected regions, even if moderately compared with the inflation surges of the twentieth century. The general lack of money was not remedied in the process.

The overall coin shortage was exacerbated by the practice of hoarding precious metal coins, often secretly to hide the money from the tax collector. Furthermore, the shortage and hoarding of coins induced recurrent phases of coin debasement. One practice was decrying the coins time and again to re-mint and re-issue them at the same face value but with lower silver content. This also happened in undeclared and fraudulent ways. The last era of intensified debased coinage was in the 1630s during the Thirty Years' War. Coin debasement in turn came with uncertain acceptance of various coins, resulting in unstable value parities between "good" and "bad" money.

This then was the background for the rise of a new type of money which occurred since the 1660s until the 1840s. That time saw the rising tide of paper money. Silver and gold remained predominant overall, but experienced a relative loss of systemic significance over the decades. Paper money offered an answer to the natural scarcity of silver and gold, to the hoarding of coins, and the recurrent debasement of coinage. Paper money need not be scarce; it can be written out or printed in any quantity.

Banknotes may have been partially covered by silver and bullion, but they do not have commodity value. And yet, to the degree banknotes are accepted in lieu of coin, they give full purchasing power. Paper money opened the door to monetary modernity by substituting a purely symbolic or informational token for the traditional commodity money. This does not contradict Keynes' view of stamped silver coins to have always been token money. With paper money, however, modern money was starting to break away from its traditional commodity substrate.

Paper money was much cheaper to produce and more convenient to handle than the cumbersome and cost-intensive mining, melting, minting and handling of coins and bullion. The related seigniorage for note issuers was accordingly much higher. Payment of larger amounts of money in banknotes carried in a wallet was more convenient than payment in coins carried in belt bags and strongboxes.

However, paper money is susceptible to counterfeiting, succeeding the previous fraudulent coin debasement. Forgery of paper money even became a way of warfare by other means, in this case as an assault on the enemy's currency. For example, English counterfeiting helped to wreck the *continental dollar* notes of the American War of Independence as well as the *assignats* of the French Revolution. The Nazis tried to do likewise in 1943/44 when they forced highly skilled concentration camp prisoners to counterfeit British pound notes. The effect, however, was not that important anymore as most large transactions had long since been cashless.

Paper money was issued by private banks, often privileged by the Crown or a local principality, and partly also by bankers and aristocrats jointly operating a note-issuing bank. Running such a bank required a licence from the government or parliament, but the operational business remained private and largely unregulated. Typical cases included the Stockholms Banco 1656/61, the Bank of England 1694, the Cologne Banco di Gyro d'Affrancatione 1705, and the Paris-based Banque Générale 1715 run by John Law.

In addition, and throughout the epoch, there were temporarily also royal and princely treasuries that used paper money of their own, pure fiat money, issued debt-free by way of government expenses for public purchases and works, civil servants and the military. Such bills were used like banknotes. They could also be used for payment of taxes which helped to make them more widely accepted in the home country. As a rule, however, it was not possible to pay with them imports from other states.

In America at the same time, and there too, due to a lack of coins, the governors of what were to become the later US Federal States issued uncovered colonial bills, also known as colonial scrip, handed out to every taxpayer debt-free, that is, free of interest and redemption. In most cases, the practice did not cause inflation, in a few cases only to a small extent. Instead, the bills triggered a surge in prosperity. The practice was restricted by British Currency Acts between 1751 and 1773. The Americans' rancour over this economically damaging restraint can be seen as one of the reasons behind the War of Independence, which began in 1775. Starting in the same year, the Continental Congress issued unbacked and debt-free paper money, known as continental dollars. They helped to finance the War of Independence from 1775–83.

Overall, the paper money of the time came as a mix of state-issued notes, state-privileged private banknotes and purely private banknotes, the mix depending on the country and time. What they had in common was that they were largely unregulated. Even treasury-issued notes were not "legal tender", a notion which only came into existence in the course of the nineteenth century. Except for the licensing of the note issue, there was no coherent idea of a monetary regime for banknotes, although everyone knew that over-issue had to be avoided. It appears that the American governors at the time were by and large successful in striking a balance between too little and too much. This did not apply to the note issue of the Banque Générale under John Law and his card-table companion, the Duc d'Orléans, nor to the *assignats* of the French Revolution.

Paper money allowed for a much increased money supply in support of the growing goods manufacture and trade of the mercantile era. However, the multitude of paper notes issued by individual banks and principalities, often of only local reach and uneven trustworthiness, meant a varied and overall limited acceptance of the banknotes. A related problem was the convertibility of notes into silver coin, which was promised but, due to the fractional base of silver coin and bullion, not always kept. The lack of universal acceptance was the Achilles' heel of unregulated paper money throughout the eighteenth and far into the nineteenth centuries. The paper money's patchy acceptance hampered the development of well-integrated national markets and also international trade.

Furthermore, and also from the beginning, the ease of issuing notes lured bankers and certain treasuries into over-issue of paper money. This in turn resulted in unstable currency exchange rates and unstable purchasing power, as well as banking crises and hitherto unknown boom-and-bust-cycles due to over-investment and under-demand. Such cycles, later on called business cycles, occurred after the Napoleonic Wars and widely established industrialisation since the 1830/40s.

5.3 1840s Until Around 1910: Rising Tide of National Central-Bank Notes, Ebb Tide for Unregulated Paper Money

The second monetary turning point in Europe occurred in 1833/44 (England) and continued through the following decades until 1914 (World War I). This era saw the rising tide of national central-bank notes and the ebb tide for unregulated paper money of all sorts. They were phased out, while central-bank notes were phased in, establishing the legal-tender note monopoly such as it stands to the present day. The transition from unregulated paper money to legal-tender notes was a process lasting decades, but in the end there were no more private banknotes in Europe, and treasury notes only to a small extent.

Central-bank notes became the dominant type of money in this period. Central-bank notes eliminated the problems of patchy acceptance and unstable parity and purchasing power of unregulated paper money. Central-bank notes proved to be a useful universal means of payment, accepted everywhere by everyone in payment of whatsoever. National banknotes were the means of choice to build nationally integrated economies.

The British Currency School of the 1830–40s had played a decisive role in establishing the central-bank note monopoly. They were opposing the private-money Banking School of the time. The legal basis for central-bank notes was created with the Bank of England Act in 1833 and the Bank Charter Act in 1844. This then became the point of reference for most European states at a Paris meeting in 1867. Central-bank notes are still about paper money, but monetarily they represent a different type of money: legal tender, reflecting the monetary sovereignty of a nation-state, issued by the national central bank on the basis of a legal mandate.

However, there was a catch, and that was the gold standard. The British bullionists and Currency School adherents had accused private banks and thereafter also the Bank of England of over-issue of notes. At their insistence, the gold standard was soon made the fundament of the central-bank note regime. The gold standard intended to limit the creation of central-bank notes according to existing gold stocks, in this way artificially reproducing the natural scarcity of precious metal coins. This was thought to be an anchor of stability, and was seen that way for a long time, even as late as 1944 in Bretton Woods when the gold-backing of the US dollar was established, rather than recognising any gold standard with Keynes as the "barbarous relic" it is.

In actual fact, the gold standard proved to be a backward-looking hindrance to providing for the expansive needs of the time (population growth, urbanisation, industrialisation, international trade). The gold standard was a potentially deflationary setback contributing to unnecessary bottlenecks in the allocation of funds and distribution of income, adding to pauperism and social-class antagonism.

In the U.S., things developed differently at first. After two discontinued attempts to establish a licensed private central bank, the US Treasury under Lincoln's presidency started to issue uncovered legal-tender notes in 1862 to pay for the expenses of the Civil War, the still famous "greenbacks". This was mirrored on the Confederate side in the issue of "greybacks". Treasury notes were also issued time and again later on, in decreasing volume until this procedure of sovereign money creation was ended in the 1960–90s. US Treasury notes are still valid legal tender side by side with Federal Reserve notes since 1914. The Federal Reserve was set up on the initiative of a group that was known at the time as "New York international bankers", and it still is a corporate enterprise. Over time, however, the Fed's most important functions—top personnel, monetary policy and seigniorage—were regulated by public law and are carried out with active Treasury participation. So, the final outcome of the developments in America and Europe was co-directional despite not unimportant institutional and legal differences.

5.4 Late Nineteenth Century Until Around 2010: Rising Tide of Bank Money, Ebb Tide for Central-Bank Notes and Reserves

The third monetary turn of tide was from the decades around 1900 and continues to the present. We live at the end of this era. It was marked by the rise of bank money, which has probably already passed the zenith of its dominance since the banking crisis of 2008, and the decline of cash, as well as the decline of central-bank reserves until the crisis of 2008.

The rise of bank money came about in two stages, the first from around 1880, still in the era of European colonialism and international free trade. This epoch ended with World War I and the Great Depression from 1929 onwards. The second surge occurred with the "economic miracle" after World War II and a new expansion of international trade and free cross-border movement of capital. The ensuing era of globalisation is likely to have reached its peak in the course of the 2010s. The era included the end of the Cold War and the rise of China.

The M1 share of bank money in Europe and North America initially rose from around 20–30% to around 55–60% in the first stage, and in the second up to 85–97% of today. Conversely, the share of cash declined from about 80% in 1870 to 60% around 1900, and further to 45–40% in the 1920–60s, and from then down to the current 10–2%.[4]

[4] The data vary from country to country by number and time, but structurally follow a co-directional path according to statistical time series material from the central banks and statistical offices of the U.S., the UK, Germany and Switzerland.

The U.S. appears to differ from the other countries in that the share of cash there is now half of M1, i.e. the same as bank money. This is deceptive. In the 1950s and 1960s,

The reason for this tidal change to the benefit of bank money was not a problem with the note monopoly. The problem was the gold standard. The artificial scarcity of money it induced was a hindrance amidst strongly growing populations, industries and commerce. As a result, the gold standard repeatedly had to be relaxed or even temporarily suspended. In addition, an amount of national government bonds were counted as part of the gold coverage without much fuss.

More importantly, as an alternative to cash and a way to bypass the constraints of the gold standard, the banking sector developed the possibilities of book money, that is, cashless payment by transfer of non-bank account balances and interbank clearing of claims and liabilities. As a general means of payment, bank money emerged in the decades before and after 1900. The bank credit theory of money dates from the 1890s.[5] In the 1920/30s cashless payment then spread more widely as chequebook economy. Chequebooks had been around for a long time, but not as the mass practice which it became with the rise of bank money.

The practice of clearing account balances dates back to the Italian banks of the Late Medieval Rinascimento. However, the practice remained limited to banks and merchant houses. Only the expansion of the practice in the second half of the nineteenth century on an ever broader basis strengthened the role of bank money. In the paper money reforms of the earlier nineteenth century, the transfer of liquid deposits as a method of payment was left unconsidered. Interbank clearing of customer account balances could thus be established as a general way of making payments, and bank money as a rising new money surrogate used by ever more firms, private and public actors, ultimately by almost everyone. Central banks themselves have contributed to this development

the cash share in the U.S. was only 20% of M1. But it has risen steadily since then, along with the rise of the US dollar as the dominant world currency. As a result, most dollar notes do not circulate in the U.S., but abroad as a parallel currency and worldwide as an underground currency. Since around 2015, the underground part has increasingly been taken over by Bitcoin and other cryptocurrencies. The stock of dollar notes has been declining since then. At the same time, the share of non-cash money is much higher in the U.S. than it appears. On the one hand, the boundaries between M1 and M2 (savings and time and time deposits) have become blurred due to the availability of M2 balances, so that the latter, if interest-bearing, are preferred. On the other hand, demand deposits in M1 were partly replaced and generally overlaid by MMF shares up to the amount of 2.4 times M1.

[5] Vgl. Ingham (2004). Foundations in Macleod (1889), Withers (1909) and Hawtrey (1919). Also see Schumpeter (1934 [1911], p. 110).

by carrying out cashless interbank payments by way of clearing between bank accounts at the central bank.

Cashless payment practices were supported by ongoing innovations in telecommunications and data processing throughout the nineteenth and twentieth centuries, from postal services, telegraph and telephone, via calculating and tabulating machines and telex, to computerisation and the internet. Cashless payment is more convenient and cheaper than payment in cash, particularly when many or large payments are involved, in wholesale banking anyway. Bank money—i.e. booking into and out of customer accounts—is also easier and cheaper to provide and handle than banknotes. The money users had advantages in terms of convenience. Bank money is also safer to store and handle than notes and coins. Account balances cannot be falsified in the same way as paper notes can be counterfeited. In terms of technical and monetary efficiency, cash cannot compete with technology-based cashless payment practices. So the path was established for the imminent final rise of bank money to full system dominance since the 1960/70s.

The spread of bank money contributed significantly to putting an end to the gold standard. The growing demand for bank money, not least because of the financing needs of the two world wars as well as the economic stimulus programmes of the 1930s, was accompanied by a more frequent suspension of the gold standard. The gold standard was followed by the gold-linked US dollar standard agreed upon in Bretton Woods in 1944. No sooner had this standard been adopted than it was softened again as a result of the Korean War of 1950–53 and the American intervention in the Vietnam War from 1965–75. In 1971, US President Nixon took the dollar off the gold peg.

Since then, a "US Treasury bond standard" has in actual fact taken its place.[6] It triggered an even greater monetary expansion since around 1980. This certainly made for continued economic growth and still increased living standards. The downside was—similar to the over-issue of unregulated paper money in the eighteenth century, but on a larger scale—overshooting dynamics in financial assets and indebtedness. The expansion of bank money came with high inflation until around 1980, subsequently disinflation and strong asset inflation, and thus increased financial vulnerability.

[6] Hudson (2003 [1972], p. 377).

5.5 Upcoming from the 2020s: Rising Tide of Digital Tokens, in Particular CBDC

At the present time, bank money has accomplished its rise to monetary dominance, even attaining para-state status. Some of the problems related to the bank money regime have been detailed in the preceding chapters. The shortening of the quantity lever of monetary policy due to the decline in cash and operationally necessitated reserves has resulted in a loss of effectiveness of monetary policy, raising the question as to whether the monetary system is still governable at all. It became obvious that the overshooting crisis-prone dynamics of the bank money regime cannot be contained by central banks. Instead, they feel compelled to act as an auxiliary body of the banking sector, accommodating the banks' demand for fractional refinancing in *all* circumstances, especially in times of self-inflicted crises. The unfortunate situation cannot be fundamentally changed as long as the bank money regime persists and bank money remains dominant.

At the same time, new types of money surrogates are emerging. Apart from MMF shares and e-money, these are primarily digital currencies, for one thing in the form of private uncovered cryptocurrencies, and most recently stablecoins backed by bank money and securities, for another thing in the form of CBDC. Effective monetary policy becomes possible again to the extent that CBDC grows to a decisive quantity. In addition, digital money generally promises more efficient and cheaper as well as convenient payment transactions as well as further long-term innovations related to the programmability of digital tokens.

Thus, the preconditions for another historical recomposition of the money supply are in place and there are indications that such a process has already set in. This will not be a revolution, but still a structural trend reversal in the composition of the money supply, including a rearrangement of the monetary and financial institutions involved (banks, shadow banks, central bank and government), comparable in character and scope to previous epochal monetary turning points.

How quickly and widely digital money will spread, and how far and how long bank money will last, depends on a number of conditions. These include the principles of the CBDC design to be implemented, but also significant changes in political-economic paradigms. According to the epistemologist Th. Kuhn, paradigm shifts hardly occur through changing convictions of the incumbents, but rather in a "biological way", which points to a time horizon comparable to previous monetary turning points.

References

Aliber, Robert Z., and Charles P. Kindleberger. 2015 [1978]. *Manias, Panics, and Crashes. A History of Financial Crises*, New York: Basic Books. 7th edition.

Davies, Glyn. 2013. *A History of Money*. Cardiff: University of Wales Press.

Ferguson, Niall. 2008. *The Ascent of Money. A Financial History of the World*, London/New York: Allen Lane.

Galbraith, John Kenneth. 1995 [1975]. *Money. Whence it Came, Where it Went*, New York: Houghton Mifflin, 1st ed. 1975.

Graeber, David. 2012. *Debt. The First 5,000 Years*, New York: Melville House Publishing.

Hawtrey, Ralph G. 1919. *Currency and Credit*. London: Longmans, Green & Co.

Hixson, William F. 1993. *Triumph of the Bankers. Money and Banking in the Eighteenth and Nineteenth Centuries*, Westport, Conn./London: Praeger.

Hudson, Michael. 2003 [1972]. *Super Imperialism. The Origin and Fundamentals of U.S. World Dominance*, new edition, London: Pluto Press.

Huerta de Soto, Jesús. 2009. *Money, Bank Credit, and Economic Cycles*, Auburn, Al : Ludwig von Mises Institute, 2nd edition (1st 2006).

Ingham, Geoffrey. 2004. *The Emergence of Capitalist Credit Money*, In: Wray, L. R. (ed.) 2004, 173–222.

Kindleberger, Charles P., and Jean-Pierre Laffargue (Eds). 1982. *Financial Crises. Theory, History, and Policy*, Cambridge University Press.

Macleod, Henry Dunning. 1889. *The Theory of Credit*. London: Longmans, Green & Co.

O'Brien, Denis Patrick. 1994. *Foundations of Monetary Economics*, Vol. IV – The Currency School, Vol. V – The Banking School, London: William Pickering.

O'Brien, Denis Patrick. 2007. *The Development of Monetary Economics*. Cheltenham: Edward Elgar.

Schumpeter, Joseph A. 1934 [1911]. *The Theory of Economic Development. An Inquiry into Profits, Capital, Credit, Interest, and the Business Cycle*, Harvard Economics Studies No. 46.

Siekmann, Helmut. 2016. Deposit Banking and the Use of Monetary Instruments, in D.Fox/W.Ernst (eds). *Money in the Western Legal Tradition. Middle Ages to Bretton Woods*, Oxford University Press, 489–531.

Simmel, Georg. 2004 [1900]. *Philosophy of Money*, ed. by David Frisby, London: Routledge.

Skidelsky, Robert. 2018. *Money and Government: The Past and Future of Economics*. New Haven/London: Yale University Press.

Withers, Hartley. 1909. *The Meaning of Money*. London: Smith, Elder & Co.

Zarlenga, Stephen A. 2002. *The Lost Science of Money – the Mythos of Money, the Story of Power*, Valatie, NY: American Monetary Institute.

CHAPTER 6

Today's Recomposition of the Money Supply

6.1 The Future of Money is Digital

In technical terms, the new era is about the digitisation of money. Digital money is any transferable currency unit in the numerical form of binary digits processed electronically. Until some years ago, digital money just referred to cryptocurrencies. Their emergence has triggered the hype surrounding anything "digital". In the meantime, the term also refers to account-based book money as well as to e-money and mobile money. In fact, virtually everything is now being digitised and electronically processed. This brings misunderstanding in that terms such as digital money, electronic money and e-money are used quite vaguely and, in particular, bank money and central-bank reserves are also said to be digital.

To avoid misunderstanding, conventional reserves are not referred to as digital money here. They are transferable account balances at the central bank, representing book money. The same applies to bank money which is book money in the form of bank-account balances. Digital money, in contrast, is to be understood as a means of payment that has the technical form of digital tokens. The tokens are taken in, stored and paid off by means of an e-wallet. Such tokens can also be understood as a kind of digital cash in the sense that it is a bearer instrument which, firstly, is fully owned by the holder, not owned or held in trust by a bank or other agency. Secondly, it is transferred peer to peer, directly from payer

J. Huber, *The Monetary Turning Point*,
https://doi.org/10.1007/978-3-031-23957-1_6

to payee. A transaction using digital tokens bypasses the intermediary payment processing by banks and other PSP involved in book money payments. This applies even if the payment infrastructure of the central banks and banks as PSP may fulfil a technical function in the transfer of CBDC—notabene, the transfer of *central-bank currency*, whereas *bank money* is no longer involved here.

Unlike cash, digital money is transferable online from everywhere to anywhere, basically also across borders and currency areas. Furthermore, and this promises to be the really innovative and groundbreaking feature, digital tokens are programmable and can be linked to so-called smart contracts.[1]

The history of digital-token transactions is recorded and documented in a system database. In the case of CBDC, the system including the database is provided and maintained by the central bank. It can be a blockchain or another transaction and storage system. The individual e-wallets have access to the database as far as own transactions are concerned. The system design can be centralised or multicentre. In any case, it has to preserve confidentiality, but must guarantee traceability if need be.

If the CBDC database is a blockchain, the system operates independently of banks or other financial actors. All the same, banks and PSP will use a respective CBDC system, either for doing proprietary business or, if applicable, in providing a service for customers, such as money exchange, borrowing CBDC from customers, extending CBDC loans to customers or execution of customer investments. If the system is more conventional and reserves-based without a blockchain, banks and PSP can be part of the system and act as payment intermediaries, albeit not transmitting bank money, but digital tokens of customers.

The current, still early stage in the development of digital money may soon be outdated in some respects. The digital tokenisation of money, though, is here to stay. There are already different types of tokens. For example, the cryptocurrency Bitcoin uses tokens of a fixed, non-divisible amount, comparable to a 100 euro note that cannot be turned into a 75 euro note. When payment is made, the token in question is deleted or marked as spent, and two new unspent tokens are created, one in the amount of 75 for the recipient and one in the remaining amount of 25

[1] OMFIF/IBM (2019, pp. 7, 26), Dt. Bundesbank (2020, 2021, p. 65).

for the payer.[2] This prevents double-spending, that is, the possibility of spending an amount twice with an identical coin copy.

Other cryptocoins, such as Ether and Ripple, can be suitably denominated. They use an account system for this purpose, through which inflows and outflows are settled real-time. While the Bitcoin type is called a token-based solution, Ether and Ripple are called account-based solutions. However, and if applied to CBDC, account-based does not refer to a conventional central-bank transaction account, i.e. not a book-money account, but a blockchain account containing CBDC, which is technically different from the conventional central-bank book money in the form of reserves.

Today's cryptocurrencies are blockchain systems. Such a system consists of the computer nodes of a distributed payment network that shares identical copies of the system database they maintain and synchronise. This database acts as a ledger or journal of the payment transactions taking place (distributed ledger technology DLT). A mutually verified or validated transaction is stored chronologically, representing final settlement in the resulting blockchain. Put differently, the distributed database representing an accounting journal exists in the form of a distributed blockchain.

The decisive elements of the distributed database are the protocols laid down in it. There are approaches, especially in the field of CBDC, that work without a blockchain. Technical efficiency and costs, legal aspects and policy preferences play a role in this question. It is not yet foreseeable which digital money and payment systems this will finally lead to.

One basic question concerns the difference between non-permissioned versus permissioned networks, that is, open public networks versus closed private networks. Non-permissioned/open is often associated with concepts such as decentralisation and anonymity. Access to a permissioned or closed system must be authorised. Such a system is more likely to be associated with aspects of centralisation or multi-centricity, controllability and non-anonymity, while still ensuring confidentiality.

Digital tokens are not only suitable for money and payments, but basically for any type of documentation, such as the management of deeds, cadastres, patents, technical standards, or schedules. Three types of tokens

[2] Zellweger-Gutknecht (2021, p. 34).

are already in use, (1) general-purpose means of payment, (2) special-purpose tokens that open access to the defined use of certain goods or services (utility tokens), as well as (3) financial security tokens that manage any kind of security on a blockchain.[3]

Different applications can also be linked to each other. In this way, it is possible to use digital tokens for programmable money and automated payment processes.[4] Programmable money includes the possibility to earmark money for certain user groups and purposes, with a fixed amount, a limited or variable quantity, in compliance with deadlines, etc. Earmarking money certainly has its limits. Tying money to specific purposes and deadlines can lead to an inflexible and inefficient use of funds, as is often the case with public budgets. For money to optimally fulfil its function as a means of payment, all revenues must be usable to pay for all kinds of expenditures.

The possibilities of programmable payments go far beyond the standing banker's orders that are possible today. A payment can be automatically linked to and triggered by the fulfilment of predefined conditions or events. Automated transactions can involve devices, machinery, vehicles, infrastructures, etc. (machine-to-machine in the internet of things, or paying per use). For example, it is possible to shop at the supermarket by going in, taking what you need and simply walking out again. The registration of items, their payment as well as the timely replenishment of supermarket stocks is automated according to interlinked algorithms. In principle, this is already possible with book money, but with digital money it will be much easier to implement.

Advantages cited in favour of digital money include easier and safer handling as well as faster transfer and lower costs than bank money and cash could previously offer. The one or other of these advantages is apparently true in certain cases, but not across the board.[5] As far as the speed of payments is concerned, banks and PSP have not missed out on some new developments. Real-time transfer of deposits within a currency area is now available. This can also be expected in cross-border transfers in a not too distant future. Ripple and other cryptocurrencies that have been used

[3] Howell et al. (2020).

[4] Slack (2022), Seidemann (2021), Dt. Bundesbank (2020), Dt. Bank (2020, parts II + III). OMFIF/IBM (2019, pp. 7, 26).

[5] Cf. Cunha et al. (2021, p. 4).

as a vehicle in cross-border transfers might lose the competitive advantage they have in this regard.

The stablecoin Libra/Diem, planned by Facebook in 2018/2019, was announced as being able to process 1,000 transactions per second (tps). Such indications, however, tend to vary considerably. About 4–7 tps are reported from Bitcoin, 15 tps from Ethereum (Ether's blockchain) until recently, but a great multiple of that as a result of Ethereum's switch from proof-of-work to proof-of-stake.[6] Transaction costs depending on transaction density can be expensive, at times considerably more expensive than bank transfers.

At 4–7 tps combined with high costs, Bitcoin-type cryptocurrencies are not competitive as a universal means of payment. Since 2016/2017, the Bitcoin community has split into different coins, or approaches to Bitcoin's further technical development, respectively. One contentious issue was Bitcoin's in-built quantity limit; more generally speaking the question of scalability, that is, possible increases in the number of tps or the quantity of coins that can potentially be generated. Apparently, this is only possible by sacrificing the absolute decentralisation and "distributedness" of the computer nodes and blockchain system involved. The *Lightning Network*, formed in this context, claims the proud possibility of instant payments "of millions to billions of transactions per second across the network".[7] However, this would include partial off-blockchain computation, which then is not that different from having payments managed by conventional computer systems of banks acting as trusted third parties in between payers and payees.

In comparison to Bitcoin and the older variety of Ethereum, traditional transfers of account balances are still competitive. PayPal averages 190–200 tps. Visa and MasterCard manage more, with 1,700–2,000 tps. In the euro area, based on the ECB's TARGET2/TIPS system, 6,000–10,000 traditional transactions take place every second.[8] The People's Bank of China reports a current capacity of 10,000 tps of its CBDC, the digital yuan. The digital yuan does not use a blockchain, but works with

[6] Ethereum.org/en/upgrades/merge. *The Economist*, 22 January 2022, 66; 1 January 2022, 55.

[7] Lightning.network.

[8] Kumar (2022), Mathew (2018), Tapscott and Tapscott (2016), Heasman (2019), van Hee and Wijngaard (2021, p. 54).

tokenised traditional central-bank balances. GNU Taler, a newly developed system which transfers digital tokens anonymously and without a blockchain, does 28,500 tps.[9]

The Bank for International Settlements and the central banks of Hong Kong, China, Thailand and the UAE have developed a blockchain for cross-border payments based on the Ethereum hyperledger Besu. Transfers are processed within seconds, not in days as is the case with bank transfers. Costs have been cut by half.[10] Speed is of immediate monetary relevance, because faster circulation of money has the same effect as an addition to the stock of money at constant use frequency.

With regard to the environment, cryptocurrencies are said to be excessively energy and CO_2 intensive.[11] How far this is true remains to be specified. If it is stated that Bitcoin at 205 TWh annually has an electricity demand like Thailand, and a carbon footprint like Kuwait, what is that supposed to say? Bitcoin is not a national endeavour. Annual electricity consumption worldwide is currently at 180,000 TWh. Bitcoin's electricity consumption is 0.11% of that. Is that a lot or a little?

A Chinese study from 2021 concluded that Bitcoin would become a "non-negligible obstacle" to achieving the country's climate goals by 2024.[12] At the time, 70% of the world's coin mining took place in China. Still, why only Bitcoin and not other industries? What is the energy consumption and carbon footprint of other financial and service sectors? Was the government looking for arguments to ban all Bitcoin trading in September 2021? Since then, Bitcoin mining has for the most part shifted to North America.[13]

Another comparison says Bitcoin produces just under a tenth of the greenhouse gas emissions of the banking sector each year.[14] How does one compare the size of Bitcoin with that of the banking sector? Perhaps by the number of transactions, if one knew. Presumably, the number of all bank transactions is currently still orders of magnitude higher than that of Bitcoin transactions. Seen that way, Bitcoin's "under 10%" look rather bad.

[9] Summer and Hermanky (2022), Chaum et al. (2021).

[10] *Bloomberg News*, 28 September 2021, *Reuters*, 28 September 2021.

[11] Reiff (2022).

[12] Guan and Wang (2021).

[13] Cuen (2021), Reiff (2022).

[14] Elmandjra (2021).

Cryptocurrency computing in North America and Iceland is now more often using climate-neutral hydropower, wind power and geothermal energy.[15] As long as Bitcoin and its ilk are mainly used as tokens in the financial casino or by the economic and political underground, costs and the environment may not be of much interest. But if a digital currency is to be usable as a regular and universal means of payment, cost efficiency is just as decisive as reasonably stable purchasing power.

The initial crypto community turned the principles of decentralisation and anonymity into an ultra-libertarian ideology. In a way, this looks like presenting telephony as a decentralised technology. Telecom corporations, however, operate gigantic networks. Phone calls are made inter-individually, but are organised multicentre and hierarchically. DLT/blockchain networks do not differ too much in this respect. In principle, all processes can be technically retraced. The computing capacity for validating Bitcoin transactions is dominated by a number of large nodes, the coin miners.

There seems to be a trade-off between centralisation, speed, less resource consumption and lower costs on the one hand, and decentralisation, less efficiency, higher resource consumption and higher costs on the other hand. The greater the number of transactions, the greater the pressure for efficiency which comes with a tendency towards bundling and centralisation. This considerably reduces the computing effort for verifying transactions, thereby also reducing costs as well as energy consumption and its carbon footprint. Future digital-token payment systems are thus likely to be multicentre rather than decentralised, with fewer but larger active computing nodes.

There are approaches promising to combine efficiency, anonymity and case-by-case verifiability, for example in a so-called dedicated computing cloud, that is, a network of individual e-wallets in which payments of anonymous amount take place without blockchain, whereby the digital tokens and the software of the system originate from the central bank, while the computer system may also be operated by the central bank or on behalf of it and under its control.[16] Other alternatives to blockchain technology include, for example, eCash software and GNU Taler software as smartphone apps using blind signatures which, furthermore, is supposed

[15] Cuen (2021), *The Economist,* 10 April 2021, p. 60.

[16] Such is the approach by van Hee and Wijngaard (2021).

to be highly secure.[17] Blockchain technology is the current state of the art, but by no means the one and only future of digital currencies.

In the end, decentralised finance might be less decentralised than imagined, just as a user ID might be less anonymous than envisaged. All electronic data transmissions leave a data trail that can be traced by authorised bodies. Blockchains are no exception. Just as in investigations of bank money transactions much depends on the willingness of banks and PSP to cooperate, so with cryptocurrencies it depends on the willingness of computer-node operators and trading platforms concerned and their place of jurisdiction.

As far as the safety of digital tokens and payments is concerned, one has to trust in the law of large numbers. There is no such thing as absolute safety. A small number of bank transfers go amiss. Banking IT infrastructures and crypto trading platforms have proven to be vulnerable to hacker attacks. Many billions of dollars have been stolen that way. In El Salvador, Bitcoin was declared legal tender in September 2021, but has found little acceptance following reports of irregularities.[18]

In reaction to problems concerning operating safety in banking with book money, ever more cumbersome security precautions have been implemented. This has spoiled the fun of online banking. Formerly, the work of account management used to be done by the banks. Online banking has led to the work being passed on to the customers. With digital money, this is the case right away.

The digitisation of money raises new questions or old questions anew, particularly governance issues related to financial privacy. Is the digitisation of money and finance compatible with freedom and privacy? Protection of data, user identity and confidentiality of payments are an important concern already under today's conditions of book money. Protective legislation in this respect will have to be developed even further in digital payment transactions than has been the case so far in IT-supported book-money transactions.

Big Brother is no longer a far-fetched dystopia, rather, in combination with some elements of *Brave New World*, a still stylised but basically possible scenario, especially in autocratic and repressive regimes. The general digitisation of the economy and society opens up possibilities

[17] See Chaum et al. (2021), Summer and Hermanky (2022).

[18] Brigida and Schwartz (2022).

of surveillance which secret services in previous dictatorships of fascist and communist parties could hardly have imagined. Non-intrusive social monitoring of individual behaviour in the public space and work space is technically feasible, including, as the case may be, the private sphere as well as private finances. Digitised social monitoring can be combined with a system of social credits, as already exists in China, rewarding conformist behaviour and sanctioning deviant behaviour. Rewards and penalties could be programmed, if applicable, into the use of digital wallets, for example by blocking the purchase of certain goods or the payable use of certain services and infrastructures.

It would surely be naïve to assume that possibilities of non-intrusive digital surveillance would not be applied under a rule of law based on civil rights and liberties. However, one should be able to assume that the use of such practices is legally restricted to well-defined exceptions to the rule of individual and private non-surveillance. Financial privacy will enjoy high priority under any liberal rule of law. One has to live up to the task, but cannot make respective problems go away. Modern society's dependence on telecommunications, computerisation and digitisation is just as problematic as its dependence on natural resources and sinks, electricity, long-distance transport, external supplies and much more. Such dependencies are part of the flip side of the benefits and advantages of ongoing modernisation. Finding a practicable and sustainable balance of interests remains a permanent challenge.

6.2 The Prospects of the Various Types of Money at a Glance

The taxonomy of money presented at the beginning of this book describes the initial situation in the current monetary turning point. With regard to new third-tier money surrogates as well as base money challengers, the situation is many-faceted. This is not untypical for structural changes in the evolution of complex systems, when a previous constellation is nearing its end, and a new constellation emerges from it. Nonetheless, the relevant lines of development and conflict in the upcoming competition between the various types of money, particularly digital money and book money, are fairly clear:

- CBDC and private digital money, be it unbacked cryptocurrencies or stablecoins, are vying to succeed bank money as the systemically dominant type of money.
- CBDC has the best prospects of emerging from the competition as the new dominant type of money, more precisely, CBDC from stable nation-states, especially if they also play a certain role in financial and economic terms, also including communities of nation-states such as the EU and the European Currency Union. Tokenised CBDC can technically do everything that private digital tokens can do. But compared to private currencies, CBDC of respective countries is the more secure money in terms of stock-safety, validity and value. Respective currencies are held as international reserve currencies. Last but not least, sovereign national currencies are backed by the full faith and credit of the nation-states concerned—which is certainly a relative factor, but likely to be decisive in competition with domestic private means of payment.
- Besides CBDC, private cryptocurrencies appear to have further development potential. However, because of their being uncovered and unwarranted they will hardly find general acceptance as a regular all-purpose means of payment. This will be particularly noticeable in difficult times of increased uncertainty. The same applies to quantity-limited Bitcoins. How much further their function as a near-money forex-like investment vehicle will extend remains to be seen.
- Stablecoins seem to have better prospects than unbacked cryptocurrencies, provided they are based on reasonably reliable 1:1 cover in money and cash equivalents. If a significant part of the cover consists of CBDC and other base money in the official home currency, stablecoins can also expect more good will from the authorities.
- Bank money competes against both CBDC and private digital monies to assert its previous position. Bank money is dominant today and will persist for a longer period of time, albeit gradually declining in importance to the extent that technical and cost advantages of CBDC and possibly also stablecoins and other cryptos will be experienced.
- Central-bank reserves will over time be going down together with bank money, or be replaced with CBDC early on.
- Solid cash does not play a systemically decisive role anymore and will sooner or later fall into disuse.

The following sections explore these perspectives in detail.

6.3 CBDC Begins Its Ascent

Provided the analysis of monetary turning points is basically right, it is in the logic of current developments that CBDC is rising to become the new systemically dominant type of money. There is the typical situation of the incumbent dominant money causing serious problems that cannot be overcome within the given framework, while at the same time promising alternatives are emerging. The situation is comparable to that of the eighteenth and nineteenth centuries, when private banknotes and treasury-issued paper money in Europe became dysfunctional and were replaced by the regulated note monopoly of central banks. In a similar way, albeit at a more complex stage of development, today's task is to rein in bank money and new money surrogates as well as financial practices based on them through a new type of sovereign money. A technical aspect of this is the replacement of previous book money by digital money. Another aspect concerns a corresponding institutional rearrangement in the relationship between banks, shadow banks and central banks. So the future of money can be expected to be digital *and* sovereign.

In the process, central banks are becoming what they had already become to a certain extent before the bank money regime has blocked the way since the middle of the twentieth century: the authority that wields a state's monetary sovereignty, the monetary power in analogy to the powers of legislature, executive and judiciary. It may still be called central bank, understood as a nation's or community of nations' monetary authority, no longer only as *bank of the banks*, but also *bank of the state*, providing the monetary endowment for the entire economy, financial and real-economic, private and public, while *not being*, however, a *financing* institution in a general fiscal, creditary and capital-market function. These aspects will be discussed in more detail in the concluding chapter on the role of central banks and monetary policy.

The brief foreshadowing of the changing role of central banks opens up the horizon against which the upcoming monetary turning point is taking place. It is about regaining a state's monetary sovereignty as a prerogative of constitutional importance, as outlined in the chapter on monetary sovereignty and the para-state status of private bank money.

Were the change not to go in the direction of defending and reinvigorating the sovereign monetary prerogatives, monetary policy in today's sense would soon no longer exist. In the current bank money regime, there may still be talk of having a *national currency* (unit of account), while *monetary* sovereignty has long since been ceded to the banking sector. It is certainly welcome that the emergence of private cryptocurrencies has created a new awareness among central bankers, politicians and the public of the importance of monetary sovereignty. However, it does not yet seem to have fully filtered through that national currency-unit sovereignty without a dominant base of sovereign money is an empty shell. It is not a balanced view of things when Facebook's Libra plan for a supranational private stablecoin was rightly seen as a threat to monetary sovereignty while the realities of conventional bank money are ignored.

To be able to fulfil their tasks as guardians of the currency, central banks *must* regain effective monetary control. They can do so by way of interest-rate policy or quantity policy *if and as far* there is a sufficiently large quantity lever of central-bank money in the public circuit (beyond the interbank circulation of reserves). How large that quantity lever must be in order to be effectual has apparently not yet been investigated. The experience with the decline of cash prima facie suggests that the leverage must amount to about half of the money in public circulation, rather more.

At any rate, the more central-bank money of safe stock expands its share, the smaller becomes the share of inherently insecure, crisis-prone bank money and the new third-tier money surrogates based on bank money. As a result, central-bank money becomes the actual primary money base again, and monetary policy wins back an effective transmission lever and thus more control over money creation and a flexible readjustment of the total stock of money.

A first research group on digital central-bank money was set up by the People's Bank of China in 2014. In 2015, D. Andolfatto, then Vice President of the Federal Reserve of St. Louis, went public with the proposal of a "Fedcoin", a government cryptocurrency, "Fedwire for everyone" as it were.[19] Starting in 2016, other central banks began to address the potentials of CBDC, notably those of Sweden (e-Krona) and England.[20] As an international central-banking institution, the Basel Bank for International Settlements championed CBDC in the years that followed.[21]

[19] Andolfatto (2015), Koning (2014).

[20] Danezis and Meiklejohn (2016), Zitter (2016), Broadbent (2016), Barrdear and Kumhof (2016, pp. 3–18), Sveriges Riksbank (2017, 2018a, 2018b).

[21] BIS (2015, 2018, 2019, 2020, 2021), Bech and Garratt (2017), Boar et al. (2020).

Preceding the official forays into CBDC, authors from the international monetary reform movement had developed concepts of sovereign money reform, which would replace bank money with central-bank money.[22] In this context, a special approach aimed at "safe accounts", meaning direct or indirect access to a central-bank transaction account for non-banks.[23] L. Kotlikoff proposed limited-purpose banking, a special variety of narrow banking. All payments should be made via fully covered cash mutual funds, separate from all other types of funds.[24] Beyond that, approaches to 100% reserve banking from the 1930s also experienced a certain revival.[25]

In the run-up to a referendum on introducing a sovereign money system in Switzerland that began in 2011, D. Niepelt, Director of the Swiss National Bank's Study Centre, spoke against ending the bank money privilege, but in favour of introducing central-bank money into the public circuit, that is, "central-bank reserves for everyone" as it was put it in the categories of the bank money regime.[26] This was then followed by the aforementioned central-bank concepts for CBDC, to be implemented in coexistence and competition with the continued existence of bank money. The CBDC approach now dominates the entire monetary reform discourse.[27]

Nonetheless, central banks remained somewhat divided on CBDC, and the matter was moving hesitantly. In old-industrial countries, there is a well-developed banking and payment infrastructure. Almost all households have a bank account. Especially since the introduction of central-bank RTGS payment systems with interbank reserve transfer in the 1990s,

[22] Huber and Robertson (2000), AMI (2010), AfJM (2021), Yamaguchi (2014), Kotlikoff (2010), Positive Money (2011), Benes and Kumhof (2012), Jackson and Dyson (2013), Sigurjonsson (2015), Of late Omarova (2021). The organisations affiliated to the International Movement for Monetary Reform have developed their own varieties of sovereign money reform, some of which are country-specific. Cf. internationalmoneyreform.org/members.

[23] Mayer (2013), Andresen (2014, 2019), Wortmann (2019).

[24] Kotlikoff (2010, pp. 123).

[25] Gomez (2010), building on Allais (1988), Phillips (1995), Kay (2009, 2015).

[26] Niepelt (2015), Schemmann (2012), Andresen (2014, 2019).

[27] Dyson and Hodgson (2016), Bech and Garratt (2017), Kumhof and Noone (2018, pp. 4–22, 35–37), Ingves (2018), Dyson and Meaning (2018), Meaning et al. (2018), IMF (2018), Mayer (2019), Niepelt (2018, 2021a). Among the more academic supporters are Bordo and Levin (2017, 2019), Bordo (2018), Eichengreen (2017), Prasad (2021).

one tends to think to have achieved a secure system of reliable final settlement. This is the reason for some to think there is no need for CBDC. RTGS systems were certainly a step forward in the conventional two-tier book-money system of banks and central banks. But it doesn't concern the fundamental question of where and how the money in the system comes from, who puts how much of what type of money into circulation, when and for what purpose, or withdraws money from circulation.

It was not until about 2020 that plans for CBDC made a general breakthrough. About 130 133 central banks of the 190 IMF member states have now jumped on the bandwagon. It is no longer a question of whether there will be CBDC, just how and when.[28] Two events have been instrumental in getting the train rolling. One was Facebook's 2019 plan for the international Libra stablecoin. All of a sudden, politicians and experts of all stripes saw monetary sovereignty under threat. The second reason was the decision of the People's Bank of China to start the roll-out of the digital yuan (e-CNY) in 23 cities, including large metropolitan areas, on the occasion of the 2022 Winter Olympics.

It is noteworthy that up to then the US Federal Reserve was rather defensive and reluctant to take a stand on CBDC.[29] However, in March 2022, President Biden issued an executive order placing the "highest urgency" on researching and developing a digital dollar.[30] US Treasury Secretary J. Yellen, former Fed Chairwoman, once more stressed the need for a digital dollar, not least in view of the wave of cryptocurrencies.[31] To J. Powell, then Fed Chairman in his second term, a digital dollar is "something we really need to explore. ... One question around CBDCs is do we want a private stablecoin to wind up being the digital dollar? I think the answer is no. ... If we're going to have a digital dollar, it should be government-guaranteed money, not private money".[32] In contrast to

[28] Cf. Cunha et al. (2021, p. 8), PwC Switzerland (2021), Smith (2021), Federal Reserve of the U.S. (2022), Dt. Bank (2020), Dt. Bundesbank (2020, 2021), Boar et al. (2020), BIS (2020), Bank of England (2020), OMFIF/IBM (2019), OMFIF (2020), ECB (2020b).

[29] Smialek (2021).

[30] www.washingtonpost.com/opinions/2022/03/13/us-should-not-rush-into-digital-dollar, by the Editorial Board, as of 19 October 2022.

[31] Braun (2022a).

[32] Braun (2022b). It may be noted here that the Federal Reserve's Board of Governors and the Federal Open Market Committee are under U.S. law and in this sense part of

Yellen and Powell, Chr. Waller, as a member of the Fed's Board of Governors, was reported to have said in a speech that a digital dollar brings no advantages over the current dollar system, and, as the report was titled, that CBDC isn't necessary for dollar supremacy.[33]

In these statements, three fault lines become clear—first, the challenge of private digital currencies to the current bank money regime, including the role of central banks in it; second, the looming conflict of interests between the future role of sovereign digital currency (or central banks, respectively) and the previous dominance of bank book money (or the banking sector, respectively); and third, the question of whether a global transition to CBDCs will support or weaken US dollar supremacy.

The latter question apparently also moves the Chinese government. It is obvious that one reason behind the early roll-out of the digital yuan is China's claim to global power status. Cryptocurrencies can facilitate cross-border payments past the established structures for international transfers of bank money and central-bank reserves. These are related to the SWIFT system, dominated by the US dollar, and used by the US government and also European governments and the EU to implement sanctions. China is certainly looking for an alternative of its own making, and the digital yuan is fundamental in any such perspective. A Chinese suggestion by official political consultants to create a pan-Asian CBDC stablecoin based on a basket of national Asian currencies fits into this context.[34]

Another reason for going ahead with a Chinese CBDC was the domestic expansion of Bitcoin mining as well as private PSP and their e-money (Alibaba Group's Alipay with 711 million users, and Tencent's WeChat Pay with 900 million users). The Chinese government and the People's Bank of China had to counter this with a sovereign digital currency and a related payment system in order to keep control. For the same reason, trading in cryptocurrencies was banned altogether in China in September 2021.

the U.S. government, whereas the 12 regional Reserve banks are private corporations of the American banking sector. Such being the case, a CBDC issued and guaranteed by the government is to be understood as a digital 'Fedcoin', not a digital 'Treasury coin', as it could also be understood and which would fit well into the American tradition of colonial bills, continental dollars, greenbacks and greybacks as well as U.S. Treasury notes.

[33] Cf. www.reuters.com/business/finance/us-central-bank-digital-currency-isnt-necessary-dollar-supremacy-feds-waller-2022-10-14. Smialek (2021).

[34] Reynolds and Rubin (2022), Caudevilla (2021).

At the beginning of the 2022 Winter Games, 261 million Chinese had a digital yuan payment app installed on their mobile phones. About 5.6 million merchants accept the digital yuan. The related transfer system is called Digital Currency Electronic Payment system (DCEP). The phone number serves as the user ID.[35] As the roll-out is still in its beginnings, the number and volume of transactions in digital yuan represent a relatively small market share, in the billions rather than trillions.[36] This is likely to change as ever more potential users learn about the new type of money and ever more major companies feel incentivised or coerced to accept and use digital yuans.

China's digital yuan was preceded by the Bahamas' Sand Dollar in 2020, the Eastern Caribbean's DCash, Bakong in Cambodia and eNaira in Nigeria in 2021. India has announced plans to introduce a blockchain-based digital rupee soon.[37] Ukraine as well as Russia (before Russia's invasion of Ukraine), also Uruguay, South Korea and a few more countries have progressed in the development of CBDC for general public use.[38] In contrast to such retail CBDC, there are interbank or wholesale CBDCs, on a pilot basis limited to the use of banks. The focus is on testing interoperability with existing payment systems and linking with retail CBDC, including across borders. Thailand, Hong Kong, Singapore, Canada, Switzerland, France/EU, South Africa and the UAE are reported to be most advanced in this respect.[39] It took China eight years to go through all R&D stages until the official launch of the digital yuan. Even the more advanced among the other central banks are likely to be ready only after the mid-2020s.

[35] Nicolle (2021), Liao (2022), Kumar (2022).

[36] Frisbie (2022). Reuters.com/markets/currencies/China's digital currency passes 100 bln yuan in spending, October 13, 2022. China-briefing.com/news/china-launches-digital-yuan-app, 22 September 2022.

[37] Cryptopolitan.com, report by Mohammad Shahid, 1 May 2022. How digital rupee will be different from cryptocurrency, *Mint*, 15 February 2022.

[38] PwC Switzerland (2021), McKinsey Global Institute (2021). https://cbdctracker.org.

[39] PwC Switzerland (2021), Niepelt (ed.) (2021, part II on country-specific projects).

6.4 The Age of Bank Money Has Passed Its Peak

According to their stated intention, central banks do not want to replace bank money with CBDC, but to introduce CBDC in parallel to bank money, in coexistence ***and*** in competition with each other, as a few earlier pronouncements made explicit. In this sense, one has opted for a partial sovereign money reform, that is, a mixed system of sovereign money and private means of payment. Full sovereign money reform with an end to the bank money privilege seemed too radical, even in view of the governability problems of an overly complex money supply consisting of cash, central-bank reserves, CBDC, bank money and various new money surrogates, including stablecoins and unbacked cryptocurrencies.

The banking organisations are certainly not enthusiastic about the situation, but see their interests preserved by the continuation of the bank money privilege. They have taken a cautiously positive position on CBDC. Only a few voices from the banking milieu do not expect peaceful coexistence between CBDC and bank money, rather a process of crowding out in which bank money is going to lose out over time in the competition with CBDC. To the extent that CBDC spreads and expands its share in the money supply, this in itself implies a loss of market share for para-sovereign bank money and other private means of payment. In fact, the long-term outlook for bank money is not favourable.

In the near term, bank money is still in a strong defensive position. There are considerable economies of scale and network effects in its favour. Institutional inertia is always strong at first in a process of change, and old habits—behaviours, routines, paradigms and attitudes—die hard anyway. New learning curves do not normally take off like rockets. Wide breakthroughs are normally made at a later stage. Yet even if this is the case and digital money and CBDC is still a rare experience for most firms and people, general digitisation has long since taken hold, and digital money is no longer just latent but emergent and already implemented in significant beginnings.

One special element in favour of bank money is seen in the fact that CBDC is conceived of by most current plans to be not interest-bearing. By contrast, bank money under normal interest-rate conditions can yield deposit interest. If, furthermore, central-bank support and government guaranties for bank money were maintained, bank money would appear to be in a good position. However, if banks still pay deposit interest (to retain customers), it will cost them extra, in addition to the efficiency and cost disadvantages of bank money compared to advanced digital tokens.

Another advantage banks can hope for is to offer credit cheaper than shadow-bank competitors, thanks to the refinancing advantages banks enjoy (only fractional reserve requirements or none at all). That could have something going for it, especially in combination with calculating a somewhat lower banking profit from the lending business. However, in view of the recent strong growth in lending by non-bank financial institutions, the banks' scope of being able to offer credit more cheaply than the competition should not be overestimated.

CBDC is often presented as a digital version of cash. That's correct as far as the comparison with cash goes, but the entire potential of CBDC goes far beyond. CBDC can do much more than cash, and also more than bank book money, for example, direct peer-to-peer transmission without payment intermediaries (which entail costs that are eliminated by using digital tokens), payment from everywhere to anywhere at any time, even across borders, simpler and faster handling, therefore lower user fees to be expected, not least programmability. The latter may not be important at the moment, but will become all the more important in the future, particularly in the internet of things. From all these aspects, bank money will hardly be able to compete with CBDC.

Bank money, as a bank account balance in the two-tier banking system, cannot be upgraded so much as to emulate the advantages of digital tokens. Digitisation has already technically replaced book money in the sense of handwritten or typewritten entries in paper books. Today, banks operate with comprehensive IT infrastructures, even downright *as* such. But this does not include the above characteristics of digital money; at least not as long as bank money is deposit money which is transferred by way of clearing or a parallel transfer of central-bank reserves. In a monetary system that is increasingly based on digital tokens, bank money and the banks in their role as trusted third parties, as creators and deleters of bank money, and as payment intermediaries of that bank money, are gradually becoming redundant. Furthermore, in an environment of heightened economic uncertainty, the demand for money will tend to turn towards safe-stock CBDC, like towards solid cash so far, turning away to that extent from bank money. The existence of bank money in a future of CBDC and also stablecoins will thus depend mainly on how far central bank and government are still willing to guarantee bank money.

On the other hand, the public remains to a certain extent dependent on banks for getting investments funded and obtaining consumer loans and overdraft. As a condition of lending, banks can require, as is often the case today, that borrowers maintain a current bank account with them. In this way, banks can still take advantage of the bank money privilege.

Shadow banks, as competitors of the banks, will not care too much. Presently, shadow banks have not much alternatives to operating on bank money. In the future, they will have the choice between bank money and CBDC as well as stablecoins. This in turn will again put pressure on banks to issue credit not only in bank money but also in CBDC. Alternatives to bank credit are already in place in the form of new money surrogates, stablecoins and other cryptocurrencies, as well as shadow bank loans. Bank lending to non-banks no longer is a unique selling proposition. The proliferation of CBDC will further intensify this development. The demand for the various types of money will no longer be largely predetermined by the banks' supply of bank money, and be increasingly decided by customer demand.

For the banks, the shadow banks are something like the viper they have nurtured in their bosom. Shadow banks now finance almost as much as the banks, including mortgage lending. The total amount of financial assets held by shadow banks is larger than those of the banks.[40] In a way, this means that shadow banks have now taken half of the lending business and of other financial market transactions from the banks. In addition, regarding payments, there is competition from PSP and fintechs. Their market share continues to grow.

For the various financial institutions beyond traditional banking (shadow banks, PSP, fintechs, insurance companies), there is no fundamental business compulsion to work with one particular type of money. Ultimately, the choice between different types of money depends on comparative advantages in terms of business-enhancement, convenience, efficiency, reliability, safety and costs. From these points of view, non-bank financial institutions will make their choice between bank money, CBDC, stablecoins and other cryptocurrencies in the same way as all other companies and private households—in the longer term increasingly to the detriment of bank money. Bank money developed through the crisis-prone practice of fractional reserve banking, exists through it and is

[40] Financial Stability Board (2020).

likely to go down with it to the extent it has to compete with CBDC as a safe-stock sovereign bearer instrument. The history of MMF shares in the last 30–40 years, often used in financial transactions instead of bank money, could provide a foretaste of what is to come.

Lest anyone misunderstand, the rise of CBDC portends a long-term decline in bank money, not however the end of banking. Banks as well as shadow banks perform many useful and partly indispensable functions in managing money, currencies and payments, lending, investment banking, and financial asset management. Banks, too, like shadow banks, can perform all these functions technically just as well with CBDC as they do with creating bank money on only a fractional base of reserves. After all, prior to the bank money regime, banks had no technical difficulties in operating on a dominant base of central-bank notes.

The difference today, to be sure, is in advantages for the money users, in enhanced monetary policy, and more stability overall, including macro-sectoral changes regarding monetary and intermediary credit, GDP finance and non-GDP finance, and better balanced macro-sectoral economies beyond. For the banks, a shift in perspective is unfolding: from being privileged and system-defining money creators to becoming monetary service providers and financial intermediaries like other financial institutions.

It might seem obvious for banks to issue digital tokens of their own. However, unbacked or insufficiently covered tokens would be out of the question. Uncovered bank tokens, after all, would be nothing more than a relapse into the times of insufficiently backed paper money in the seventeenth and eighteenth centuries, using digital tokens in lieu of paper notes. Bank tokens without bonding to central-bank money and without smooth interbank cooperation would be individual solitaires. They would pose the same acceptance problems as the then banknotes of individual banks not guaranteed by a third party. Bank tokens would face problems to maintain 1:1 parity with the official currency.[41] They might then have a floating exchange rate, as is the case today with national currencies or with cryptocurrencies. In view of this, central banks and supervisory authorities are unlikely to tolerate digital tokens from banks that are eligible for central-bank refinancing and whose book money enjoys government warranty.

[41] Cf. Bjerg (2018).

If, instead, central banks were to require cover for digital bank tokens, what form should this take? Should it be in central-bank reserves or in cash equivalents? Should it be full 100% cover or only fractional cover? A fractional reserve would be as inappropriate for digital bank tokens as it has always been for bank money. Apart from that, a reserve for tokens is functionally different from a reserve for bank deposit money. Bank tokens would not circulate through the central-bank RTGS payment system, nor by way of interbank clearing.

Incidentally, today's minimum reserves, if they still exist at all, are largely unavailable und only marginally usable as liquidity reserves. They were once intended as a control instrument to either curb or facilitate the banks' creation of deposits (bank money). But it never satisfyingly worked that way. One reason is that the minimum reserve requirement has to be fulfilled by the banks in their function as recipients of external customer payments, not by those banks whose credit creation issued the bank money in the first place.

As far as digital bank tokens are concerned, a reserve in CBDC to be held by the issuing bank could basically indeed serve as a safety cushion, provided the reserve is close to 100%. The digital bank tokens would thus be stablecoins. Otherwise, there can easily be a bank run with a crash of the tokens' value and the collapse of the issuing bank. The reserve would indeed have to consist of CBDC rather central-bank reserves, because non-banks cannot obtain such reserves. An involuntary redemption of the tokens in bank money would certainly not be acceptable, as this would again be similar to the situation with private banknotes of the eighteenth and nineteenth centuries.

Stablecoins based on a 100% CBDC reserve do double the money supply, but the quantity of CBDC reserves in question is deactivated. Macroeconomically this does not make a difference. For the issuer, however, this is somewhat pointless. Even if the central bank were to pay a small deposit interest on CBDC held as coverage—which is rightly not envisaged—the banks' profit from issuing a digital coin would remain only moderately lucrative. With a fallow cover reserve, the issuers would have to charge user fees, possibly as expensive as with bank money. Or the issuers could engage in profitable data mining which, however, conflicts with data protection requirements.

The matter would be even more problematic if the cover of a bank stablecoin consisted of cash equivalents and other securities, with only a smaller share of CBDC. For the banks concerned, of course, this could be profitable. Securities normally yield interest and may gain in value. For any issuer of money surrogates, the interesting point is using the cover funds for doing proprietary business by lending and investing the funds short-term and even long-term. The higher the coverage in cash equivalents and other tradable assets, the greater the prospect of earnings, but possibly also losses. Which is to say, the more a bank stablecoin, like any stablecoin, is covered by securities, the more risky and crisis-prone such a stablecoin is.

A syndicate of major banking corporations might be in a position—assuming the central bank's acquiescence—to launch a stablecoin in its own currency, scalable and possibly also programmable. Nonetheless, these would be stablecoins like those of any other issuers, without refinancing privilege and without support from central bank and government. Such a syndicate would no longer be a monetary banking institution in the sense of today's fractional reserve banking. It would be a large financial institution with a 1:1 reserve requirement in whatever composition.

Considering today's bank money privilege, issuing digital tokens is not really an interesting option for banks, unless the cover share of interest-bearing securities were high and deposit interest was paid on CBDC reserves. But the full financing of the cover of digital bank tokens alone would contribute to ending the current banking business model, which is based on fractional refinancing. Basically, it does not make much sense to exchange one type of bank liability for another with comparable risk. This is all the more true since cover assets may not be sufficiently stable in value, and the banks cannot assume their bank tokens to enjoy the same support and guarantee from central bank and government as bank money has enjoyed up to now.

The banks are in a quandary here. When they operate on new types of money—CBDC, MMF shares, stablecoins or other cryptocoins—they feed the competition to their bank money. Sooner or later, banks might come to the conclusion that it is better to put the role of bank money into perspective and part from it instead of going down with it. It is an indication of this when American banking corporations such as JPMorgan, Wells Fargo, Morgan Stanley and others start to include cryptos in their business, for example by accepting crypto payments by their customers. The banks are cooperating with US providers of e-wallets and crypto trading platforms. Customers can link their credit and debit cards to their e-wallets and pre-set their preferred means of payment. During transactions, cryptos are automatically exchanged for dollars or, conversely, dollars are exchanged for the respective cryptocurrency. Some banks also launch crypto funds, and some banks give a small reward in cryptocoins for using their credit or debit card. The banks do not issue the cryptocoins, but accept and trade them. The banking corporations are thus reacting to deposit and investment outflows from customers who are shifting some part of their bank money into crypto investments.[42]

6.5 What Will Be of Central-Bank Reserves?

Will CBDC make central-bank reserves redundant or will both continue to exist side by side? In the current system, central-bank reserves serve as the monetary base of bank money, in that cashless interbank payments are made in reserves. Since bank money is to exist in parallel with CBDC, the function of central-bank reserves remains as long as bank money remains.

Initially, and in some cases still today, CBDC were not necessarily thought of as digital tokens, but often as reserves for everyone, implying access to a central-bank account for everyone. The Swedish CBDC approach originally left open whether the e-krona should be reserves or digital tokens. It was soon heard from other quarters that it was not technically possible to expand the existing RTGS payment systems for general public use. This may have been an excuse, even though expanding central-bank payment systems for public retail payments would certainly entail additional costs.

Besides, it became clear that central banks don't consider managing accounts for everyone, even if the public were only given indirect access to CBDC through banks running CBDC omnibus accounts at the central bank for their customers. In the meantime, in most cases the die has been cast in favour of tokenisation of CBDC. Digital tokens, however, are transferred directly from one e-wallet to another. A central-bank transaction bank account is not needed for this, and accordingly no more reserves for the transfer of bank money in interbank transactions.

At the same time, it is possible to transfer CBDC back and forth in interbank transactions instead of transferring central-bank deposits back

[42] Birch (2022), Umar (2021).

and forth as before. In fact, CBDC can both fulfil the previous function of central-bank reserves in interbank transactions *and* serve as a universal means of payment in the public circuit. From this point of view, account-based reserves could basically be abolished upon the introduction of CBDC.

One probably won't want doing that for the time being because of well-rehearsed procedural routines, and also because of not-yet-existing broad-based CBDC transaction routines. So the existing central-bank reserves will continue to exist separate from CBDC for an indefinite period. If, however, for the sake of interoperability of old and new types of money, central banks will convert reserves and CBDC into each other according to bank demand, it can be assumed that reserves do not remain in use for as long as bank money.

6.6 Cash—On Its Way to the Money Museum

For over two thousand years, coins were the only form of money, except for medieval tally sticks of limited use. Paper money has existed for almost four hundred years, first as private banknotes and princely treasury bills, then for nearly two hundred years as central-bank notes, sometimes also as treasury notes as in the U.S. The state-run mints and the central banks take care to make the coins and notes aesthetically pleasing and the notes as counterfeit-proof as possible.

Although cash is being used decreasingly, many people feel attached to cash, so much that indignant "save the cash" campaigns have come up in many places. Politicians and central bankers hasten to affirm they are in no way thinking of abolishing cash. Nevertheless, the gradual disappearance of cash without making a modern equivalent like CBDC available has led, strictly speaking, to an unlawful state of affairs. For one thing, cash is legal tender, but ever more actors, including state bodies, even the tax office, refuse to be paid in cash. For another thing, the laws require account balances to be withdrawable in cash, completely and without unreasonable effort. Today, however, this is only possible to a very limited extent. Cash withdrawals beyond what is usual are definitely impossible, banks have made larger withdrawals cumbersome, and in many countries there are caps on withdrawable amounts of cash.

Some activists demanded, even in court, to be able to pay their taxes or public broadcasting fees in cash. This was meant as a political campaign to raise awareness of the fact that public bodies refuse to accept legal tender and instead demand payment in private bank money, and that when there is no more cash, bank money will have the monopoly in the public circuit—basically a highly relevant message, but cash on its way to the money museum is apparently an unsuitable vehicle for it. Not many really cared.

The demand to preserve cash is rationalised by the fear of Big Brother. Cash is seen the only remaining haven of financial privacy and freedom. This is grossly exaggerated, especially in view of already existing restrictions on the use of cash. That aside, today all cash is withdrawn from a bank account, a process that leaves its electronic trace, and what the money is spent on must be declared to the tax office to a considerable extent by both payers and payees.

Beyond rationalisations, cash apparently touches sensation and emotional attachment, even if increasingly nostalgic in nature. Whenever Europe has been about replacing the national currency with the euro, it became clear that national identity was also at stake. Whether consciously or not, for very many people cash, haptically and visually, is part of their national and thus also personal identity, similar to the passport. One's bank account may be reassuring or worrisome, but a bank statement is certainly not part of national identity; the national currency, however, is.[43]

The decline in cash payments may also be due to the fact that central banks stop issuing large banknotes. The largest denomination of US Federal Reserve notes is 100 dollars since 1969. The ECB decided to stop issuing 500 euro notes in 2016. Payments above a threshold of a few thousands must be made cashless. These measures are intended to counter financing of terrorism, money laundering and undeclared work. How effective this is remains unclear. Illicit payments, especially when larger amounts change hands, are now increasingly made in the form of cryptos instead of handing over briefcases stuffed with banknotes, as portrayed in older mobster films.

For most companies, administrative bodies as well as private households, the rejection of cash payment has obvious practical reasons. Carrying a lot of cash around is unsafe, and cash payment—even if just locally—can be inconvenient, time-consuming and expensive for all

[43] In the EU, nationalist and populist forces like to instrumentalise the euro as an "external" scapegoat. Nevertheless, 70% of the national populations concerned now identify with the euro (according to Flash-Eurobarometer No. 429, 12–14 October 2021).

parties involved. For tax offices and other public agencies, payroll and pension offices, utilities, telecom companies, broadcasters, mail order companies, etc., cash payment is simply not a viable option. At the same time, it is people themselves who increasingly prefer non-cash payment by card or online banking to cash payment.[44]

Digitisation will sooner or later put an end to the remaining cash, not necessarily everywhere in the coming years, but over time it will disappear in the course of changing payment behaviour and corresponding changes in the demand for the various types of money. If the maintenance of the necessary cash infrastructure, including ATMs, becomes a subsidy business for ever more banks and businesses, the circulation of cash will come to an end anyway.[45]

However—and this is probably not entirely clear to either the aforementioned instances or many cash activists—with the gradual disappearance of cash, bank money has de facto been given a sole-reign position in the public money circuit, with far-reaching implications for the (in-)effectiveness of monetary policy and the (in-)stability of the financial economy. It is indeed high time to launch CBDC as a modern sovereign means of payment in succession to traditional cash.

6.7 The Outlook for Unbacked Cryptocurrencies

6.7.1 *Essentially an Empty Promise*

Except for stablecoins, cryptocurrencies are unbacked. Some part of the latter cannot be created by discretion, but, like Bitcoin, only by way of a computational process called mining. Nevertheless, these cryptocoins are uncovered and unwarranted, meaning that there are no other funds or assets behind them, and no government or private entity vouches for them. Their value stands or falls on the extent and steadiness of demand for them, similar to the value of works of art or other collectibles.

How much and for how long cryptos are worth something, depends primarily on their standing and goodwill, and also the critical mass of those who use a cryptocurrency. If several large corporations accept a coin as a means of payment and thousands of firms and tens of thousands of people want to pay with it, then the coin in question certainly serves as a

[44] ECB (2020a, 2020b).

[45] Cf. Prasad (2021).

means of payment. However, the price of cryptocurrencies, and thus their purchasing power, has so far been more volatile than stable, and there is no indication that the crypto market will soon enter more stable waters.

Beyond currency speculation and the underground economy, why use an unbacked coin when there are less unreliable stablecoins and even reliable CBDC as alternatives? Seen from this angle, one would not expect unbacked digital tokens to stand a chance of becoming regular money of wide use in the presence of private stablecoins and sovereign CBDC.

Accordingly, it would be idle to think about potential problems of a mass exodus from official money into unbacked cryptocurrencies. If that kind of currency substitution had to be seriously considered, it would be a problem, because it would be another big step towards the loss of monetary sovereignty and the irrelevance of monetary policy.[46] In actual fact, however, there is no reason to fear large-scale currency substitution of that kind. In weak-currency countries, however, the situation is different, and there have indeed been recurrent problems of currency substitution, more often referred to as capital flight, whether as a flight into other national currencies or now also into cryptocurrencies.

Basically, all private means of payment that cannot rely on central-bank support and government guarantee have difficulties in finding general acceptance among a broad public and in developing into a universal means of payment. This is illustrated by many examples from the monetarily bumpy periods of coin deterioration and unregulated paper money. That was only brought to an end by the introduction of nationally standardised central-bank notes as legal tender. This time, the analogous solution is to introduce standardised CBDC. This is also supported by the fact that currencies get into crises sooner or later, whether self-made or caused by some general crisis environment. Private means of payment without government warranty are unlikely to survive severe crises.

6.7.2 *Bitcoin and Ether*

The situation of uncovered cryptocurrencies seems to be different for two of them, namely Bitcoin with 640 billion US dollar market value

[46] Adrian and Mancini-Griffoli (2021, p. 76).

and Ether with 280 billion. All other coins are at most in a low double-digit and single-digit billion range.[47] The peculiarity of Bitcoin is that its mysterious developer by the pseudonym of Nakamoto has designed the mining algorithm in such a way that the computation of new coins becomes ever more laborious, approaching a definite cap at 21 million Bitcoins. Over 90% of that limit has already been generated.

The quantitative delimitation of Bitcoins has led to their being compared or even equated with gold. Such an equation is nonsense. The reason is that gold in fact has a residual monetary back-up function and is also a valuable commodity. Gold has real-use value in many industrial and craft applications. Bitcoin has nothing of the sort.

The improper comparison with gold has also led to the assumption that Bitcoin might protect against inflation.[48] It is debatable to what extent gold fulfils this function. The assumption is based on the classical theory according to which the value of money, like that of any other good, depends on its scarcity. But who cares about the scarcity of uncovered Bitcoins not backed by assets nor by important guarantors and devoid of real-economic use value? This is indeed like art. The value of works of art is maintained as long as the number of buyers is large and solvent enough. This can quickly change if there are uncertainties or even a crisis. But compared to the volatility of cryptos so far, the art market is a model of stability.

Basically like any currency, Bitcoin can protect against inflation perhaps indirectly, by getting out of a depreciating currency to get into Bitcoin, assuming Bitcoin were stable or rising in a given case. This turns the matter into another aspect of currency competition and currency speculation, which is already happening to a considerable extent between different cryptocurrencies, including the pro-cyclical buying and selling of Bitcoins against less volatile stablecoins. For the same reason, there is a flurry of buying and selling of cryptos from weak-currency countries, as an easy and comparatively cheap alternative to a currency flight into the US dollar as a safe haven.

Overall, the chances for Bitcoin becoming a universal means of payment are much less than some people have assumed so far. Bitcoin and its ilk are certainly to be reckoned with in the foreseeable future, but

[47] Coinmarketcap.com, 22 February 2022.

[48] Cf. Karau (2021).

only as a special option, as a kind of special-purpose instrument for very special user groups.

The chances for Ether, the second largest cryptocurrency, may look different. Ether has a special feature which Bitcoin lacks. The blockchain system Ethereum is not only used for payment transactions with Ether, but, unlike Bitcoin, also offers the aforementioned programmability of digital tokens. Ethereum's programming language can be used to develop Ether tokens encoded as smart contracts and other applications. Ether is thus not only a money surrogate, but also has use value as a management tool for contracts, other documents, tangible and intangible goods. If this proves to be successful in the longer term, Ether would have a decisive competitive advantage over Bitcoin and other unbacked currencies. That advantage, however, can also be combined with stablecoins. It's just a question of design.

There remain some disadvantages and shortcomings of highly distributed and public - blockchains, prototypically applying to Bitcoin. These disadvantages include inadequate efficiency due to an overdone libertarian ideology of decentralisation and anonymity, coming with unsustainable high-energy consumption, and resulting high costs that are only partially competitive.

Ether sets itself apart from this. Its developer community has been working for some years to radically streamline the process of verifying and documenting transactions. In the previous consensual proof-of-work procedure, all computer nodes (miners) have to reach agreement on all sides, which is costly in terms of time, energy and money. In contrast, the proof-of-stake procedure newly introduced by Ether, randomly selects a few large computer nodes from participants that must fulfil certain criteria. This is said to lead to a reduction in computational effort and energy consumption of up to 99.9%.[49] Accordingly, the velocity of payments strongly increases and the costs decrease accordingly. The system also achieves higher operational security and, unlike blockchain, scalability, and it still remains public with open access. It thus appears that Ether has a considerable competitive advantage over other cryptos. Whether, however, it will also become a widely used means of payment, depends on other, non-technical monetary and political-economic factors still to be discussed.

[49] Ethereum.org/en/upgrades/merge.

6.8 Stablecoins as Competitors to Be Taken Seriously

6.8.1 *If Any, It's Stablecoins*

Compared to unbacked cryptocurrencies, and from the money users' viewpoint, stablecoins have an important advantage which is their having coverage and the promise of 1:1 parity with the official currency. Similar to MMF shares, one stablecoin is equal to, for example, one US dollar in bank money or Fed reserves or Fed CBDC. In the EU, 1:1 coverage is already mandatory (by analogy with e-money). In the US, the upcoming regulation will probably also amount to full coverage, howsoever this is composed.

The advantage of stablecoins is amplified when they use the Ethereum programming language or a comparable other one. A stablecoin thus achieves multi-purpose programmability. This is also an advantage in competition with bank money, in addition to the already mentioned advantages of digital tokens over book money, such as instant transfer directly from payer to payee, easy handling and basically also lower costs.

For the U.S., stablecoins and other cryptos are particularly relevant in the foreseeable future. This is because most cryptos are traded for US dollars, and stablecoins are pegged to the US dollar. The dollar peg of stablecoins is suitable for strengthening the dominant currency position of the US dollar, provided the cryptocurrency is adequately regulated and does not represent a new cluster risk.

It may have been precisely the aspect of dollar dominance that prompted the Federal Reserve and the US Treasury to reject Facebook's multi-currency Libra stablecoin project, while taking a more positive stance towards dollar-denominated stablecoins.[50] This may nevertheless be surprising, in that the trend towards digital tokens suggests a weakening of existing international payment networks designed to manage transfers of bank-account balances (book money) and dominated by US Fed dollars and American bank dollars. All the same, the global use of US dollar-linked stablecoins is likely to expand the dollar dominance or at least maintain it.

Despite the advantages that can be cited in favour of stablecoins, the question remains as to why a digital surrogate should be used when the

[50] Federal Reserve of the U.S. (2022, p. 11).

digital original in the form of CBDC is readily available. Issuers of stablecoins will have to offer benefits that CBDC does not. Initially, these advantages are likely to be transfer speed and cost advantages, as well as programmability of advanced cryptos and stablecoins. Current CBDC concepts seem to be lagging behind developments in this regard.

6.8.2 *Potential Problems also with Stablecoins*

One should be aware that private cryptocurrencies possibly lead to the same problems and crises as bank money. Uncovered cryptos are in any case exposed to a high run risk. To a degree, this also applies to stablecoins. Backing second-tier or third-tier money with other money surrogates is of questionable security. The same holds true for securities coverage, because the value of such financial assets fluctuates, so that the relevant reserve positions of a stablecoin gain or lose value. This would become more entrenched if stablecoins were subject over time not only to passive, but possibly also active issuance. This happens, for example, if a stablecoin issuer does not sell new tokens by way of ICO, but buys securities directly with new tokens (as far as the sellers of securities accept payment in a respective stablecoin).

While stablecoins are subject to e-money regulation in the EU, the coverage of stablecoins is not yet consistently regulated in the U.S. So far, the 1:1 coverage of stablecoins is largely a voluntary commitment. Actual coverage can differ considerably. For example, the stablecoin USDCoin is backed by dollar-denominated bank money. In this way, it follows a kind of narrow-banking approach, that is, it tends to be fully backed by money, in this case by bank money, not central-bank reserves.[51]

It is different with Tether, currently the largest stablecoin, and with a market value of USD 70 billion the third largest cryptocoin behind Bitcoin and Ether.[52] Tether's cover consists of securities and receivables. The receivables are claims on creditors to whom *Tether Limited*, Tether's operating organisation, has extended loans. For decentralised finance actors, Tether is an important source of liquidity.[53] Another part of the Tether cover consists of Bitcoins, because mainly these are traded by

[51] Vandeweyer (2021, p. 83).

[52] Coinmarketcap.com v. 23 February 2022.

[53] McKinsey Global Institute (2021, p. 4).

institutional and professional traders against Tether.[54] How stable can a stablecoin be if the 100% coverage consists of risky and unstable cover assets? According to the US government and a recommendation of the Federal Reserve, stablecoin trading should be classified as a systemically relevant banking business and regulated accordingly.[55]

Even after such regulation, there remains a certain potential for stablecoins not to meet 100% coverage. It is also possible that in the course of a prolonged period of financial relaxation, politicians and authorities may once again be persuaded to agree to even a fractional reserve. As a result of this as well as fluctuating currency values, fractional reserve banking might continue with stablecoins. A run on stablecoins can occur, analogous to a run on bank money. The more uncovered cryptos and covered stablecoins spread and become systemically relevant, the more the problems of *too big to fail* and *too interconnected to fail* is reproduced. If stablecoins of weight get into a crisis, central banks and governments are under pressure to secure the existence of these systemically relevant private funds in order to prevent worse.

6.8.3 Stablecoins in Competition with Bank Money and Central-Bank Money

The political uproar over the Libra/Diem project has made it clear that stablecoins with wide distribution and international use are seen as a threat by banks and central banks. Stablecoins compete with both bank money and central-bank money.

As far as the competition with bank money is concerned, stablecoins are not legal tender as CBDC is, and, unlike bank money, stablecoins are not guaranteed by central bank and government, and nothing of the kind is envisaged so far. Under conditions of uncertainty, the reliability of stablecoins might be considered less certain than is that of safe-stock CBDC and even para-sovereign bank money. Stablecoins will thus not be as strong a competitor for bank money as CBDC. But stablecoins are advantageous enough to normally put bank money under pressure.

[54] Lopatto (2021).

[55] Press Release of the President's Working Group on Financial Markets (PWG), the Federal Deposit Insurance Corporation, and the Office of the Comptroller of the Currency, 1 November 2021. Davis Polk, *Insights*, U.S. regulators speak on stablecoin and crypto regulation, 12 November 2021.

No matter how hard banks try to speed up transfers and otherwise promote digitisation, the banks' book money cannot replicate the above-mentioned advantages of digital tokens regarding handling, efficiency, costs and programmability.

Moreover, a proliferation of stablecoins will intensify the general trend of shifting financial transactions away from banks to shadow banks, at the expense of traditional banks and partly also the use of bank money by shadow banks. The banks themselves have helped to bring about and finance this development, either through separate subsidiaries under the umbrella of the own banking corporation or through co-financing external financial institutions. Banking corporations have become increasingly active in areas such as investment banking, asset management and brokerage, while hitherto non-bank financial institutions are active in money exchange and payment services as well as in lending and investment banking in a broad sense.

Some big banks are now reversing course by concentrating more on business clients and investment banking, as they once did, and leaving the mass business with smaller retail clients to other providers. Such restructuring and overlaps between banks and shadow banks continue to develop. In view of the new third-tier monies, the distinction between monetary and non-monetary financial institutions becomes blurred.

The fact that stablecoins also compete with central-bank money may be less obvious. How the competitive coexistence of CBDC and stablecoins will turn out is uncertain for the time being.[56] Central-bank money is indeed base money, but central-bank cash isn't systemically decisive any more, while central-bank reserves, as a quasi subset of bank money, are limited to the interbank circuit. By introducing CBDC, this will change. But how soon or late CBDC will be usable for retail transactions, and when it will have reached the critical mass necessary to make a difference, remains to be seen. Meanwhile, the crypto sector and stablecoins continue to develop.

Even once CBDC is widely used, stablecoins will compete with CBDC in the same sense that bank money has competed with cash. Bank money has marginalised cash and pushed back operationally necessitated excess reserves. Bank money thus has become systemically relevant and finally

[56] Cf. McKinsey Global Institute (2021).

dominant. The central banks turned into re-active and subordinate all-time refinancers of bank money. Having a sovereign currency unit without determining important stocks of sovereign money is an empty shell indeed.

It cannot be excluded from the outset that what bank money has done to cash and reserves, stablecoins might do in a comparable process to CBDC. It doesn't have to be that way, especially since CBDC has the advantage over stablecoins of being the base money that need not be redeemed in other types of money, the legal base to which other types of money refer—but only as long as the central banks and other relevant state bodies act accordingly and make sure that there is a large supply of technologically high-powered CBDC in the overall composition of the money supply. Of particular importance in setting the course of that matter is the design of CBDC, as discussed in the next chapter.

References

Adrian, Tobias and Tomaso Mancini-Griffoli. 2021. How will Digital Money Impact the International Monetary System? In Niepelt (Ed.) 2021, pp. 73–79.

AfJM (Alliance for Just Money). 2021. American Monetary Reform Act, update of AMI 2010.

Allais, Maurice. 1988 [1977]. *L'Impôt sur le capital et la réforme monétaire*. Paris: Hermann Éditeurs des Sciences et des Arts, Nouvelle édition.

AMI (American Monetary Institute). 2010. *Presenting the American Monetary Act*. Valatie, NY: American Monetary Institute, http://monetary.org/wp-content/uploads/2011/09/32-page-brochure.pdf.

Andolfatto, David. 2015, February 3. Fedcoin: On the Desirability of a Government Cryptocurrency. *Macromania*.

Andresen, Trond. 2014. The Central Bank with an Expanded Role in a Purely Electronic Monetary System. *Real-World Economics Review* 68 (2014): 66–73.

Andresen, Trond. 2019, October. Initiating a Parallel Electronic Currency in a Eurocrisis Country. Why it Would Work. *Real-World Economics Review* (89): 23–31.

Bank of England. 2020, March. Central Bank Digital Currency. Opportunities, challenges and design, *Discussion paper*.

Barrdear, John and Michael Kumhof. 2016, July. The Macroeconomics of Central Bank Issued Digital Currencies, Bank of England. *Staff Research Paper* No. 605.

Bech, Morten and Rodney Garratt. 2017, September. Central Bank Cryprocurrencies, Basel Bank for International Settlements. *BIS Quarterly Review*, 55–70.

Benes, Jaromir and Michael Kumhof. 2012. The Chicago Plan Revisited. *IMF working paper*, 12/202 August 2012, revised draft February 2013.

Birch, Kate. 2022, January 6. How Large Enterprises are Driving Digital Currency Adoption. *Business Chief*.

BIS. 2015, November. *Digital Currencies*, prep. by the BIS Committee on Payments and Market Infrastructures. Basel: Bank for International Settlements.

BIS. 2018, March. *Central Bank Digital Currencies*, prep. by the BIS Committee on Payments and Market Infrastructures. Basel: Bank for International Settlements.

BIS. 2019, January. Proceeding with Caution. A Survey on Central Bank Digital Currency, Written by Christian Barontini and Henry Holden. *Bank for International Settlements Papers,* No. 101.

BIS. 2020. *Central Bank Digital Currencies: Foundational Principles and Core Features*, publ. by BIS and the central banks of Canada, EU, Japan, Sweden, Switzerland, England and USA. Basel: BIS.

BIS. 2021. *CBDC: Opportunity for the monetary system.* BIS Annual Economic Report, 65–95.

Bjerg, Ole. 2018, August. Breaking the Gilt Standard. The problem of parity in Kumhof and Noone's design principles for Central Bank Digital Currencies. *Copenhagen Business School Working Paper*.

Boar, Codruta, Henry Holden and Amber Wadsworth. 2020, January. Impending Arrival – A Sequel to the Survey on Central Bank Digital Currency. *BIS Papers*, No. 107. Basel: Bank for International Settlements.

Bordo, Michael D. 2018. *Central Bank Digital Currency. The Future Direction for Monetary Policy?* Shadow Open Market Committee, E21 Manhattan Institute, March 9, 2018, http://shadowfed.org/wp-content/uploads/2018/03/BordoSOMC-March2018.pdf.

Bordo, Michael D. and Andrew T. Levin. 2017, August. Central Bank Digital Currency and the Future of Monetary Policy. *NBER Working Paper Series*, No. 23711.

Bordo, Michael D. and Andrew T. Levin. 2019, January. Digital Cash: Principles & Practical Steps. *NBER Working Paper Series*, No. 25455.

Braun, Helene. 2022a. Janet Yellen Stresses Need for Central Bank Digital Currency Work. *CoinDesk*, October 13, 2022a, https://www.coindesk.com/policy/2022a/10/13/yellen-stresses-need-for-central-bank-digital-currency, as of October 18, 2022a.

Braun, Helene. 2022b. Powell Says Fed Plans Recommendation to Congress on CBDC. *Reuters*, June 23, 2022b, www.coindesk.com/markets/2022b/06/23/powell-says-fed-plans-recommendation-to-congress-on-cbdc, as of October 18, 2022b.

Brigida, Anna-Cat and Leo Schwartz. 2022, March 15. El Salvador's Bitcoin gamble is crumbling. *The 2022 Rest of the World Reader Survey.*

Broadbent, Ben. 2016. *Central Banks and Digital Currencies*, Speech at the London School of Economics documented by the Bank of England, www.bankofengland.co.uk/publications/Pages/speeches/default.aspx.

Caudevilla, Oriol. 2021, January 4. A Pan-Asian Digital Currency would bring many opportunities to China. *Macau News Agency Opinion.*

Chaum, David, Christian Grothoff and Thomas Moser. 2021. How to Issue a Central Bank Digital Currency. *SNB Working Papers*, 3/2021. Bern: Swiss National Bank.

Cuen, Leigh. 2021, March 21. The Debate About Cryptocurrency and Energy Consumption. *Join TechCrunch+.*

Cunha, Paulo R., Paulo Melo and Helder Sebastião. 2021. From Bitcoin to CBDC: Making Sende of the Digital Money Revolution. *Future Internet* 13: 165. www.mdpi.com/journal/futureinternet.

Danezis, George and Sarah Meiklejohn. 2016. *Centrally Banked Cryptocurrencies.* http://www0.cs.ucl.ac.uk/staff/G.Danezis/papers/ndss16currencies.pdf.

Dt. Bank. 2020, January. *The Future of Payments*, Corporate Bank Research.
Part I – Cash: the Dinosaur Will Survive … For Now.
Part II – Moving to Digital Wallets and the Extinction of Plastic Cards.
Part III – Digital Currencies: The Ultimate Hard Power Tool.

Dt. Bundesbank. 2020, December 21. Money in Programmable Applications. Report of the Working Group on Programmable Money. Frankfurt.

Dt. Bundesbank. 2021, April. Digital Money: Options for Payments. *Monthly Report*, 57–75.

Dyson, Ben and Graham Hodgson. 2016. *Digital Cash. Why Central Banks should start Issuing Electronic Money.* London: Positive Money.

Dyson, Ben and Jack Meaning. 2018, May 30. Would a Central Bank Digital Currency disrupt monetary policy? *Bank Underground.*

ECB. 2020a, December. *Study on the Payment Attitudes of Consumers in the Euro Area (SPACE).* Frankfurt.

ECB. 2020b, October. *Report on a digital euro.* Frankfurt: ECB.

Eichengreen, Barry. 2017, October 30. Central Bank-Issued Digital Currency is the Future, Not Cryptocurrency. *CNBC The Fintech Effect.*

Elmandjra, Yassine. 2021, June 29. Debunking Common Bitcoin Myths. *ARK Invest.*

Federal Reserve of the U.S. 2022, January. *Money and Payments: The U.S. Dollar in the Age of Digital Transformation, Research & Analysis.* Board of Governors of the Federal Reserve System.

Financial Stability Board. 2020. *Global Monitoring Report on Non-Bank Financial Intermediation 2020*. www.fsb.org/2021/12/global-monitoring-report-on-non-bank-financial-intermediation-2021.

Frisbie, Sonnet. 2022, June 13. Widespread e-CNY Adoption in China is Coming. *Morning Consult*.

Gomez, Christian. 2010. 100%-Money. *Osons Maurice Allais*, Juin 2010, https://osonsallais.wordpress.com/2010/02/22/christian-gomez-100-money.

Guan, Dabo and Shouyang Wang. 2021, April 7. Environmental Science: Climate Impacts of Bitcoin Mining in China. *Nature Communications*.

Heasman, Will. 2019, December 6. The Worrying Truth Behind China's Digital Currency. *Decrypt*.

Howell, Sabrina T., Marina Niessner and David Yermack. 2020, September. Initial Coin Offerings: Financing Growth with Cryptocurrency Token Sales. *The Review of Financial Studies* 33 (9): 3925–3974.

Huber, Joseph and James Robertson. 2000. *Creating New Money. A Monetary Reform for the Information Age*. London: New Economics Foundation.

IMF. 2018. Casting Light on Central Bank Digital Currency. *IMF Staff Discussion Note*, written by T. Mancini-Griffoli et al., Washington D.C.: International Monetary Fund.

Ingves, Stefan. 2018. *The e-Krona and the Payments of the Future*, Speech by the Governor of the Swedish Riksbank, Stockholm.

Jackson, Andrew and Ben Dyson. 2013. *Sovereign Money – Paving the Way for a Sustainable Recovery*. London: Positive Money.

Karau, Sören. 2021. Monetary Policy and Bitcoin. *Dt. Bundesbank Discussion Paper*, No. 41/2021.

Kay, John. 2009. *Narrow Banking. The Reform of Banking Regulation*, publ. by the Centre for the Study of Financial Innovation, London.

Kay, John. 2015. *Other People's Money*. London: Profile Books.

Koning, J. P. 2014, October 19. Fedcoin. *JP Koning Blog*.

Kotlikoff, Laurence J. 2010. *Jimmy Stewart is Dead. Ending the World's Ongoing Plague with Limited Purpose Banking*, Hoboken, NJ: Wiley.

Kumar, Ananya. 2022, March 1. A Report Card on China's Central Bank Digital Currency: The e-CNY, *Atlantic Council Blog Econographics*.

Kumhof, Michael and Clare Noone. 2018, May. Central Bank Digital Currencies – Design Principles and Balance Sheet Implications. *Staff Working Paper*, No. 725. London: Bank of England.

Liao, Rita. 2022, January 22. China's Digital Yuan Wallet Now Has 260 Million Users. *Join TechCrunch+*.

Lopatto, Elizabeth. 2021, August 16. The Tether Controversy Explained. How Stable are Stablecoins? *The Verge*.

Mathew, Neil. 2018, November 12. Bitcoin Cash Surpasses Paypal's Transaction Speed. *Newconomy*.

Mayer, Thomas. 2013, July. A Copernican Turn in Banking Union Urgently Needed. *CEPS Policy Brief*, No. 297.

Mayer, Thomas. 2019. A Digital Euro to Compete with Libra. *The Economists' Voice* 16 (1): 1–7.

McKinsey Global Institute. 2021, November. *The Rise and Rise of the Global Balance Sheet*.

Meaning, Jack, Ben Dyson, James Barker and Emily Clayton. 2018, May. Broadening Narrow Money: Monetary Policy with a Central Bank Digital Currency. *Bank of England Staff Working Paper*, No. 724.

Nicolle, Emily. 2021, November 16. Why CBDC are Facing an Identity Crisis. *The Fintech Files*.

Niepelt, Dirk. 2015, January 21. Reserves for Everyone – Towards a New Monetary Regime? *VOX CEPR's Policy Portal*.

Niepelt, Dirk. 2018. Central Bank Digital Currency. What difference does it make? In *Do we need central bank digital currency? Economics, Technology and Institutions*, eds. Gnan, Ernest and Donato Masciandro, 99–112. Vienna: SUERF Conference proceedings.

Niepelt, Dirk. ed. 2021a. *Central Bank Digital Currency. Considerations, Project, Outlook*, Centre for Economic Policy Research. London: CEPR Press 2021.

Niepelt, Dirk. 2021b. 'Reserves for All': Political Rather Than Macroeconomic Risks. In Niepelt (Ed.) 2021, pp. 39–44.

Omarova, Saule T. 2021, October. The People's Ledger: How to Democratize Money and Finance the Economy. *Vanderbilt Law Review* 74 (5): 1231–1300.

OMFIF. 2020. *Digital Currencies – A Question of Trust*. Written by Bhavin Patel and Pierre Ortlieb. London: OMFIF.

OMFIF/IBM. 2019. *Retail CBDCs, the Next Payments Frontier*. London: Official Monetary and Financial Institutions Forum / Costa Mesa, CA: IBM Blockchain Worldwire.

Phillips, Ronnie J. 1995. *The Chicago Plan & New Deal Banking Reform*, Foreword by Hyman P. Minsky, Armonk, NY: M. E. Sharpe Inc.

Positive Money. 2011. *Bank of England Creation of Currency Bill*. London: Positive Money.

Prasad, Eswar. 2021. *The Future of Money*. How the Digital Revolution is Transforming Currencies and Finance: The Belknap Press of Harvard University Press.

PwC Switzerland. 2021, April. *PricewaterhouseCoopers' CBDC Global Index*, authored by Adrian Keller and Bastian Stolzenberg.

Reiff, Nathan. 2022, July 9. The Environmental Impact of Cryptocurrency. *Investopedia*.

Reynolds, Sam and James Rubin. 2022, October 17. First Mover Asia: A Pan-Asian Digital Currency? *CoinDesk.*

Schemmann, Michael. 2012. *Liquid Money – The Final Thing. Federal Reserve and Central Bank Accounts for Everyone*: IICPA Publications.

Seidemann, Wolfram. 2021, July 27. CBDC Systems Should Focus on Programmable Payments. *OMFIF News.*

Sigurjonsson, Frosti. 2015, March. *Monetary Reform. A better monetary system for Iceland.* Icelandic Parliament, submitted to the Committee on Economic Affairs and Trade.

Slack, Andrew. 2022, January 24. CBDC Must Preserve Defining Features of Physical Money. *OMFIF News.*

Smialek, Jeanna. 2021, August 5. Dividing Lines Harden as the Fed Contemplates Issuing a Digital Dollar. *New York Times Daily Business Briefing.*

Smith, Tyler. 2021, November 26. Digital Tokens. *The Fintech Times.*

Summer, Martin and Hannes Hermanky. 2022. A Digital Euro and the Future of Cash, Austrian National Bank. *Quarterly Review of Economic Policy*, Q1–Q2 91–108.

Sveriges Riksbank. 2017, September. *The Riksbank's E-Krona Project*, Report 1, Stockholm.

Sveriges Riksbank. 2018a, October. *The Riksbank's E-Krona Project*, Report 2, Stockholm.

Sveriges Riksbank. 2018b. Special Issue on the e-Krona. *Sveriges Riksbank Economic Review*, 3.

Tapscott, Don and Alex Tapscott. 2016. Blockchain Revolution – How the Technology Behind Bitcoin is Changing Money, Business, and the World. New York: Penguin Random House.

Umar, Ismail. 2021, September 24. Two-Sided Integration Between Fiat and Crypto. How Banks are Gearing Up to Move into Digital Currencies. *Tearsheet.*

van Hee, Kees and Jacob Wijngaarden. 2021, December. A New Digital Currency System. *Central European Review of Economics and Management* 5 (4): 33–60.

Vandeweyer, Quentin. 2021. Stablecoins as Alternatives to CBDC. In Niepelt (Ed.) 2021, pp. 81–85.

Wortmann, Edgar. 2019. *Public Depository: Safe-Haven and Level Playing Field for Book Money*, Ons Geld, Nederland.

Yamaguchi, Kaoru. 2014. *Money and Macroeconomic Dynamics. An Accounting System Dynamics Approach.* Awaji Island: Muratopia Institute/Japan Futures Research Center. www.muratopia.org/Yamaguchi/MacroBook.html.

Zellweger-Gutknecht, Corinne. 2021. The Right and Duty of Central Banks to Issue Retail Digital Currency. In Niepelt (Ed.) 2021, pp. 31–38.

Zitter, Leah. 2016, March 28. The Bank of England's RSCoin – An Experiment for Central Banks or a Bitcoin Alternative? *Bitcoin Magazine.*

CHAPTER 7

CBDC System Design Principles

This chapter deals with questions that are being discussed as CBDC design principles, such as, for example, questions of system architecture, whether digital tokens are managed by way of distributed ledgers (blockchain) or by advanced traditional payment infrastructures, or how CBDC enters into circulation, how the interaction between CBDC and bank money should work, whether there is an increased danger of bank runs due to CBDC and whether the central bank and the government should continue to guarantee bank money to the same extent as hitherto.[1]

It is in the nature of these things to be not only about operational functionality, but also about political and paradigmatic aspects. The latter are difficult for those who fear politicising of money. But portraying monetary policy as something apolitical and purely technocratic is misleading. Monetary policy *is* about politics as a matter of fact. This is not to be feared, but to be met in a transparent way.

[1] A variety of approaches to CBDC design principles inter alia in IMF (2018), Kumhof and Noone (2018), Ingves (2018), Sveriges Riksbank (2017, 2018a, b), Meaning et al. (2018), Barrdear and Kumhof (2016), and Bindseil (2019).

J. Huber, *The Monetary Turning Point*,
https://doi.org/10.1007/978-3-031-23957-1_7

7.1 What System Architecture for CBDC?

At the present stage, any attempt to typify system architectures of CBDC retains a somewhat provisional character.[2] Certain basic structures can nevertheless be identified, basically three:

- conventional account-based
- digital tokenised
- hybrid.

The conventional end of the spectrum is characterised by CBDC based on standard central-bank accounts, that is, CBDC as reserves for everyone. This is conceivable, for example, by way of *direct* access to an individual central-bank account. This would be a transaction account as some public institutions have, not a credit or refinancing account as banks have. Transaction accounts for everyone can be docked to the banks' payment infrastructure, with the account balances, however, directly owned by the customers and existing outside a bank's balance sheet. The execution of payments remains a pure service for customers, similar to a securities account, except that there are no securities or bank money in the account, but central-bank reserves. Another variant would be *indirect* access, in that banks or PSP maintain an omnibus account at the central bank for their customers, to which the customers have credited their individual share. This could well be set up for conventional online banking.

Approaches to a sovereign money system until the mid-2010s, before the digitisation trend as a result of cryptocurrencies had reached monetary policy, have proposed direct as well as indirect varieties. This was in part also considered by central-bank research staff. Conventional account-based CBDC would still be a considerable step forward, but with the disadvantage of leaving out the technical potential of tokenisation of CBDC. Notwithstanding, a conventional account-based approach is unlikely anyway, for central banks do not want to act as payment service providers for everyone. This is at least true for direct access to an individual central-bank account.

[2] As for instance in Cunha et al. (2021, p. 9).

At the other end of the spectrum of CBDC varieties—on the front line of technical progress, so to speak—are digital tokens. These tokens are a bearer instrument that is directly in the possession and at the disposal of a respective holder, and transferred directly payer-to-payee when a payment is made. Digital tokens may be programmable and are not only transferable between natural persons and legal entities (institutions, firms), but also between machines, products or other artificial-intelligence actuators in the internet of things.

A permissioned blockchain system with authorised access can serve as the payment infrastructure and overall database. Due to aspects of efficiency, energy consumption and costs, it will be a more or less centralised system or multicentre system, with large-scale servers acting as network nodes to manage the commonly shared database.

The systems currently developed or already implemented by central banks are neither purely conventional account-based nor fully tokenised, but hybrid approaches combining elements of both sides.[3] An e-wallet, for example, may handle programmable tokens or simply the balance of a conventional account, with the possibility of viewing the account history. Access is obtained through a mobile phone or landline app, for some functions also through a customary plastic card with an electronic chip.

The payment infrastructure can be conventional or a DLT/blockchain system, or in fact both.[4] For example, for the transfer of digital euros as envisaged by the ECB, the TIPS system, an extension of the reserves-based interbank RTGS system, is to mediate payments in digital euros between payer and payee.[5] TIPS allows near real-time transmission 24/7.[6] The planned Swedish e-krona project also envisages using the Eurosystem's TIPS platform.[7] A test run by the Swiss National Bank

[3] Auer et al. (2020, 2021, p. 157), Fatas (2021, p. 52), and Auer and Böhme (2020).

[4] ECB (2020b, p. 26), Maechler and Wehrli (2021, p. 150) and Auer et al. (2021, p. 157).

[5] TIPS = TARGET Instant Payment Settlement. TARGET = Trans-European Automated Real-time Gross settlement Express Transfer system.

[6] ECB (2020b, p. 38).

[7] Flodén and Segendorf (2021, p. 103).

and the Basel Bank for International Settlements has shown that traditional RTGS systems and DLT/blockchain platforms are both suitable for making final payments with digital tokens.[8]

The Chinese digital yuan, the largest CBDC realised so far, is still relatively close to a conventional account-based system. The central bank lends digital yuan to specific accounts at six major state banks and two major internet banks (WeBank, MYBank). Individual customers can apply there for a digital yuan account in the form of an e-wallet. Digital yuans have the same legal-tender status as cash.[9] Access to the digital yuan e-wallet is based on asymmetric cryptography with a public and a private key. With digital yuan, users can basically pay for everything and also use the services of banks and PSP. However, traditional bank accounts and digital yuan accounts/e-wallets remain separate. For now, digital yuan can only be exchanged for bank deposits or vice versa via the eight major banks that issue digital yuan into public circulation.[10]

7.2 Objectives Pursued and Benefits Expected

Central banks associate a number of objectives and expectations with the introduction of CBDC. The most important ones are summarised here.[11]

7.2.1 Monetary Connectivity (Interoperability, Convertability)

According to the central banks, CBDC should be added to the existing types of money, not replace them. This means that CBDC and the digital wallets, transmission channels and data bases used for it must be technically connectable to the payment systems of existing types of money. This requirement of interoperability primarily concerns the existing central-bank RTGS systems in connection with bank money and e-money based on bank money. Interoperability does not seem to be

[8] Maechler and Wehrli (2021, p. 150).

[9] De Bode et al. (2021).

[10] www.db.com/media/news?tags=asiapacific, 14 July 2021. *The Economist*, May 8th, 2021, pp. 61–62.

[11] Georgieva (2022), Federal Reserve (2022), McKinsey Global Institute (2021, p. 7), De Bode et al. (2021), BIS (2021, pp. 65–95), Fatas (2021), Adrian and Mancini-Griffoli (2021), Boar et al. (2020, p. 4), OMFIF and IBM (2019, pp. 6, 13), and BIS (2019, p. 9).

a serious obstacle, but it does require additional technical effort, which comes with corresponding costs.

The requirement of interoperability between payment systems makes sense if and because the different types of money are to be convertible, that is, CBDC exchangeable into bank money or cash, and vice versa. If there is to be no convertibility of money, there is no need for interoperability of payment systems.

As far as interoperability and convertibility of stablecoins and other cryptocurrencies are concerned, central banks and banks have not given it much concern so far. Maybe private cryptos are in many cases still seen as unwelcome competition one would rather keep out. Crypto platforms will gladly fulfil the sought-after conversion function, with corresponding profits that central banks and banks will miss out on as long as they do not care.

7.2.2 *Efficiency Increase, Cost Reduction*

At the core of expected CBDC benefits are efficiency gains in managing money and payments. This includes the promise of more convenient handling of digital wallets compared to cash and bank money. Offline use in addition to online use would also be suitable to fulfil the promise. A main element of the expected increase in efficiency is faster execution of payments with the aim of real-time finalisation of payments, and this, in perspective, also across currency areas. In all of this, the security of digital wallets and secure money transfer must be guaranteed.

Increased efficiency is supposed to result in reduced costs, particularly by eliminating a number of intermediate stages in the current interbank payment process via current accounts. That sounds plausible. But interoperability and convertibility generate new costs. It remains to be seen to what extent cost reductions materialise at the bottom line.

7.2.3 *Increased Utility*

Beyond efficiency gains and cost reductions, CBDC is also supposed to increase use value, especially through the foreseeable programmability of digital tokens and the associated expectation of financial innovations related to smart contracts and the internet of things.

Another example would be automated interim credit. This means that excess funds can be made available to others as a micro-credit line within a self-defined framework, or that one can make use of such services oneself. It may be noted here that CBDC, like cash, represents a positive-numbered stock of money. It cannot be turned negative by overdraft of a current account. But of course, a dispo-credit line can be granted on the basis of existing money, or money made available according to the situation. Money-lending customers who enter into an automated credit arrangement must know that this means an investment, bearing interest, but also a certain risk. Unlike with fractionally covered bank money, there is no reason for the claims and liabilities involved to be government-guaranteed.

7.2.4 *Social Inclusion*

Expected cost reductions are also linked to the intention of facilitating social inclusion. In this case, this means making payment transactions with CBDC and basic financial services accessible to the hitherto unbanked. In newly industrialised countries, this still affects many people, in many developing countries the majority. In this respect, digital wallets used via mobile phone apps can support catch-up development.

7.2.5 *Safeguarding Financial Privacy, Verifiability and Legality*

CBDC needs to meet a number of legal requirements. This is already difficult today because of conflicting goals and the necessary balancing of legally protected interests. With CBDC, the situation is certainly not getting any easier.

For one thing, CBDC must maintain financial privacy and data protection, especially confidentiality of funds and payments, and anonymity to the extent practicable and legally permissible. At the same time, payment transactions must be traceable and verifiable in given cases, certainly with the corresponding authority or upon official order. Banks, PSP and other financial institutions involved must be able to exercise know-your-customer duties and help detect money laundering, tax evasion and other illicit action. Such obligations already exist, even if there may be enforcement deficits.

A welcome side effect of CDBC is that counterfeiting of banknotes will become even more obsolete than it already is due to cashless payment transactions. According to widespread expert opinion, counterfeiting of digital tokens should be impossible because of their cryptographic peculiarity and instantly verified singular identity. Theft of tokens, however, can occur, so far especially on crypto exchange platforms. Preventing this is likely to collide with the protection of the respective user identity.

7.2.6 *Improved Effectiveness of Monetary Policy, Increased Financial Stability*

Most central banks expect CBDC to improve the effectiveness of monetary policy and thus contribute to enhanced stability and resilience of the monetary and financial system. This in turn is supposed to strengthen general confidence in the monetary system and central banks.[12]

As a result of wide circulation of CBDC, improved effectiveness of monetary policy can certainly be expected thanks to a stronger quantity lever, thus improved transmission of policy impulses—the more CBDC, the more effectual; the less CBDC, the less effectual. By implication this means that today's monetary policy is insufficiently effectual, and that the bank money regime is unstable and not crisis-resilient of its own making.

Officially, central banks do not justify the necessity of CBDC with the obvious problems of the bank money regime and the far-reaching loss of effectiveness of conventional monetary policy. Usually one merely invokes the mandate to supply the population with central-bank money (legal tender). In view of the shrinking use of cash, this seemed reason enough.[13] The problematic system dynamics behind the disappearance of cash remains unspoken. Recently, however, Chr. Lagarde, ECB President, and F. Panetta, ECB Executive Board, have publicly stated that without digital currency, central banks face marginalisation and that the field must not be left to private payment instruments alone. Rather, monetary stability needs "a strong monetary anchor" in the form of CBDC.[14]

[12] BIS (2019, 2020), OMFIF and IBM (2019), and OMFIF (2020).

[13] This was already the rationale of the Swedish e-krona. See Sveriges Riksbank (2017, 2018a, b). On CBDC as a continuation of cash in digital form, also see Zellweger-Gutknecht (2021, pp. 31–36).

[14] Lagarde and Panetta (2022).

7.3 Disintermediation, Substitution and the Competitive Coexistence of CBDC and Bank Money

Among the topics at the forefront of discussing CBDC is the question of disintermediation. It is easy to talk past each other here, because the term disintermediation is used with two different meanings. One of them should rather be called substitution, since this is about the consequences of replacing bank money with CBDC to a certain extent.[15] The other issue—from which the term disintermediation derives—is the supposed function of banks as financial intermediaries, erroneously assuming that commercial banks use customer deposits as loanable funds for doing proprietary business. In this respect, it is feared that by exchanging bank money into CBDC, "the ability of banks to pro-actively issue primary credit" would be impaired.[16] In other words, CBDC would "undermine the deposit-funded lending of banks".[17]

As already explained, with the rise of the bank money regime, the notion of funding banking operations by using customer deposits has generally become inaccurate and misleading. Intermediation by banks only takes place with the remaining cash. It does not apply to the lion's share of bank money (customer account balances), for banks do *create* the bank money; they do not draw it from somewhere else to pass it on.

In contrast, financial intermediation takes place on a large scale in the shadow banking sector. Shadow banks, PSP and other financial institutions, however, will not conduct their business with CBDC any differently than with bank money. Accordingly, the introduction of CBDC does not mean that (non-existent) bank money intermediation by banks could be impaired, but exactly the opposite, that intermediation with CBDC is made possible or required of the banks. "Disintermediation" is a fictitious problem, a cognitive smokescreen.

Things are different when it comes to the question of substituting CBDC for bank money. To expect such money substitution—as a shift in the quantity ratio between bank money and central-bank money—could not be more realistic. The only question is to what extent it will happen,

[15] Assenmacher and Bindseil (2021, p. 115).

[16] Broadbent (2016, p. 5).

[17] Selgin (2021) and Niepelt (2015).

whether over time it will bring an absolute decline in bank money or only a relative loss of share, and whether it will happen faster or slower. In the process, the banking sector does not lose loanable funds, because in the current bank money regime banks need only a relative small amount of loanable funds anyway (cash and reserves). For the most part, there are no pre-existing funds, because bank money, as a second-tier surrogate on a base of fractional reserves, has taken the place that actually belongs to sovereign base money.

With the introduction of CBDC, the privilege of fractional funding—the bank money privilege—is in fact being taken back to the extent that CBDC spreads in relation to bank money. As far as bank money continues to be used, the banks retain their privilege. However, to the extent that CBDC replaces bank money, banks need to fully finance their operations in CBDC, just as they needed to fully finance the disbursement of cash in the past. To the same extent, the banks also lose the quasi-seigniorage that comes with bank money creation. This is about a special comparative advantage arising from the lower financing costs of banks compared to the financing costs of non-monetary financial institutions and all other non-banks. Non-banks cannot normally use a money surrogate they have created themselves and must therefore have fully funded all their transactions.

All the talk about disintermediation is solely about the foreseeable partial loss of the banks' (re-)financing privilege. But full financing of bank transactions in CBDC does not pose a functional problem, precisely because bank money can be substituted by CBDC. Substituting CBDC for bank money may somewhat curtail banking profits deriving from bank money creation. As far as the financeability of bank credit and investment is concerned, however, substituting CBDC for bank money is functionally neutral.[18]

Competition between CBDC and bank money arises inevitably. Initially, this had been made explicit in central-bank working papers. But then one tended to play down the foreseeable competition, or portrayed it as peaceful coexistence. In the long run, this is unrealistic. CBDC will certainly not spread overnight. Most people tend to be conservative money users, not calculating costs and benefits of payments too precisely. Rather, certain companies will first discover the advantages of the new

[18] See Brunnermeier and Niepelt (2019) and Niepelt (2021).

money. So the substitution of bank money by CBDC is likely to happen on occasion over time. As long as there is no increased uncertainty or even financial crisis, and as long as the central banks guarantee the liquidity of the banking sector as well as the government guarantees the customers' bank money, customers will have no particular reason to turn their backs on bank money in favour of CBDC.

As far as bank money is nevertheless replaced with CBDC, the banks obtain the CBDC they need from the very sources that are generally available as sources of funding. The respective sources include payments or repayments by customers in CBDC to their bank; interest-bearing CBDC deposits by customers with banks; short- and long-term CBDC borrowing on the open money market from other banks and shadow banks; CBDC bond issue; and finally, as necessary, central-bank financing through credit lines, regular funding tenders and open-market operations. All of this applies to CBDC as much as to cash hitherto.

To bank money today, the relevant sources are partly less yielding, for example with regard to customer payments to a bank made in bank money. If the payment is made by an external customer, the bank obtains additional and usable reserves. If, by contrast, the payment is made by an internal customer, this results in a corresponding deletion of that bank's liabilities rather than in usable funds for that bank. Reserves, cash and, in the near future, CBDC are loanable funds for the banks (the reserves, however, only for interbank lending and for the initial purchase of government bonds). Insofar as customers will provide CBDC to a bank, this is an interest-bearing loan to the bank.

The banks have recently received trillions in excess reserves as a result of QE policies. The unfounded worries about bank financing would be rendered pointless from the outset if the trillions in question were to be made available to the banks as CBDC and thus made accessible to the public via the banks. This would take the wind out of the sails of both the substitution issue and the fictitious disintermediation issue, as well as the bank run issue yet to be discussed.

7.4 Implications for CBDC Design Principles

CBDC is now underway. It seems, however, that many central bankers have rushed ahead of their long-held convictions. Central banks are not publicly thinking about how they could circulate CBDC quickly and on a large scale. Instead, their published thinking revolves around how to limit and slow down the introduction of CBDC so as not to run any risks that are rightly or wrongly suspected (disintermediation, substitution, bank run). Existing major risks of the current bank money regime, to which experts and people have become accustomed, are talked down. Risks related to CBDC that do not yet exist and are likely to be much smaller are projectively exaggerated.

7.4.1 CBDC Issuance According to Market Demand

As CBDC succeeds central-bank cash, one implication of this is that banks should be obliged to meet customer demand for CBDC, analogous to today's obligation to convert bank money into cash according to customer demand. In practice, such an obligation to provide CBDC according to customer demand should not play a major role, because shadow banks will certainly be happy to offer CBDC credit, and so banks will do likewise in order not to lose still more business to the shadow banking sector. Since under normal conditions there is no cause for concern that substitution of bank money by CBDC will occur in a landslide, settling this matter can be left to market demand.

7.4.2 CBDC Accessible and Usable Without Restriction

Because of the defensive attitude of many central banks towards their own initiative, the plan everywhere for now is not to leave the introduction of CBDC to market demand, but to restrict the matter administratively. For example, some central banks are developing CBDC not for everyone (retail), but only wholesale for banks, PSP, shadow banks and large companies with extensive payment transactions. This obviously contradicts the rationale of CBDC as a kind of modern cash in general use. As the beginning of a gradual introduction of CBDC, as a test of practicability under reality conditions with continued technical optimisation, an initial restriction to large payers may be plausible. The perspective remains to introduce CBDC as a universal means of payment in public circulation as soon as possible. This is an indispensable part of the project, not only because CBDC is a modern successor to traditional cash, but also in the sense of the financial inclusion that CBDC aims to achieve in newly industrialised and developing countries. Therefore, CBDC must be universally accessible and universally usable, literally for everyone and everything. Put differently, CBDC must be available on a retail basis, irrespective of all possible wholesale uses.

Some CBDC developers, however, aim to limit the available quantities of CBDC. For example, the Swedish Riksbank has considered applying today's legal limits for cash payments to the planned e-krona. This would be a restriction of each payment to a maximum of 250 euros or dollars.[19] Alternatively, the amount of bank money that can be exchanged in CBDC in a given period can be limited, or the total amount of available CBDC can be limited, for example to 10% or 20% of M1. This would correspond to the share of traditional cash in the past two to three decades.

These are recognisably protectionist measures to shield bank money from competing with CBDC. In terms of monetary policy, such strong quantity restrictions would be useless, as they wilfully retain the dominance of bank money and thus hardly change the relative ineffectiveness of monetary policy. For monetary policy to become truly effectual again, the share of CBDC would gradually have to reach a critical order, say, towards half of M1 and beyond.

Another concern relates to the use of CBDC by foreigners.[20] This is a well-known problem of dominant reserve currencies, but not a problem which would be specifically related to CBDC. It is possible, however, that the problem will be exacerbated by digital money as the modern successor to traditional book money. The problem exists as currency flight from weak-currency countries into dominant or reserve currencies. For strong-currency countries, this is a double-edged advantage, today mainly concerning the US dollar, also Switzerland, Singapore and a few others. The advantaged countries may be caught in the Triffin dilemma, which is that the additional creation of US dollars for foreigners has so far been accompanied by a deficit in the US current account—which, in a sense, is a luxury problem.

The current restrictions on the amount of cash, or limited usability of cash, conflict with the legal claim for cash to be unrestricted legal tender. It is certainly not among the objectives of CBDC to continue the limited usability of cash. Rather, one goal is to overcome the unfortunate monetary restrictions on the public use of central-bank money due to the declining use of traditional cash. Therefore, it is a guiding design principle

[19] Sveriges Riksbank (2017, p. 21). Also ECB (2020a, b, p. 28).

[20] Assenmacher and Bindseil (2021, p. 116).

not to administratively restrict the use of CBDC, neither in quantity nor in purpose. Instead, CBDC is to be made available as a universal means of payment according to general market demand. Only then will CBDC be unrestricted legal tender, which is one of the fundamental purposes for introducing CBDC. Otherwise, one might as well leave things as they are.

7.4.3 *Should CBDC Be Interest-Bearing?*

One measure banks can take to counteract the substitution of bank money by CBDC is to pay deposit interest on account balances. That would certainly work in favour of bank money. The question is whether the banks can afford deposit interest in competition with digital money, especially CBDC. Probably not.

Apart from that, deposit interest on bank deposits would not help much if central banks too pay interest on CBDC. Some CBDC working papers had envisaged this.[21] In addition, tiered interest rates paid on CBDC have been suggested, for example, paying a certain interest rate on CBDC holdings below 3,000 euros, and a lower interest rate above that threshold.[22] Central banks have occasionally already used tiered interest rates on conventional reserves.

Meanwhile, the majority of CBDC developers are of the opinion that CBDC, being base money, should not be interest-bearing. Another reason is that interest on CBDC is probably only practicable where it is in the form of conventional central-bank account balances. In this case, a central bank could, for purely pragmatic reasons, consider paying a similar interest rate on reserves-based CBDC as banks might pay on customer deposits. This would counteract any fluctuations in the use of bank money and CBDC.

The situation is different when CBDC exists in the form of tokens in the digital wallets of individuals, financial institutions, companies, etc. It would be rather effortful for a central bank to access individual digital wallets, if at all permissible under data protection laws. As with bank account numbers, people will have no choice but to disclose the address

[21] For example Kumhof and Noone (2018, p. 8), Bordo and Levin (2017, 2019), and Adrian and Mancini-Griffoli (2021, p. 75).

[22] Bindseil (2020, p. 22).

of their digital wallet to the tax office. To the central bank as well? Rather not, and central banks themselves are unlikely to want that. Independently, for reasons of proper division of functions, the tax office should not be used as a service provider for the central bank. The banks, for their part, are out of the game as far as CBDC is concerned, since they no longer have anything to do with the monetary management of CBDC customer wallets, unlike previous customer bank accounts.

Traditional cash cannot be credited or debited with interest. The same ought to apply to modern digital currency. Apart from that, money was and is not an interest-bearing financial contract, but a widely used means of payment for very many purposes. As it says succinctly on US dollar notes: *This note is legal tender for all debts public and private.*

This points to an essential reason for not paying or demanding interest on holding money. The inscription on dollar notes does not read: *This note is transferable credit and debt*. Money, the means of payment, the bearer instrument, also for paying out credit and to settle debts, is itself not credit and debt and should thus not be interest-bearing. Interest is only justified by a credit relationship. Interest is paid by a debtor to a creditor. The widespread view in today's economics of the identity of credit and money ("credit money" or "debt money") is a false identity. It is true that credit is provided by central banks and banks in the form of central-bank account balances and bank account balances, that is, non-cash money created specifically to pay out a loan or make an investment "out of thin air". But the payment instrument created in this way is not the credit relationship. The equation of account balance and credit, or of credit amount and credit, respectively, is an understandable verbal simplification but nevertheless misleading and confusing.

This does not contradict deposit interest on bank account balances. Banks have a good credit reason when they pay deposit interest. However, that interest is not paid on the payment instrument, but on the credit involved, "disbursed" in bank money. That bank money is a surrogate for the actual disbursement of the loan in central-bank money. The account balance at a bank entails the promise to pay out the balance in cash at the customer's request or to transfer it in the form of reserves to the recipient bank of another customer. Bank money is associated with a cash loan from the customers as creditors to the banks as cash debtors (and reserve debtors in the case of bank money transfers to other banks).

Central-bank money, in contrast, may be issued in disbursement of a loan from the central bank to a bank, but this does not establish a *mutual* credit relationship like bank credit. A respective bank owes principal and interest to the central bank, while the central bank owes nothing more to that bank. Since the end of any kind of gold peg, central-bank base money stands for no other monetary value than itself. Cash, reserves and CBDC are the forms of base-level fiat money, neither required to be covered in other types of money nor redeemable in assets of the central bank. Therefore, a central bank cannot become formally illiquid in its own currency. At most, the forms of central-bank money can be exchangeable for each other, such as reserves for cash. Or worn-out banknotes can be exchanged for new ones. In credit terms, however, the central bank only owes its borrowers disbursement of base money in the form of cash, reserves and soon also CBDC. Other than that, the central bank owes nothing to the banks and non-bank users of central-bank money, just as holders of cash, reserves and CBDC have no claim on the central bank.

The CBDC design principle that follows from this is that properly handled CBDC is not interest-bearing. This has always applied to central-bank notes, and should have applied also to reserves. Zero deposit interest on reserves has indeed been practiced by some central banks, while others—unfoundedly—did and do pay deposit interest.

7.4.4 CBDC as "Good Money", Bank Money as "Bad Money"

Bad money drives good money out of circulation. This is a rule of experience formulated by Th. Gresham and N. Copernicus in the sixteenth century. At that time, this meant that good coins, those with a regular silver content, were held back by their owners as far as possible, while bad coins, those that were worn out or deliberately degraded with a lower silver content, were to be disposed of as soon as possible. Often, the difference between good and bad coins was associated with a change in the parity of prices. The consideration could also apply to modern bank money and central-bank money insofar as reserves and CBDC represent high-powered "good money", while money surrogates—insufficiently covered and thus vulnerable bank money as well as the new money surrogates (MMFs, e-money, cryptocurrencies)—are in the role of "bad money".

Wouldn't this mean that banks need not worry about their bank money, and that central banks might have reason to worry about hoarding of CBDC? The question remains hypothetical for now. As long as the central bank and the government guarantee the existence of bank money, the question will not arise in practice and the 1:1 parity of bank money to central-bank money will not be in doubt.[23]

Unlike silver and gold, modern token money has no commodity value. Instead, the question is of how safe stock and stable value the money is. From this point of view, central-bank money is usually the safer and more stable money. Where this is not the case, there is the problem of currency flight and parallel currencies. But where there is a reasonably stable currency, safe central-bank base money will have an advantage over unbacked or insufficiently backed or securities-backed private currencies.

The advantage of base money is today transferred to a considerable extent to the actually private and lowly covered bank money, in that central bank and government guarantee the bank money to a large extent and thus the existence of systemically relevant banks. Whether and to what degree that transfer of trust also applies to third-level money surrogates (MMF, e-money, stablecoins) as far as they work with bank money, is questionable, especially if the coverage consists for the most part of securities. However, to the degree there are doubts about the ability of central bank and government to actually maintain the functioning of the bank money regime—and this happens to a lesser or greater extent in a crisis—a move away from bank money and from new monetary surrogates is to be expected, or currency flight altogether.

In a futurist scenario, this would then also threaten the acceptance of bank money and its 1:1 parity with CBDC, thereby also that of new money surrogates based on bank money. As a result, bank money and new money surrogates could circulate below par to central-bank money. Hedge funds could start speculating on this, the way Soros speculated against the British pound.[24] But here, too, things are not as clear-cut as they might seem. In Chile, for example, contrary to what might be expected, many goods often command a higher price when paid for in cash, or, respectively, a lower price when paid for cashless with bank money by credit card or bank transfer.

There is a model of a general trilemma of monetary policy, based on, but not to be confused with the more specific Triffin *di*lemma of the US dollar as the world's reserve currency. The general *tri*lemma of monetary

[23] The problem of CBDC parity with other types of money is discussed in Bjerg (2017, 2018, pp. 6, 9, 18).

[24] Bjerg (2018, p. 14).

policy is based on three objectives: free cross-border mobility of capital, free exchange rate of the currency and autonomous monetary policy. The trilemma states that only two of these three objectives can be achieved at a time, while the third must be abandoned.

For example, if international capital mobility is unrestricted and the exchange rate is free, the only thing a central bank can do is to fulfil the market dynamics of these two variables and largely forego other monetary policy goals and measures—or else to take measures that restrict capital mobility or manage the exchange rate, so that these would no longer be free.

O. Bjerg has transferred the monetary policy trilemma to the coexistence of central-bank money and bank money.[25] The three corresponding objectives are

- 1:1 parity between bank money and central-bank money
- unlimited convertibility of the two types of money into each other
- monetary policy autonomy of the central bank.

How far an analogous trilemma is given here is left open. But it is plausible that the more one wants to achieve one or two of the three objectives, one has to make concessions to the others. If the central bank wants to retain maximum control over the relationship between bank money and CBDC, it cannot unlock exchangeability. However, limited exchangeability or limited access to digital CBDC may jeopardise the 1:1 parity of bank money, and it is not certain that the government guarantee of CBDC will eliminate this danger in a crisis situation. If, on the other hand, free exchangeability is to be ensured, the central bank must supply CBDC to the extent it is in demand.

7.4.5 *Phasing Out State Support for Non-legal-tender Means of Payment*

Governments can contribute to the spread of CBDC in their own ways. One effective measure, for example, is for government and other public sector entities to gradually move towards preferring CBDC rather than

[25] Bjerg (2017, p. 29, 2018, p. 7).

bank money in their own payment transactions. This aspect of substituting CBDC for bank money should be an explicit design principle for establishing and promoting CBDC.

Another CBDC design principle, one of fundamental systemic significance, is to reduce government guarantees on bank deposits. Deposit insurance of banks should gradually be fully privatised. Similarly, to recapitalise or temporarily nationalise private banks in distress should no longer be considered an obvious option of government intervention.

As for the role of central banks, their de facto liquidity guarantee to banks needs to be restricted and reconsidered in more detail. A change already results from the fact that the share of bank money in the public money supply M1 decreases when the share of CBDC increases. In this respect, the banks' need to fully finance in CBDC or fractionally refinance in reserves open up certain policy options for the central banks.

Such measures on the part of the government or the central bank can be taken to the extent that CBDC spreads. Put more generally: The spread of CBDC requires and enables the gradual withdrawal of central-bank support and state warranty of money surrogates, or non-legal-tender means of payment, respectively. Even if government and central bank tolerate private money—bank money, MMF shares, e-monies, stablecoins and uncovered cryptocurrencies—it by no means follows that central bank, government, taxpayers and bank customers (through bail-in) are held liable for it.

7.5 Bank Run—A Problem of Bank Money, Not of CBDC. Further Implications for CBDC Design Principles

Today's successors to the Banking School doctrine claim that introducing CBDC would destabilise the monetary and financial system. There would be a landslide shift in money holdings.[26] Quite a few bankers and central bankers are indeed worried that the substitution of bank money could happen too quickly on too large a scale. This would be tantamount to a general bank run with the risk of a collapse of the entire payment system. About 82% of central bankers surveyed harbour this concern.[27]

[26] For example Selgin (2021).

[27] OMFIF and IBM (2019, pp. 28, 30).

Concerns of this kind are once again an implicit admission of the instability and crisis-proneness of the existing bank money regime. It is remarkable how the bank-run problem is ignored or at least played down in the existing fractional-reserve system, while it is grossly overstated in the context of CBDC. A bank run does not occur under normal conditions, but is imminent only in a crisis situation of a single bank or the entire banking sector. With CBDC, this will not change abruptly, especially if there were deposit interest on bank money and the central banks continue—to a degree—to act as lender and broker-dealer of last resort. Nevertheless, in crisis mode, runs on bank money in favour of cash or CBDC are likely. The worse the crisis and the larger the share of bank money in the total money supply, the more massive the bank run.

But where does the problem come from? Is it caused by CBDC? No. Bank run is the collapse mechanism inherent in the fractional reserve base of the bank money regime. In an emergency, the obligation to redeem bank money in cash or CBDC can only be fulfilled to a small extent and thus not reliably. There must be no ambiguity: Bank run has been the problem of bank money ever since it existed. Bank run is the writing on the wall of the bank money regime. Central-bank money, by contrast, knows no run problem for it is sovereign base money, not a promissory second-tier or third-tier money surrogate.

What can happen, of course, is a run on the official currency in the form of flight into other national currencies. This can arise on the occasion of a banking or debt crisis, or it may sometimes be the case, even chronically, in countries with weak economies or, independently, poorly managed national monetary systems as part of government mismanagement. In any case, where there is a problem of currency flight, it affects bank money as much as central-bank money.

However, as far as the relationship between bank money and central-bank money is concerned, central-bank money is the stabilising factor, while bank money is the factor of uncertainty and instability. The more CBDC there is, and correspondingly less bank money and other monetary surrogates, the lower the risk of bank runs, and the lower also the severity and damage potential of crises in the banking and financial sector.

Once again, it follows as a CBDC system design principle to make CBDC available on demand, rather than restricting it administratively and withholding it from the public in large quantities. Three principles can be formulated in more detail, concerning the convertibility of bank money and CBDC:

> First, CBDC and bank money must generally be interchangeable. The convertibility of bank money into central-bank money (cash so far) has always been, and continues to be, an essential precondition for the general acceptance of bank money. It is also a prerequisite for the parity of bank money and central-bank money.[28] This will apply in the same way to the convertibility of bank money into CBDC.
>
> Second, the matter is made easier for all concerned if—in interbank transactions as well as between banks and the central bank—traditional reserves and CBDC are convertible into each other, and if CBDC can also be used for fulfilling the previous reserve functions.
>
> Third—and this is of considerable importance in preventing bank runs—the central bank should issue a standing conversion guarantee to the effect that the exchange of bank money into CBDC is possible at any time through the central bank providing adequate CBDC funds.

Today, central bank and government have to bail out the banks and now even relevant non-bank financial institutions, in order to save the bank money. This is a constraint of a certain blackmail character, because the bank money of the customers, their bank account balances, are held hostage on the banks' balance sheets. Central-bank money, in contrast, does not need to be saved. It is of safe stock and safe to hold, no matter what happens to the banks and the financial markets.

Recent QE rescue measures flooded bank and non-bank finance with liquidity, entailing a mostly unsolicited glut of reserves in the banking sector. Low and even zero interest rates were thus entrenched for a long time, which in turn promoted asset inflation, financial market and real-estate bubbles as well as much increased social inequality and political unrest. This has intensified with asset inflation turning into strong real-economic inflation, triggered by runaway housing prices, the COVID-19 pandemic, Russia's war against Ukraine, and further geopolitical troubles resulting in runaway energy prices, supply chain disruptions and partial supply shortages. The latter developments can certainly not be directly attributed to the flood of reserves. But it is clear that huge amounts of money redirected from non-GDP finances to

[28] Ingves (2018, pp. 2, 9).

GDP finances and output-related expenditure contribute to a huge hike in real-economic inflation.

The reserves can be converted into CBDC according to demand. In the presence of sufficient quantities of CBDC, bank money can be exchanged for CBDC. The certainty that the central bank can provide enough CBDC, and would do so in an emergency, makes it likely that a feared run on bank money will not happen at all. Who can be sure of claims being met, or more precisely, who can trust to be able to redeem bank money in CBDC at any time, does not need to panic.

This has proven true in the crisis after 2008. A big bank run did not occur (except for Cyprus) thanks to government pledges to guarantee customers' bank money. Depending on the country, governments today guarantee bank money up to 100,000–250,000 dollars per account. This would add up to many billions or several trillions in an emergency. In reality, government and parliament could not have raised such sums in a short time. The central bank basically can, irrespective of regular issuing practices. If in a crisis situation a change from bank money to CBDC would still occur, this would not alter the existing volumes of money, credit and debt, unlike today, where in such a case there is a sudden and problematic expansion of respective balance sheet items of both banks and central banks. What would change, of course, is the composition of the money supply by substituting CBDC for bank money.

Incidentally, it cannot be ruled out that in a bank run situation the 1:1 parity of bank money to central-bank money would pose problems, particularly if the central banks, in an attempt to seal off bank money, were to strictly ration the supply of CBDC despite significantly increasing demand for CBDC. Those who believe that different market prices when paying with different types of money are impossible today could be wrong. Different interest rates on financing in different types of money cannot be entirely ruled out either.

As long as there is bank money and other money surrogates that need to be backed up in various ways, the bank run problem will continue to exist. CBDC is suitable for limiting the potential for damage from a bank run. And once more the question arises as to why one should expose oneself to the problem of unsafe and insecure money at all. Credit and investments will never be truly safe. One should not want that either. Capital bears interest, dividends, other returns or appreciation, while at the same time always carrying some risk. Money, however, as the fundamental instrument of the financial and real economy, should not itself be subject to such risks. Money must be as stable in value as possible and, above all, its stock must be absolutely secure. That's why money itself, its creation as well as its flexibly re-adjustable stock should not be an undistinguishable part of the risky credit business and the financial economy in general.

7.6 Putting CBDC into Circulation

Current CBDC concepts envisage putting CBDC into circulation in the same way as hitherto cash and reserves, thus as credit-and-debt money against collateral. In the case of central-bank credit to banks, the collateral consists of eligible securities, primarily sovereign bonds. In the case of bank credit to clients, it will be a disbursement in CBDC against bank-accepted collateral, preferably pledges of housing property or other client assets. That way, money creation remains determined by pro-active primary bank credit, even though the credit is now partly paid out in CBDC, depending on customer preferences. As with cash, a bank must have the required amount of CBDC completely available, or borrow it on the money market or from the central bank, possibly also by converting reserves into CBDC. The banks receive most of the required CBDC through redemption payments from customers or through savings and term investments from customers. As already mentioned, it is advisable to make the QE-induced reserves glut available to the banks in the form of CBDC.

Another obvious possibility is central-bank open market operations, as has been practiced for almost a hundred years now, usually buying up already issued government bonds from private holders. The practice can be expanded, in that it would no longer be an injection of reserves into the banking sector (and crediting of bank money to the bond-selling non-banks). Instead, it can be about a more widespread open-market issuance of CBDC, beyond banks to other financial institutions and actors.

A subsequent next step ought to be the direct but limited purchase of newly issued government bonds by the central bank, bypassing to that extent primary dealers and bond markets, but doing so according to the sole discretion of the central bank, without any involvement of the government. Put differently, even direct bond purchases should be made under "monetary dominance", not "fiscal dominance". In the eyes of many neoclassical economists, this still borders on a taboo. Historically, however, it was by no means off limits, and also today it is considered in certain crisis situations.[29]

In the US, the direct purchase of Treasury bonds by the Fed was a common practice to ensure continued government liquidity until 1935, when Congress prohibited the practice. During WW2, the prohibition was suspended. Since 1975, there has been an exemption for Short-Term Cash Management Bills. In 1981, the prohibition expired altogether. Since then, nonetheless, Federal Reserve banks have *not directly* purchased US Treasury bonds, although this would basically be possible if Congress, Treasury and the Fed agreed accordingly.[30]

In Britain, there have been the ways-and-means advances, a standing government overdraft facility with the Bank of England, of £0.4 billion since 1968. During EU membership 1973–2020 Britain, the UK had reserved the right to maintain that instrument. With the 2008 crisis, the overdraft was expanded to £19.9 billion.[31]

The Bank of Canada offers another example of established practice. It acts as an auctioneer of government bonds, thereby directly absorbing itself 13–20% of newly issued government bonds past primary dealers and government securities distributors.[32] This works smoothly and no one finds it particularly remarkable.

In the EU, by contrast, *direct* sales of government bonds to the ECB or its national member banks are outright prohibited under Art. 123 TFEU (Lisbon Treaty). However, open-market purchases of sovereign bonds by the ECB remain unrestricted. This comes down to indirect or retroactive monetary (re-)financing of government spending. The initial purchasers of government bonds, the primary dealers, are a consortium of banks. They sell on the greater part of the bonds to other banks, funds, insurance companies, etc. Prior to the introduction of the euro, some euro countries, too, had direct central-bank credit to the government, at least as a bridging loan to cover gaps between expenditure and revenues. The Lisbon Treaty has radically prevented even such small things.

[29] Cf. Adrian et al. (2021, p. 29).

[30] Garbade (2014).

[31] HM Treasury and Bank of England announce temporary extension to Ways and Means facility, Bank of England 09 April 2020.

[32] Becklumb and Frigon (2015).

The rationale for this ban was mainly a feared lack of budgetary discipline in public finances, while blinding out that it has always been banks and bond markets that have financed excessive sovereign debt, and that banks and shadow banks are recurrently prone to excessive exuberance in other private financial markets too. One thing is certain: government debt is a thriving business for bond traders and bond holders. Why should primary bond dealers, pension funds and other institutional and individual bond holders have a birthright to the entire, ultimately tax-funded cake of sovereign bonds?

As a CBDC design principle, it follows from the above to circulate CBDC not only through bank credit to non-banks, or in exchange for bank money, but also, to a limited extent, through regular open market purchases of government bonds by the central bank, through government overdraft facilities with the central bank, through direct underwriting of government bonds by the central bank and, in the future—and still to be explained—through debt-free genuine seigniorage to the public purse. The CBDC design principles developed so far are summarised in Box 7.1.

Box 7.1—Top ten CBDC design principles

1. CBDC to take the form of digital tokens transferred directly from a payer's digital wallet into that of the recipient, rather than traditional central-bank reserves (book money).
2. CBDC to be unrestricted legal tender, both in terms of access to CBDC as well as its usability, for non-banks as well as for banks and other financial institutions, for private customers as well as for business customers.
3. Provision of CBDC according to market demand. No administrated quantity limits.
4. CBDC not interest-bearing.
5. As CBDC spreads, gradual phase-out of government guarantees for bank money. No central-bank and government support for third-tier money surrogates and uncovered private monies.
6. Gradual expansion of CBDC use in payment transactions of state bodies and other institutions under public law.

7. Substitutability of conventional reserves by CBDC in interbank transactions and at the central bank.
8. Mutual convertibility of CBDC and bank money in non-bank transactions.
9. Standing conversion guarantee by central banks to provide CBDC according to demand, especially in prevention of a possible bank run.
10. Issuance of CBDC not only by way of bank credit to nonbanks or through the exchange of bank money into CBDC, but also, to a limited extent, through open-market purchases of government bonds by the central bank and through government overdraft facilities with the central bank.

    Additional recommended issuance channels are the direct underwriting of a share of newly issued government bonds by the central bank as well as issuance through debt-free genuine seigniorage to the public purse.

7.7 Coverage for Stablecoins and Other Third-Tier Money Surrogates

Beyond CBDC design principles there is the question of how to deal with new third-tier money surrogates and unbacked cryptocurrencies.

Issuers of new money surrogates are often thought of as narrow banks. The term narrow banking originated from of the concept of 100% reserve banking which was developed in response to the banking crisis after 1929. According to this concept, bank money should be 100% backed by base money from the US Treasury or the Federal Reserve. To prevent the new monetary surrogates of the last three decades—initially MMF shares and e-money—from repeating fractional reserve banking, the narrow-banking principle was applied early on. As stated in the introductory taxonomy of money, the principle of 1:1 coverage is anchored in the regulation of MMFs and e-money, with modifications depending on the country.

E-money from banks, PSP and other licensed e-money institutes must be backed 1:1 by bank money, whereby a certain part may also be held in government bills, subject to the requirements of the financial supervisor.[33] Banks' e-money is held in a corresponding pool of customer balances, but without 100% reserve coverage. A 100% guarantee by central bank and government is apparently implied here, as part of the bank money privilege.

Unlike e-money, MMF shares were originally not intended as a means of payment, but as a money-market security. Paid-in money flows entirely into short-term bonds, repo transactions, etc. MMFs are obliged to invest only in best-rated assets. MMFs promise their clients to manage the investments in such a way that 1 fund unit is always worth 1 or 10 currency units and can be redeemed accordingly. Regulation of the same kind is currently underway with regard to stablecoins. A contentious question relates to whether the issuers of stablecoins should be regulated like banks, that is, as monetary credit institutions creating a cryptographic money surrogate, or as a kind of shadow bank or PSP or other financial institution.

Banks are associated with the idea that they are more strictly regulated and supervised than non-bank financial institutions. However, this cannot always be said. It is true that the banks have had to buy the retention of their privileged status by accepting over time a myriad of bureaucratic requirements. But the very core of the bank money privilege—the fractional reserve—has never been restricted in the process; instead, reserve requirements were abolished or reduced ever further and became a subcategory of tier-1 banking core capital of at least 6% of risk-weighted assets. This sounds like something, but in fact it is far too little in an emergency, and implicitly continues to rely on the helping hands of the central bank and government. Under this aspect, the already existing as well as the still to be expected regulation of the new money surrogates is more coherent and stricter than banking regulation is.

Another contentious question relates to the means of coverage for the new money surrogates. Should the coverage be in base money (conventional reserves, future CBDC) or also in bank money? Or should both be permissible, also in combination? Should broad or narrow bounds be set to issuers regarding the question of whether a larger or only a small portion of the paid-in money can be lent on the interbank or shadow-bank money market? Or by allowing cash equivalents and other

[33] Oliveros and Pacheco (2016) and Hess (2019).

investments as cover funds? If several or all of these options are to be possible, in what proportions should it be permissible?

Such questions now mainly concern stablecoins. Who is actually liable for their continued existence and stable value? Should they be rescued in an individual or sectoral crisis like bank money and the banks? For example, prior to the 2008 banking crisis, MMF shares were considered completely safe; until September of that year, when, as a result of losses from the Lehman Bank, the shares of the Reserve Primary Fund fell to 0.97 dollars, thus less than 1 dollar. This triggered a general run on MMF shares. The US Treasury felt compelled to set up a *Temporary Guarantee Program*, which guaranteed investors 1 dollar per share. So far, this remained an isolated case, but perhaps a precedent. It became clear that third-tier money surrogates, even with a 100% cover reserve, are just as safe or as unsafe as the cover funds in question.

Would it not be more correct to tell the users of new money surrogates from the outset that they are using private money for which the central bank and the government do not guarantee in case of emergency? This is what is being advocated here: A state warranty of third-level means of payment as well as unbacked private cryptocurrencies is to be completely ruled out, as is any support or rescue of issuing companies by the central bank or the government. Otherwise there is a danger that the new money surrogates will repeat the long history of crises and bankruptcies of bank money, and that central bank and government are compelled to come to their rescue.

As far as cryptocurrencies and stablecoins are concerned, the EU Commission considers them in part as securities covered by the EU Financial Markets Directive. This is especially true for trading in Bitcoin and other uncovered cryptos. On the other hand, as far as stablecoins serve as a means of payment outside the crypto market, they are treated as e-money, which falls under the EU Electronic Money Directive.[34]

The 2021 Report on Stablecoins by a commission of the US President recommended regulating American stablecoin issuers as federally insured depository institutions. This includes depository banks (commercial banks) and savings banks.[35] The proposed classification as depository banks would make stablecoin issuers members of the US depository

[34] European Parliament (2021).

[35] President's Working Group (2021, p. 16).

insurance scheme and the stablecoin issuers eligible for Federal Reserve standard benefits, in an emergency also for liquidity assistance from the Federal Reserve and the US Treasury. In this way, stablecoins would be guaranteed by the state in the same way and to the same extent as bank money. The recommendation thus repeats a basic mistake of banking regulation, which is central-bank and government warranty of private means of payment.

At the same time, the *US President's Report on Stablecoins* has failed to make a proposal on how to cover stablecoins. The de facto criterion for stablecoins is to have sufficient bank money as well as Bitcoins and securities that can be readily liquidated in order to meet the ongoing exchange of the stablecoins back into bank money or Bitcoins. In exchange for the issuance of 1 stablecoin, the issuer takes in 1 dollar or an equivalent amount in Bitcoins. How the sponsoring entity deals with these revenues as cover funds has so far been left up to it. However, if a stablecoin issuer promises redemption in US dollars at any time, it must prove to the supervisory authorities that it is able to do so. Otherwise, it would be a case of brochure fraud.

In contrast to the *President's Report on Stablecoins*, another expert paper rejected the classification of stablecoin issuers as depository banks and instead proposed specific coverage requirements.[36] These demand stablecoin issuers to be given a status as a special-purpose investment company similar to that of MMFs. The purpose is to issue stablecoins whose monetary value is anchored or synthetically pegged to the US dollar. The legislative proposal includes the following coverage requirements: At least 10% of the coverage consists of liquid US bank money or overnight repos; at least 20% are to be held in liquid bank money or securities with a residual maturity of 7 days or less. Only high-grade securities are eligible. No more than 5% of the cover reserve may come from the same issuer. This spreads the debtor risk.

These requirements place the emphasis on the proportional allocation of the cover reserve to overnight bank money (in future also CBDC), near-money and other cash equivalents. But the proposal is obviously designed for undisturbed business as usual. In the event of a crisis, these requirements are likely to be too low, involving a high risk of illiquidity and insolvency.

[36] Michel and Schulp (2021).

Overall, regulatory principles for stablecoins should include the following:

- Stablecoins must be denominated in their own name. They may not be denominated in the respective official currency, or have a composite name that includes the name of the official currency, even if they peg their exchange rate to it.
- Stablecoins, MMFs and e-money must be issued on a 1:1 basis against bank money and/or central-bank reserves and CBDC.

  As CBDC proliferates, the proportion of funds collected by the stablecoin issuer shall represent the proportions of bank money and CBDC in M1.

  All other means of payment are excluded for the purchase of third-level money surrogates, in particular unbacked cryptocurrencies such as Bitcoin (currently a large and volatile cover of stablecoins).
- The money paid in, as well as any assets acquired with it, must be denominated in home currency and issued by financial firms or government bodies located in that currency area.
- Issuers must guarantee 100% value coverage of their stablecoins at all times. If, in addition to money, the coverage includes cash equivalents, more than half of the coverage must be CBDC and overnight bank money according to their share in M1; a smaller part can be cash equivalents, and the smallest part also longer-term highest-rated securities.
- Only a small part of the coverage in cash equivalents and securities, for example a maximum of 5%, may come from one and the same issuer (debtor).
- Any support and warranty of third-tier money surrogates by central bank and government is expressly excluded on a statutory basis.

If the above conditions are met, central-bank monetary policy will reliably be transmitted to the new money surrogates. What, however, should happen to unbacked cryptocurrencies, assuming, contrary to expectations, they would reach critical volumes?

A ban on trading cryptocurrencies like in China is unlikely to happen in the Western world in the foreseeable future. In smaller countries, it is questionable anyway whether a ban could be practically enforced if crypto platforms continue to operate abroad and there is unimpeded access to the World Wide Web. For the same reason, it hardly seems possible to limit the quantity of uncovered cryptocurrencies.

However, it is not a foregone conclusion that precautions against uncovered cryptos become relevant at all in the very presence of CBDC and stablecoins. This is because CBDC and, to some extent, bank money and stablecoins are likely to be more in line with the interests of the vast majority in a halfway predictable value of money than uncovered and volatile-unstable cryptocurrencies.

If in a free market economy people and companies accept payment in cryptos, this should not be stopped without good reason. Monetary sovereignty, monetary and financial stability as well as preventing illicit finance *are* good reasons. But currently prevailing interests are apparently unwilling to see it that way. As long as there is no internationally agreed legal handling of unbacked cryptos, this market is likely to remain a volatile trouble spot, a vehicle for exalted speculation as well as for the underground economy, money laundering and tax evasion.

The bottom line remains that a permissive regulation of stablecoins will bring about a new variety of unstable reserve banking, not necessarily a fractional reserve, but an inadequately secured one. To regain monetary sovereignty and effective monetary policy, it is indispensable not only to have 1:1 coverage of new money surrogates, but a coverage the greater part of which consists of CBDC and bank money according to the composition of M1. For a while, this contributes to some extent to the retention of bank money, but will not prevent the rise of CBDC and the related recomposition of the money supply.

References

Adrian, Tobias, and Tomaso Mancini-Griffoli. 2021. How Will Digital Money Impact the International Monetary System? In *Central Bank Digital Currency. Considerations, Project, Outlook*, ed. Dirk Niepelt, pp. 73–79. London: CEPR Press.

Adrian, Tobias, Christopher Erceg, Simon Gray, and Ratna Sahay. 2021. Asset Purchases and Direct Financing. International Monetary Fund, DP/2021/023.

Assenmacher, Katrin, and Ulrich Bindseil. 2021. The Eurosystem's Digital Euro Project: Preparing for a Digital Future. In *Central Bank Digital Currency. Considerations, Project, Outlook*, ed. Dirk Niepelt, pp. 111–118. London: CEPR Press.

Auer, Raphael, and Rainer Böhme. 2020. CBDC Architectures, the Financial System, and the Central Bank of the Future. VoxEU/CEPR, 29 October.

Auer, Raphael, Giulio Cornelli, and Jon Frost. 2020. Rise of the Central Bank Digital Currencies: Drivers, Approaches and Technologies. BIS Working Papers, No. 880, August.

Auer, Raphael, Giulio Cornelli, and Jon Frost. 2021. Central Bank Digital Currencies: Taking Stock of Architectures and Technologies. In *Central Bank Digital Currency. Considerations, Project, Outlook*, ed. Dirk Niepelt, pp. 155–162. London: CEPR Press.

Barrdear, John, and Michael Kumhof. 2016. The Macroeconomics of Central Bank Issued Digital Currencies, Bank of England. Staff Research Paper No. 605, July.

Becklumb, Penny, and Mathieu Frigon. 2015. *How the Bank of Canada Creates Money for the Federal Government*, Publ.No. 2015-51-E. Ottawa: Library of Parliament, 10 August.

Bindseil, Ulrich. 2019. Central Bank Digital Currency—Financial System Implications and Control. ECB Working Paper, ECB Directorate General Operations, 30 July.

Bindseil, Ulrich. 2020. Tiered CBDC and the Financial System. ECB Working Paper Series, No. 2351, January.

BIS. 2019. Proceeding with Caution. A Survey on Central Bank Digital Currency, Written by Christian Barontini and Henry Holden. Bank for International Settlements Papers, No. 101, January.

BIS. 2020. Central Bank Digital Currencies: Foundational Principles and Core Features, publ. by BIS and the central banks of Canada, EU, Japan, Sweden, Switzerland, England and USA. Bank for International Settlements, Basel.

BIS. 2021. CBDC: Opportunity for the Monetary System. BIS Annual Economic Report, 65–95.

Bjerg, Ole. 2017. Designing New Money—The Policy Trilemma of Central Bank Digital Currency. Copenhagen Business School Working Paper, June.

Bjerg, Ole. 2018. Breaking the Gilt Standard. The Problem of Parity in Kumhof and Noone's Design Principles for Central Bank Digital Currencies. Copenhagen Business School Working Paper, August.

Boar, Codruta, Henry Holden, and Amber Wadsworth. 2020. Impending Arrival—A Sequel to the Survey on Central Bank Digital Currency. BIS Papers, No. 107, Bank for International Settlements, Basel, January.

Bordo, Michael D., and Andrew T. Levin. 2017. Central Bank Digital Currency and the Future of Monetary Policy. NBER Working Paper Series, No. 23711, August.

Bordo, Michael D., and Andrew T. Levin. 2019. Digital Cash: Principles & Practical Steps. NBER Working Paper Series, No. 25455, January.

Broadbent, Ben. 2016. Central Banks and Digital Currencies. Speech at the London School of Economics documented by the Bank of England. www.bankofengland.co.uk/publications/Pages/speeches/default.aspx.

Brunnermeier, Markus K., and Dirk Niepelt. 2019. On the Equivalence of Private and Public Money. *Journal of Monetary Economics* 106: 27–41.

Cunha, Paulo R., Paulo Melo, and Helder Sebastião. 2021. From Bitcoin to CBDC: Making Sende of the Digital Money Revolution, *Future Internet* 13: 165. www.mdpi.com/journal/futureinternet.

De Bode, Ian, Matt Higginson, and Marc Niederkorn. 2021. CBDC and Stablecoins: Early Coexistence on an Uncertain Road. McKinsey & Company, October 11.

ECB. 2020a. Study on the Payment Attitudes of Consumers in the Euro Area (SPACE), Frankfurt, December.

ECB. 2020b. Report on a Digital Euro. ECB, Frankfurt, October.

European Parliament. 2021. *Briefing on Stablecoins—Private-Sector Quest for Cryptostability*. Brussels: European Union.

Fatas, Antonio. 2021. Can Central Bank Digital Currency Transform Digital Payments? In *Central Bank Digital Currency. Considerations, Project, Outlook*, ed. Dirk Niepelt, pp. 51–55. London: CEPR Press.

Federal Reserve of the U.S. 2022. Money and Payments: The U.S. Dollar in the Age of Digital Transformation, Research & Analysis. Board of Governors of the Federal Reserve System, January.

Flodén, Martin, and Björn Segendorf. 2021. The Role of Central Banks When Cash Is No Longer King. A Perspective from Sweden. In *Central Bank Digital Currency. Considerations, Project, Outlook*, ed. Dirk Niepelt, pp. 99–109. London: CEPR Press.

Garbade, Kenneth D. 2014. Direct Purchases of U.S. Treasury Securities by Federal Reserve Banks. New York Federal Reserve Staff Reports, No. 684, August.

Georgieva, Kristalina. 2022. The Future of Money—Gearing up for CBDC. IMF Speech, 9 February.

Hess, Simon. 2019. 100% E-Money and Its Implications for Central Bank Digital Currency. SSRN Working Paper, 26 June.

IMF. 2018. Casting Light on Central Bank Digital Currency. IMF Staff Discussion Note, written by T. Mancini-Griffoli et al. International Monetary Fund, Washington, DC.

Ingves, Stefan. 2018. The e-Krona and the Payments of the Future. Speech by the Governor of the Swedish Riksbank, Stockholm.

Kumhof, Michael, and Clare Noone. 2018. Central Bank Digital Currencies—Design Principles and Balance Sheet Implications. Staff Working Paper, No. 725. Bank of England, London, May.

Lagarde, Christine, and Fabio Panetta. 2022. Key Objectives of the Digital Euro. *The ECB Blog*, 13 July.

Maechler, Andréa M., and Andreas Wehrli. 2021. How to Provide a Secure and Efficient Settlement Asset for the Financial Infrastructure of Tomorrow. In *Central Bank Digital Currency. Considerations, Project, Outlook*, ed. Dirk Niepelt, pp. 147–153. London: CEPR Press.

McKinsey Global Institute. 2021. The Rise and Rise of the Global Balance Sheet, November.

Meaning, Jack, Ben Dyson, James Barker, and Emily Clayton. 2018. Broadening Narrow Money: Monetary Policy with a Central Bank Digital Currency. Bank of England Staff Working Paper, No. 724, May.

Michel, Norbert J., and Jennifer J. Schulp. 2021. A Simple Proposal for Regulating Stablecoins. Cato Briefing, No. 128, November 5.

Niepelt, Dirk. 2015. Reserves for Everyone—Towards a New Monetary Regime? VOX CEPR's Policy Portal, 21 January. http://voxeu.org/article/keep-cash-let-public-hold-centralbank-reserves.

Niepelt, Dirk. 2021. "Reserves for All": Political Rather Than Macroeconomic Risks. In *Central Bank Digital Currency. Considerations, Project, Outlook*, ed. Dirk Niepelt, pp. 39–44. London: CEPR Press.

Oliveros, Rosa M., and Lucia Pacheco. 2016. Protection of Customers' Funds in Electronic Money: A Myriad of Regulatory Approaches, BBVA Research. Financial Inclusion Watch, 28 October.

OMFIF. 2020. *Digital Currencies—A Question of Trust*. Written by Bhavin Patel and Pierre Ortlieb. OMFIF, London.

OMFIF and IBM. 2019. *Retail CBDCs, the Next Payments Frontier*. London: Official Monetary and Financial Institutions Forum and Costa Mesa, CA: IBM Blockchain Worldwire.

President's Working Group. 2021. Report on Stablecoins, November (Full authorship: The President's Working Group on Financial Markets, the Federal Deposit Insurance Corporation, and the Office of the Comptroller of the Currency).

Selgin, George. 2021. CBDC as a Potential Source of Financial Instability, *Cato Journal* 41 (2) (Spring/Summer).

Sveriges Riksbank. 2017. The Riksbank's E-Krona Project. Report 1, Stockholm, September.

Sveriges Riksbank. 2018a. The Riksbank's E-Krona Project. Report 2, Stockholm, October.

Sveriges Riksbank. 2018b. Special Issue on the e-Krona. *Sveriges Riksbank Economic Review* 2018: 3.

Zellweger-Gutknecht, Corinne. 2021. The Right and Duty of Central Banks to Issue Retail Digital Currency. In *Central Bank Digital Currency. Considerations, Project, Outlook*, ed. Dirk Niepelt, pp. 31–38. London: CEPR Press.

CHAPTER 8

Central Banks and Monetary Policy Under Conditions of CBDC

8.1 Objectives of Monetary Policy. To Be or Not to Be in Control of Money Creation, Inflation, Interest Rates, Growth and Employment

Dealing with CBDC and the development of the monetary system would be incomplete without reflecting on the development of central banks. As a rule, they are the issuers of CBDC and the governing body of the monetary system, or at least they should be. Their role has evolved since they have existed, professionally and politically controversial, over a spectrum ranging from a narrow delineation of tasks to a broad mandate.

Depending on the country and history, central banks may differ in terms of institutional arrangement and monetary policy stances. All the same, they share certain responsibilities. They are seen as guardians of a nation's monetary sovereignty and custodians of the official currency. This includes preserving the currency's purchasing power as far as this can be attributed to monetary factors, which in turn includes taking care of the currency's foreign exchange rate. However, the guardians of national currencies have long neglected *money* sovereignty in terms of being in control of the national stock of money (the means of payment), the composition of the overall money supply and the provision of sovereign money in an amount that makes monetary policy effectively possible in the first place.

J. Huber, *The Monetary Turning Point*,
https://doi.org/10.1007/978-3-031-23957-1_8

In view of the central banks' pronouncements and public discussion of monetary policy, the impression could arise that a central bank's task is to control inflation and the level of interest rates, whereas supplying money to the economy and exerting control over the stock of money in general does not really seem to be part of a central bank's business. Under current conditions this isn't entirely beside the point, but a misapprehension of why there are central banks it is nonetheless. What central banks can do without direct administrative intervention, is, first, create central-bank money (notes, reserves, future CBDC) and, second, set the interest rates on central-bank money. That's what they can do in actual fact, everything else they can only try—in particular, try to influence the creation of bank money and other money surrogates, as well as try to influence the external value of the currency and the levels of inflation and interest—but whether and to what extent they succeed in doing so often remains unclear.

The original task of central banks and the reason for their emergence was to issue money, paper money at the time, central-bank notes. Systematic refinancing of the banks and the provision of central-bank book money exclusively for the banks (reserves on central-bank account) were only gradually added from the last decades of the nineteenth century onwards. From the very beginning, the issuance of central-bank money was inevitably linked to the question: How much central-bank money? How much money can there be without causing unwanted side effects, especially inflation?

Hence, money creation is in the context of a monetary quantity theory, going back to J. Bodin's inflation theory from the sixteenth century, formulated on the occasion of the Spanish silver inflation. According to this theory, inflation arises from an overshooting money supply. That basic approach to inflation continued throughout the centuries until the last and extreme variety of quantity theory, which was monetarism according to M. Friedman. Monetarism was widespread in the 1960–1980s, as a counter-concept to then prevailing Keynesianism. Friedman postulated inflation as "always and everywhere a monetary phenomenon".[1]

In this simplistic view, more money means more demand, and consequently a higher inflation rate if the increased demand is not matched by a simultaneous increase in supply. The conclusion for monetary policy

[1] Friedman (1991, p. 16, 1992, p. 198).

is that in order to fight inflation, the growth of the money supply must be curbed, or even fixed at, say, a reserve stock of bullion, or a fixed annual growth rate (Friedman proposed 3% or 4% p.a.), or 21 million Bitcoins. Curbing or even fixing the growth in money supply has been tried quite so often. It never worked for good. Most recently, the main reason was the unfolding of the bank money regime which came with a corresponding loss of central-bank control over money creation. Setting limited central-bank reserve positions for the banks did not limit the creation of bank money. The initiative for money creation is with the banks, not the other way round. The supply of central-bank money does not act as a limiting multiplier base, but results as a factual constraint on central banks to refinance the banks, whereby the re-actively required central-bank base money (fractional reserve) as a percentage of bank money became ever smaller over time.

Interest-rate policy is an alternative to monetary quantity policy. Banks have remained dependent, albeit decreasingly, on refinancing in central-bank money (notes and reserves), be it on the interbank money market or directly by central-bank credit. It is assumed that an increase/decrease in central-bank interest rates results in the same increase/decrease in interbank rates and will dampen/encourage the commercial banks' borrowing of reserves, and thus indirectly also the banks' lending and generation of bank money for non-bank financial institutions and the public.

Such interest-rate policies have worked just as poorly as quantity policies. This is due again to the fact that the fractional cash and reserve base to be refinanced is much smaller than the total amount of bank money, and furthermore that the banks' interest margin almost always remains high enough, that is, the interest rates the banks can take on their bank money loans are normally higher enough than the central-bank and interbank rates the banks pay on the money market for reserves (which the banks only necessitate at a fraction of the bank money they create).[2]

[2] The terminology on interest rates is not entirely uniform internationally. The following applies here: *Central-bank rate* is the interest banks pay on borrowing from the central bank, also called *bank rate* for short as well as rediscount rate. *Interbank rate* is the interest on reserves banks pay on loans to each other, also called overnight rate. *Banking rate* is the interest charged by banks for loans to non-bank customers, also referred to as annual percentage rate (APR) as well as, misleadingly, base rate. *Capital-market rates* are, for example, those on bonds and other securities and long-term lending by banks and other financial institutions.

The thesis of low effectiveness of interest-rate policy will be countered by saying that changes in the central-bank rate are given a great deal of attention by the markets and also play a role in the banks' projective calculations of their own banking interest rates on lending bank money. But why should banking interest rates and, one step further, capital-market interest rates mechanically follow central-bank and interbank interest rates, when the bank money involved in the banks' customer business and on the capital markets represents a large multiple of the comparatively small amounts of central-bank money involved in central-bank and interbank lending? Neither the central-bank rate on loans to banks nor the interbank overnight rate on reserves do mechanically determine banking rates, less so capital-market rates.

As far as transmission takes place here, it remains unclear whether this is about a communicative mechanism of sector-wide policy leadership, rather than the workings of a market mechanism determined by flexible price setting in the context of actual supply and demand. The mechanism is known as cognitive "reduction of complexity", something which bankers and other financial players apparently appreciate, far from seeing it as the soft sort of "central planning" it could actually appear to be.

Quite interesting in this respect are cyclical turning points such as the transition from inflation to disinflation, from rising to falling interest rates, or vice versa from falling to rising inflation and interest rates. For example, in the reversal from 2020, it may have looked as if central banks had set the new direction, not major market players. But the rapidly accelerating inflationary push was not expected and certainly not wanted by the central banks. The triggering circumstances, apart from real-estate asset inflation caused by QE, cannot be blamed on the central banks (i.e. the intricate mix of crisis developments including the Covid-19 pandemic, Russia's war on Ukraine, disturbed geopolitics and supply-chain disruptions).

Things are even clearer with the reversal in interest rates. The ECB, unlike the Fed and the Bank of England, actually wanted to continue the politics of financial repression central banks had been pursuing procyclically. For banks and other financial institutions, however, it had become ever more difficult to operate on low to zero interest, causing their margins to shrink. Negative interest rates in the euro area and elsewhere proved counterproductive. Not least, central banks had finally to counter asset inflation especially in real estate, while various financial actors had begun to raise interest rates on their own.

The causations between (1) central-bank rates, (2) interbank rates, (3) banking rates and (4) capital-market rates involve complex two-way dynamics rather than being a simple one-way road that starts at the central bank. In the overall set of given feedback loops, the decisiveness even of central banks remains limited. It often remains undiscernible whether central banks are action leaders or opinion leaders, and more often than not they tend to be the latter, in the hope markets will follow their guidance, whereas in the preponderant impulse direction the central banks follow the factual lead of the markets.

So as not to be misunderstood, central banks are of course weighty market participants. It's not that central-bank policy doesn't make a difference. On the contrary, the question is whether central-bank interest rates (on a short lever of central-bank money supply) are able to induce an overall better balanced development of the money supply and optimal interest rates at all, or whether they do not rather trigger overinterpretations and financial and creditary overreactions of one kind or another.

One can read the succession of approaches to monetary policy since around 1930 as a history of unsuccessful attempts to master the increasingly dominant bank money regime. The approach of a 100% reserve from the 1930s/1940s in America was intended to regain control over the development of the money supply, or over monetary credit extension, respectively. The attempt was politically averted in favour of a separate banking system of little relevance. What remained was monetary policy as mere interest-rate policy, of decreasing effectiveness the more the bank money regime unfolded.

The monetarism that followed did focus again on the money supply. However, the attempt to control bank money creation through reserve positions, that is, through the quantity of available central-bank money, was of diminishing effectiveness in the same way, as were the attempts to regain more control through central-bank rates. The reason was that the share of central-bank money in the composition of the money supply was on the decline, while the increasingly dominant share of bank money continued to expand. The policy of "unconditional accommodation", to put it bluntly, which then began and which continues to this day, made the central banks the auxiliary body of the banking sector.

The weak transmission of monetary policy can be overcome to the degree bank money is replaced with central-bank money, making CBDC the dominant money supply and thus also central-bank rates the lead rates indeed. Even then, however, the idea that monetary policy should determine the levels of prices and interest rates is politically misguided as it fails in reality.

Monetarism had a simplistic and deterministic view of the connection between money supply and price levels. Accomodationism by contrast has tended to discard monetary quantity theory altogether. But pretending there is no connection at all between the money supply and price levels, a claim which was to be heard more often until 2021/2022, has no real foundation, neither in theory nor empirically. The fundamental substance of monetary quantity theory should not be called into question. What is urgently needed, however, is its up-to-date proper differentiation and relativisation. Such an endeavour would include, among others, the following three elements.

First, formally deactivated money (for example, in the form of bank deposits in M2/M3/M4, or similarly aggregated) as well as factually inactive money (for example, in the form of redundant central-bank excess reserves) have no effect in terms of demand-induced inflation. They are of little relevance in this respect. "Lots of money" do not create inflation per se. Just actively circulating money is to be taken into account. Inflation occurs to the extent there is a structural excess of effective demand over actual supply. However, the existence of "lots of money" on the demand side certainly favours the chances of pushing through higher price intentions from the supply side.

Second, following the distinction between GDP finance and non-GDP finance, there are GDP-impacting and non-GDP-impacting uses of money, and accordingly real-economic inflation (CPI) as well as asset inflation, each to different degrees. Exploring the relationship between CPI and asset inflation in more detail would be of considerable significance for macro-sectoral monetary policy.

Third, beyond inflation for monetary reasons there can be numerous non-monetary causes of inflation. The latter arise primarily from structural shortages in the factor supply, for example the supply of labour, skills and qualifications of the workforce, or the supply of resources, energy, transport, housing and so on. The issue as such is well known, but this does not seem to apply to the consequences monetary policy draws from it. If, for example, one reacts to a rise in inflation due to factor shortages with higher interest rates, this leads straight to stagflation, exacerbating rather than eliminating the factor supply shortages. It may also be that interest rate hikes are passed off as a measure against inflation, while it is more about the foreign exchange rate of the currency.

What has been said so far on the ability of monetary policy to influence the dynamics of prices and interest rates can also be said mutatis mutandis about another main objective of central banks, which is the support of real-economic development and employment. With regard to promoting the economy by means of monetary policy, it is clearer from the outset that a central bank can contribute to the business cycle but does not normally control its reversal points.

The EU Lisbon Treaty (Art. 127 TFEU) has subordinated the economic-policy task of the central bank to the objective of price stability. In the U.S. and most other currency areas, there is no such fixed prioritisation. Either way, one should expect neither from parliaments, governments and courts nor the central banks to do things they cannot do. Money is certainly the monetary base of economic activity. But it cannot be concluded from this that prices, interest rates, financial cycles, business cycles, employment levels, etc. can be decisively controlled from the monetary base.

Central banks should not bear primary responsibility for matters they can only partially and indirectly influence. However, they should assume full responsibility for what they can do, that is, creating money in their own currency and circulating it in sufficient quantities and in a suitable way. The most basic task of central banks is in fact to supply the economy with money (not with income, but with the money whose circulation generates income). This is what central banks can do, or should be able to do comprehensively: create the money supply, or at least a dominant base-money supply, and operate payment systems for it, while keeping tight control of money surrogates. Today, this is largely not or only seemingly the case.

If central banks were in control of a dominant share of CBDC in the overall money supply, monetary policy with a loose or tight supply of CBDC, or alternatively with raising or lowering the central-bank rate on CBDC, would influence the financial and real-economic course of events much more effectively than is the case today. Even then, monetary quantity and interest-rate policies cannot and should not be all determining, but they can be effectual. The strength or weakness of policy transmission depends on the large or low weight of the central-bank money supply in general public circulation as well as in non-bank finance and the interbank circuit. With CBDC in increasing quantities, monetary policy will become more effectual. This is because the transmission lever of both central-bank rates and the quantity of CBDC is stronger the greater the share of CBDC in the overall money supply is.

8.2 Independence of Central Banks—Both from the Government as Well as Banking and Finance

8.2.1 Bank of the Banks? Bank of the State?

According to a common distinction, central banks are described as *bank of the banks* as well as *bank of the state*. In this respect, too, the situation has changed fundamentally. Central banks once began as *bank of the state*, in Sweden in 1668, England 1694, France 1800, Austria 1816, and other countries, then most often as private lenders to kings and princes, endowed with the privilege of circulating paper money denominated in the national currency unit, which, of course, did not exclude lending to banks and other private borrowers. Today, by contrast, most central banks have become state-run national monetary authorities, but acting almost exclusively as *bank of the banks*, while contributing little or in fact nothing to the direct financing of government expenditure.

In the course of past financial crises, monetary policy has now developed in a way that goes beyond the framework set out in this way. For one thing, central banks purchase government bonds on the open market on a large scale. In this way, central banks refinance bond-holding banks and shadow banks, thereby indirectly also refinancing a government's previous debt-funded expenditure. Central banks were doing so long before 2008, and with the QE crisis policies since then all the more so.

For another thing, the central banks' role as bank of the banks has expanded. Their interventions no longer only concern the banking sector, but also, directly and indirectly, shadow banks and the private financial sector as a whole. It has become an additional function of central banks to ensure the liquidity and solvency of systemically relevant non-bank financial institutions, not by statute, but de facto. The functional expansion results from the fact that shadow banks operate on the basis of bank money and in part also with new money surrogates based on bank money, having reached business volumes that equal or even exceed that of banks.

From this angle, one can say the expanded role of central banks is to be *bank of private finance* as well as, indirectly for the time being, *bank of public finance*. Bank of the banks—in the sense of refinancing a fractional reserve for the banking sector—the central banks remain to the extent and as long as there is bank money. The circle of financial institutions eligible to central-bank (re)financing is likely to expand over time. Likewise, the distribution of CBDC into the public circuit is likely not to remain the exclusive remit of banks. As bank money loses its dominance, this kind of privilege will not last either.

Labels like *bank of private finance* or *bank of public finance* should not be misunderstood to mean the central bank should be a universal lending institution for everyone and everything. Certainly not. The sole issue is the limited *monetary* mandate of the central bank. A central bank is responsible for the management of its own currency and an optimal overall money supply to the entire economy. To the extent central-bank money comes into circulation by way of credit and debt, this is done through central-bank credit to banks and, where appropriate, non-bank financial institutions and government bodies, as well as through purchases of public and, in some cases, private bonds, be it in direct initial purchases or indirectly on the open secondary market.

Central-bank credit is monetary base credit which increases the money base, whereas redemption of central-bank credit reduces the money base. There should be as much base money in the form of cash, reserves and CBDC as the central bank deems appropriate for *monetary* policy reasons. Everything else must be left to the lending and investment activities of banks, shadow banks and other financial institutions, that is, money and capital markets in general, especially if intermediary credit is involved. A central bank will not normally participate in these markets, at most to the extent necessary for monetary policy, as in open-market operations. Nevertheless, a central bank must reserve the right, if necessary, to intervene indirectly or even directly where *monetary* credit, i.e. credit that creates covered or uncovered money surrogates, is granted by private parties.

8.2.2 Independence in Relation to Fiscal and Budgetary Functions

By the share of CBDC in M1 reaching significant proportions, central-bank money and monetary policy will become monetarily more decisive than today. Already today, though, the increased importance of central banks almost reflexively evokes in some commentators the image of a central bank as overpowering bureaucratic behemoth. The image of the leviathan-like monetary authority, even central financial *planning* authority, is an unreal projection. The role of central banks is overstated and partly distorted, often in connection with criticising public finance, while the decisive role of the banking sector and the special role of non-GDP finance tend to be downplayed or ignored.

A high share of CBDC, indeed even a hypothetical money monopoly of the central bank, does not involve competence to issue specific directives. The focus of central banks is on the *monetary* framework of the economy. In this respect, central banks bear co-responsibility. But of course this is not about directive interventionism, but rather monetary macro-conditioning by setting the monetary framework conditions. Central banks must have power over their currency and the money denominated in that currency, but not beyond, without prejudice to necessary and desirable interfaces between central banks, private financial institutions and public finance.

In constitutional states based on the principle of checks and balances among state powers, the statehood of central banks as much as their independence was established. This may seem paradoxical, but is entirely consistent, in a way comparable to the independence of the judiciary. Given the developments of modern money and central banks, it is no longer appropriate to think of them as part of the state executive, such as an upper authority within the realm of the ministry of finance.

More clearly than before, central banks are becoming national monetary authorities in the exercise of a state's monetary sovereignty, in fact the fourth, monetary power of the state, complementing the executive, legislative and judicial branches. In this function, monetary policy must be independent, comparable to the independence of jurisdiction. The independence of a central bank relates to monetary policy matters in general and the control over money creation and the overall money supply in particular. In these matters, a central bank must not be subject to government directives, and be able to make monetary policy decisions on its own, albeit on the basis of a legal mandate that regulates the central bank's objectives and powers precisely enough. Current legal foundations of central-bank activity are not yet sufficiently elaborated. To set price stability as the primary or even sole objective, and leaving it to the interpretive arbitrariness of a central bank's governing board what this may or may not include, and by what means it might be achievable, is not yet a proper arrangement.

The central bank's monetary independence from the government, in particular the treasury, comes with a role division between the two. The central bank bears *monetary* responsibility, it has no *fiscal* and *budgetary* competence and no co-responsibility for financing government expenditure.[3] Fiscal responsibility lies solely with the government and parliament. The regular financing of government expenditure is through taxes, levies, other revenues and borrowing. Monetary financing of government spending by the central bank can also play a role, but, in the interest of sound finances, only to a limited extent, and subject to monetary policy, not budgetary and fiscal policy.

Monetary policy must be *monetarily* determined, complying with the principle of *monetary dominance*. This is less trivial and less tautological than it sounds. The explicit meaning is that monetary policy should not come under *fiscal dominance* and unilaterally serve only public finances for better or worse. Nor must monetary policy unilaterally come under *banking-sector* dominance, or more generally, *financial-market* dominance.

Independent and monetarily determined monetary policies do not exclude central-bank credit to the government, nor transfer of future genuine seigniorage to the treasury, as far as applicable. The central bank's profit from forex transactions, refinancing banks and open-market transactions—that is, interest-borne seigniorage—is rightly transferred to the treasury. The gain from central-bank sovereign money creation that may arise beyond the crediting activities of the central bank—that is, genuine seigniorage—cannot have any other destination. The point is that the central bank alone decides on monetary base credit and genuine seigniorage, not the cabinet or parliament. With a growing share of CBDC in the money supply, the gain from central-bank sovereign money creation—interest-borne or genuine—will increase.

Within the framework of independent monetary policy, it can and must be made possible again for a central bank to contribute to public finances in special ways. Beyond seigniorage this includes a good-sized central-bank overdraft facility for the treasury. Another example is a limited share of direct underwriting of newly issued government bonds. This is to be limited to a framework that is formally defined and utilised by the central

[3] Also see Buiter (2007, 2014b).

bank on the basis of purely monetary considerations, including the decision on which channels to use to put how much central-bank money into circulation. Exceptions must be possible in a state of emergency.

The separation of monetary from budgetary and fiscal responsibilities implies that a central bank is not responsible for financing government programmes or linking monetary policy to special purposes of government policies, no matter how much these purposes may be in the public interest, e.g. socially, environmentally or technologically. A number of civic campaigns have been calling for the "greening of monetary policy" or even for central-bank co-financing of, for example, an unconditional basic income or environmental programmes in energy, agricultural and so on.[4] A central bank would thus become too much entangled in the responsibilities of the governing cabinet and the parliament, while also interfering too much in capital markets.

Of course, a *government* can use central-bank credit and seigniorage for funding such programmes, because unlike money creation, the use of money is a matter for the markets and the government and is in principle none of a central bank's business, apart from a few macro-framework borderline cases. This also applies to the popular question of what the central bank's interest-borne and genuine gain from sovereign money creation should be used for—current expenditure, reducing public debt, tax cuts, a citizens' dividend or climate policies. All this, however, remains a matter for the parliament, the governing cabinet and specifically involved ministries. Just as courts should not be there to make up for inadequate legislation, a central bank should not be there to assume insufficiently accomplished government tasks.

8.2.3 *Independence in Relation to Banking and Finance*

The independence of central banks has another dimension, which is independence in relation to the banking sector and private finance in general. A central bank must be as independent from these as it is from the respective government. Today, however, within the bank money regime, independent action by central banks vis-à-vis the banking sector and now also shadow banks is completely illusory. The central banks have literally

[4] On using central-bank money creation to finance a universal basic income, see Crocker (2020, pp. 42–68). On greening monetary policy cf. Jourdan and Beckmann (2021) and Jourdan and Kalinowski (2019).

condemned themselves to act as an auxiliary body of the banking sector. The monetary initiative is predominantly with the banks. They create the monetary facts which the central banks have no choice but to accommodate. It cannot stay that way. To the extent that a recomposition of the money supply through CBDC and possibly stablecoins takes place, the bond between banks and central bank will loosen; the higher the share of central-bank money in the total money supply, the more so.

The independence of monetary policy in relation to the immediate requests of banking and private finance implies a corresponding division of functions also in this case, which is between *monetary policy* functions (including *foreign exchange* policy) and *general creditary and financial-market* functions. Presently, lines are blurred is in this respect. On the monetary side, money creation by way of monetary credit (as distinct from intermediary credit) is not the sole prerogative of the central bank, but is primarily carried out today by banks as well as the issuers of third-tier money surrogates and cryptocurrencies. On the financial side, central banks cannot always avoid interfering with the general credit and financial markets. Open-market operations of central banks may be required for monetary reasons, but interfere with the bond markets. Another, certainly only exceptional reason for central-bank intervention in the general credit and financial markets are crises like the one from 2008 onwards. The QE measures taken were intended to stabilise private and public finance in general. Ironically, in such cases bankers, financial markets and finance ministers are all happy about the behemoth called the central bank whose support they obviously take for granted.

The central bank is—or should be, respectively—responsible for the macro-management of the money supply. The present system, however, rests on the false identity of money and credit, in that the creation of money is closely linked to the lending and investment activities of the banking sector and other issuers of money surrogates. A central bank should retain macro-control of that entire monetary realm—but in fact monetary control has been slipping away from central banks for decades. This is mainly due to the false identity of money and credit. Given this Janus-faced bonding, central banks could only keep control of the money supply if they would also control the financial activities of private institutions that extend monetary credit or issue private monies in other ways. Since one rightly does not want central banks to exert such far-reaching financial control, they inevitably lose control of the overall money supply under generalised conditions of private credit-and-debt money.

For these reasons, it can be rather tricky under present conditions to discern the monetary from the financial. Nevertheless delineation can be drawn to the effect that a central bank is responsible for monetary policy on the basis of providing base money, setting central-bank rates and exerting macro-control of the entire money supply. By contrast, intermediary money markets as well as capital markets and the financial economy in general are basically not a central bank's business. However, as long as central-bank money is issued by way of lending or purchasing sovereign bonds (rather than by debt-free genuine seigniorage), the central bank remains partly active as a capital-market actor, especially in sovereign bond markets.

Credit is linked to quantities, terms, interest rates and repayment conditions. Moreover, credit is almost always tied to specific purposes (except for overdraft). Such earmarking of credit by banks and shadow banks would not be seen as an expression of a, say, planned banking economy. Central-bank credit, too, may involve cases in which the lending to banks is linked to a macro-structural purpose, referring here to economic macro-sectors (GDP and non-GDP finance, private and public finances). This still falls under monetary framework conditioning, far from any kind of central planning.

An example of macro-conditions tied to central-bank credit is the TLTRO programmes of the ECB (Targeted Longer-Term Refinancing Operations). With these, bank loans to firms are refinanced at preferential conditions, if the loans finance real-economic expenditure and investment. The total amount of these earmarked central-bank loans had reached 2.2 trillion euros in mid-2021.[5] The programme is a successful part of QE policies, specifically designed as "QE for the real economy", so as not to remain "QE for non-GDP finance" like most of the rest.

It is possible to apply the principle to Green TLTROs, that is, the refinancing of bank loans going into the ecological modernisation of energy, agricultural, transport, construction, mining, water management, etc.[6] It is banks and shadow banks that finance such projects. The central bank just grants preferential refinancing conditions according to certain macro-sectoral criteria—in this case the preferential funding of the

[5] Barbiero et al. (2021).

[6] Cf. van't Klooster and van Tilburg (2020) and Jourdan et al. (2021). ECB president Chr. Lagarde has explicitly spoken out in favour of Green TLTROs.

environmental economy as a broad-based cross-sector of the economy. Beyond such macro-structural specifications, however, a central bank should not influence the banks' and other financial institutions' lending and investment.

8.3 Reference Variables and Instruments of Responsive Monetary Policies

With regard to a monetary policy that is responsive to the situation, and can be accommodative without having to be, three aspects can be distinguished—(1) relevant reference variables, (2) the type of monetary policy and (3) instruments.

The reference variables comprise a range of figures on monetary and financial stability, economic development and employment. Monetary policy measures result from the analysis and assessment of the development of these key variables. It has become clear that central banks can no longer avoid expanding the range of issues and indicators that are relevant to them and also the range of instruments to be used. The ECB, however, has increasingly narrowed its mandate to consumer price stability, although EU law provides for the ECB to also support economic policy to the extent this is compatible with monetary and financial stability (TFEU Art. 127). The policy of the US Federal Reserve places much greater emphasis on its monetary support for economic policy.

The most important reference variables of monetary policy include

- the foreign exchange rate of the currency
- real-economic prices
- interest rates
- business cycle and real-economic growth, structural change and employment
- asset prices
- financial cycles and possible asset inflation and bubbles.

The money supply, or the quantity of money, is not a reference variable. Monetary policy should *not* set money supply targets. This may sound counter-intuitive. But the money supply itself is not a target, not an end in itself, but an *instrument* of monetary policy, a means to attain goals. The money supply must result from certain reasons and factors. It is futile trying to predict or prescribe relevant quantities of money. This was a basic error of monetarism as well as the calls for a new gold standard. The economic situation is ever changing. Monetary policy must be able to flexibly take into account the ever-changing dynamics of supply and demand, sometimes pro-cyclically, sometimes decidedly counter-cyclically.

For the longest time, central banks have not officially considered the development of asset prices and non-GDP finance as particularly relevant to monetary policy. They have certainly monitored runaway asset prices, but not specifically and expressly reacted to monetary overshooting in financial cycles. The fact that financial cycles and real-economic business cycles can be relatively independent of each other and not necessarily synchronous is not yet as widespread a realisation in economics and monetary policy as it should be. This has changed somewhat with the crisis policies since 2008. Asset prices and quantities of financial assets are obviously highly relevant to monetary and financial stability.

The inclusion of asset inflation requires a broader analytical toolkit. Some of this is already available, for example empirical methods of bubble spotting, while some other analytical tools still need to be developed, for example approaches to determine limits to the monetary absorptive capacity and financial carrying capacity of the economy.

The reference variables should first be understood as indicators. As target values to be aimed at they need only be quantified temporarily. The variables in question always remain, well, variable. Monetary policy should not embarrass itself by having its policy measured "exactly" against quantified targets when it can neither convincingly substantiate the target nor credibly promise to deliver. The mathematician and computer scientist John von Neumann preferred to be "about right rather than exactly wrong".

The reference variables relevant to monetary policy are partly at odds with each other and require appropriate weighing up. On the basis of the ongoing analysis and assessment of the variables' dynamics, the decision-making board will decide whether and to what extent and by means of which interest-rate and quantity measures it will tighten or loosen its monetary policy. This cannot be calculated mathematically or simulated by algorithms, at least not reliably. Monetary policy, too, is an art of the possible, certainly something for experts, but not an office to be exercised technocratically, as is often thought in misjudgement of the complex and political nature of the matter. However, it is imperative for a central bank to publicly explain its deliberations and decisions. The public would presumably better understand the meaning and purpose of such deliberations than a seemingly concrete, but in fact abstract target fetish such as "inflation at or near 2%" that eludes precise implementation.

Inflation rates have certainly always been a matter of concern. In the 1970s, J. Tobin had recommended an inflation "grease rate" of about 3%, particularly with regard to employment and economic growth.[7] Targeted inflation rates, however, did not exist in monetary policy before the end of the 1980s. Meanwhile, central banks set an "exactly" specified inflation target, generally 2% CPI, and let themselves be measured against it. At the same time, they cannot dependably bring the targeted development of prices and interest rates to pass, either pro-actively or re-actively.

What central banks should be able to do instead, is keeping an eye on the aforementioned parameters and adjust central-bank rates and/or the base-money supply in response. A central bank can wield influence both through the base-money supply (thereby also influencing interest rates) as well as through its central-bank rate (thereby also influencing monetary quantities). Since the 1980s, however, central banks have given up trying to control the money supply and pursuing monetary quantity policy, because as long as bank money is dominant and system-defining, conventional quantity policy (through reserve positions) is practically impossible, while, however, interest-rate policy too remains of limited efficacy.

The purchases of government bonds since 2008 and the associated flood of reserves for the banks, as well as the flood of bank money for the securities-selling shadow banks, represented massive monetary quantity policy as a matter of fact. But this was a kind of "unconventional" act of desperation. But also under normal conditions of monetary policy, a growing supply of CBDC should bring monetary quantity policy back into focus. With a dominant CBDC supply, basically both approaches—central-bank interest rates as well as CBDC quantity policy—are effectual.

For a central bank, the money supply in its home currency is, so to speak, its core business—which is a matter of fact, not a normative dictum. Creating central-bank money and setting the accompanying central-bank interest rate is what a central bank can definitely do and what it can bring to bear all the more effectively the weightier CBDC in the overall money supply is. The toolkit of monetary policy is in place. As the CBDC share grows, it regains its effectiveness, concerning quantity and interest

[7] Tobin (1972).

tenders, standing credit facilities and open-market policy. This can be expanded by providing credit facilities not only to banks and buying up government bonds not only from banks and other financial institutions, but also by making loans to the treasury and absorbing bonds from it directly.

8.4 Monetary Financing, Neutralisation of National Debt, Helicopter Money

8.4.1 Monetary Financing of Government Expenditure

In reaction to the 2008 crisis, and continuing since then, proposals are being made for monetary financing, that is, the central bank contributing to funding government expenditure. Among the first proponents were A. Turner, then head of the British Financial Services Authority, and the London based New Economics Foundation.[8] To overcome the Great Depression of the 1930s and during the Second World War, monetary financing had already been practiced.

In fact, after 2008, central banks have started to contribute to government expenditure indirectly and ex post facto by way of large-scale purchases of sovereign bonds previously held by banks, investment funds and insurance companies. Attempts to declare this practice inadmissible as a non-statutory transgression of Article 123 TFEU (Lisbon Treaty), which prohibits direct monetary financing, have failed at the European Court of Justice.

The mechanism is for the government to raise money by emitting new bonds, and for the central bank to promptly buy up a portion of these government bonds from respective holders. In such a *paso doble* between a state's treasury (bond-financed government spending) and the central bank (buying up government bonds on the open market and thus refinancing the banks' and shadow banks' financing of the government bonds), desired quantities of money can be made available at any time. Hence the conclusion is that a national government, that can borrow in domestic currency with the help of the national central bank, need not become insolvent. Of course, this should not be misinterpreted as a

[8] Cf. Turner (2016, pp. 227–240), Buiter (2014a), Buiter and Kapoor (2020), Jackson and Dyson (2013), Ryan-Collins (2015), and Ryan-Collins and van Lerven (2018).

licence for unrestrained debt-making, for this would trigger high inflation rates and ruin the forex value of the currency, thus bankrupting the country as a whole.

Central-bank purchases of government bonds on the open market refinance the previous bond holders, not the treasury. In contrast, monetary financing strictly speaking involves *direct* contributions by the central bank to government spending, whether through a standing overdraft facility or other central-bank credit to the government, or through the direct purchase of government bonds.

With central-bank purchases of government bonds, the government relieves itself of a corresponding part of its debt burden owed to private creditors. As far as government bonds are held by the home central bank, interest rates are basically irrelevant, because interest paid by the treasury to the central bank flows back to the treasury as part of the central bank's operating profit. However, the treasury also has to repay the principal to the central bank at maturity. Otherwise the central bank would have a corresponding loss and would soon operate on negative equity.

8.4.2 Neutralisation of National Debt

What the treasury can do instead, is to revolve maturing bonds, in that it redeems the bonds in question, but at the same time issues new bonds, part of which the central bank in turn buys up on the open market. A more far-reaching step by the central bank would be to reschedule the government bonds at maturity as *zero-coupon perpetual consols*, that is, non-interest-bearing bonds without fixed maturity.

The zero-interest perpetuals on the central bank's balance sheet are thus not redeemed, but neutralised, put on ice, as it were. The bonds remain a debt of the state to the central bank, and a claim of the central bank on the government, as well as a monetary balance-sheet liability of the central bank (= central-bank money). The amount of central-bank money corresponding to the consolidated government debt is thus not reduced and remains in circulation. Sovereign bonds held privately by banks, funds and individuals are not affected and are serviced conforming to emission terms. Over a longer period of time, the amount of debt is put into perspective by long-term price increases, even if these are comparatively small by the year. The U.S. has never reduced its national debt in absolute terms since 1835.

Basically, revolving the public debt as well as its neutralisation (consolidation) can be continued indefinitely, at least as long as it is not overdone, inflation remains moderate and orthodox economists don't get too excited about it, see Japan since 1980/1990, the U.S. to a lesser extent decades longer, likewise some European countries prior to the introduction of the euro, as well as the ECB's purchases of government bonds since 2009/10. In 2018, the share of sovereign bonds held by the home central bank was 25% in the U.S. and 50% in Japan. For long-term government bonds (10–30 years), the shares are significantly higher. As a result of the additional government spending due to the COVID-19 pandemic from 2020 and Russia's war on Ukraine since February 2022, government bonds held by central banks have once again increased sharply. Around 50–75% of new government bonds issued since then have been promptly bought by the respective central banks.[9]

Seen from this angle, the calls for monetary financing have long since been fulfilled. The function of the central bank as lender of last resort has in fact been supplemented by the function of broker-dealer of last resort, or market maker of last resort, in government bonds and to some extent also corporate bonds.[10] In this respect, too, it seems that many central bankers are now far ahead of their previous convictions.

It is about time to get honest about public debt. As M. Hudson put it: "Debts that can't be paid won't be paid".[11] This is a statement of fact, and a call for adapting financial form to reality. The counterpart to the expansion of the central-bank balance sheet through Quantitative Easing (QE) is Quantitative Tightening (QT), a contraction of the central-bank balance sheet. Such tightening is problematic. Even a balanced budget policy can leave serious investment deficits. On a larger scale, austerity policies or, put differently, contractionary policies are highly counterproductive because their effects are akin to deflation.

The problematic nature of QT policies is also evident in the difference between *monetary* credit (creating money) and *intermediary* credit (reusing existing money). Intermediary credit may involve, for example, someone putting part of their bank balances in an investment fund.

[9] Lennkh et al. (2019). fred.stlouisfed.org/series/TREAST. *The Economist*, June 20, 2020, p. 62. In the U.S., state-sponsored real-estate financiers Fannie Mae and Freddie Mac as well as other public bodies also hold government bonds on a large scale.

[10] Mehrling (2011, p. 132), Buiter (2014b), and Lennkh et al. (2019).

[11] Hudson (2018, p. xxiv).

The fund (which is not a bank) invests the bank money in bonds. If the bonds are sold or redeemed, the fund receives a payout in bank money, which remains available for further transactions. Likewise, when the customers sell their fund shares they get back the equivalent in bank money. The bank money in question is not lost. It keeps circulating among non-banks. Monetary credit, as extended by central banks and banks, is different. Each repayment of bank loans results in a deletion of the bank money from the respective bank balance sheet. Each repayment of central-bank credit results in a deletion of the amount of base money from the central-bank balance sheet.

Thus, in the present system of credit-and-debt money, each net repayment of monetary credit reduces the money supply. This does not apply to intermediary credit, but intermediary credit requires precedent monetary credit, in short: monetary credit debts gone, money gone, thereby less expenditure and investment, less income, etc. Therefore, within the existing system, and with public spending ratios of 40–60% of GDP, any reduction of government debt which is funded by monetary credit is problematic.

This is all the more true as the reduced public debt cannot be expected to be offset by increased private borrowing. After all, a considerable part of the national debt is compensatory, due to the fact that private borrowing, investment and consumer spending falter cyclically. A certain restraint in incurring public debt is certainly reasonable. But rigid austerity and mechanical debt brakes are harmful to the whole economy.

As an alternative to redemption, cancellation of public debt is occasionally called for, most often with regard to the foreign debts of developing countries, but since the euro sovereign debt crisis of 2010/11 also with regard to highly indebted industrialised countries.[12] However, debt relief is only possible to the degree that creditors (financial institutions, banks and central banks) have a sufficient cushion of equity capital. Writing off receivables from debtors means a loss of assets, while the liabilities—credit money in circulation—remain, regardless of whether a bank itself has created that book money or, as a rule, has received it from outside in customer payment transactions. The balance-sheet loss initially does not reduce the money supply but the equity capital of creditors—until

[12] Cf. Goodhart and Hudson (2018).

it is gone, which leads to balance-sheet trouble and even bankruptcy, whereupon the bank money would disappear as well.

What remains as an immediately viable path is the neutralisation of government debt on the central bank's balance sheet. Zero-interest perpetuals are not a satisfactory solution in the long run. But within the framework of existing commercial accounting and balance-sheet practices, there is no sound solution, just default with austerity hardship for debtors and capital losses for creditors. Consolidation of public debt on the central-bank's balance sheet is a pragmatic way of making the problem non-harmful until a real accounting solution is available. The final chapter discusses one such possibility.

In the meantime, monetary financing continues to make inroads. Financial repression has been stretched to its limits until 2020. The wave of strong inflation and interest rate hikes that has since set in will cause problems for many debtors, including public households given their high levels of indebtedness. What then? Then what has already begun will have to be continued. Rather than reducing sovereign-bond purchases as intended, central banks will feel compelled to continue buying an important share of government bonds.

Alternatively, countries outside the EU go straight to shaking off the Banking School taboo of direct monetary financing as in the examples already mentioned—the basically free hand of the US Congress, Treasury and Fed to do what they deem necessary in this regard, in the UK the government's standing overdraft facility with the Bank of England, in Canada the direct underwriting of a portion of new government bonds by the Bank of Canada. If one refuses to expand these or similar routes, sooner or later a major financial and economic collapse is likely to occur. This is one reason why the prohibition of direct monetary financing of government spending according to Art. 123 TFEU ought to be amended or repealed altogether. That Article does not stand up to realities and prohibits what is functionally reasonable.

Frequently voiced fears regarding monetary financing are about immoderation and abuse, resulting in inflation and currency devaluation. That problem should not be talked down. However, the problem applies to privately induced money creation at least as much as to state-induced money creation. It has nothing to do with monetary financing per se. Nevertheless, it is appropriate to caution against adding excessive state-induced money creation to cyclically excessive private money creation.

This applies all the more as the first uses of sovereign debt serve predominantly to finance real-economic expenditure. By contrast, most of private money creation in the recent past went directly into non-GDP finances, causing asset inflation and bubble formation, combined with increased inequality of financial income and wealth.

8.4.3 Helicopter Money

Since the mid-2010s, helicopter money has been discussed as an unconventional measure of monetary policy.[13] The idea goes back to C. H. Douglas' concept of a citizens' dividend.[14] One proposal is that helicopter money should go directly to private households as a citizens' dividend. The central bank should distribute one-off payments to everyone, like manna from heaven, or, according to a metaphor by M. Friedman, like dollar notes raining down from a helicopter. Unlike monetary financing by credit (indirect or even direct), the aim of helicopter money is to distribute central-bank money non-repayable and directly to the people, bypassing not only the banking sector and the bond markets, but also the government budget.

Friedman used the helicopter metaphor in 1969, when inflation rates were rising steadily. It was meant to be a thought experiment to make plausible that such a measure would only lead to additional inflation without having any effect on output. In contrast, in the mid-2010s, when inflation and interest rates were very low, the crisis-ridden financial world considered helicopter money to be a worthy option. The BlackRock Investment Institute, for example, proposed helicopter money in anticipation of a next crisis when government budgets would no longer have room for manoeuvre as interest rates would rise again. Monetary policy would then have to replace fiscal policy by "going direct".[15]

Distributing helicopter money directly to the people touches on a delicate point. How should cooperation between monetary policy and fiscal policy in this case look like without blurring the fundamental separation of the two functions and preserving the independence of monetary policy?

[13] For example Buiter (2014a), Ryan-Collins and van Lerven (2018), Diessner (2020), Jourdan (2020), Gali (2020), and Martin et al. (2021).

[14] Douglas (1974 [1924]).

[15] BlackRock Investment Institute (2019).

And how can a citizens' dividend be paid out at all? Would it be possible via the banks or via the tax office? Today, no money postman can be sent anymore. Above all, it remained unclear how helicopter money would be accounted for and represented on a central-bank balance sheet. Even B. Bernanke, chairman of the US Federal Reserve until 2014, did not give an answer to this when he mused about helicopter money as a last resort in an acute crisis situation.[16]

8.5 Problems of Monetary Accounting

8.5.1 *What Has Not Been Correct in Monetary Accounting for Long*

Some suggest the central bank should transfer the money to the treasury as genuine seigniorage. However, according to the existing rules it cannot be done "just like that". For one thing, it is prohibited as direct monetary financing in a number of countries, including the euro area and Japan (not however the U.S. and the UK). For another reason, it is not possible "just like that" under current Generally Accepted Accounting Principles (GAAP) and International Financial Reporting Standards (IFRS).[17]

Private banknotes from the late seventeenth to much of the nineteenth century were issued to customers in connection with extending bank credit, as a liability of the note-issuing bank. This made sense, because the banknotes were not yet money by sovereign fiat, but promissory notes, a kind of bearer debt instrument that promised to pay out the amount in silver currency at the request of the bearer. With the beginning of the central banks' note monopoly in the course of the nineteenth century and the associated establishment of the gold standard, national paper money was then based on the principle of coverage by a national gold hoard. But at the latest when US President Nixon in 1971 abolished the gold backing of the US dollar, which was no longer credible and only a hindrance, the Goldfinger myth of Fort Knox was ended once for all.

The illusory cover of central-bank money and any obligation to redeem it in other assets have officially ceased to exist since then. Today's central-bank money is no longer backed by anything monetary. It is pure fiat money. Bank money, too, is covered by little more than a normally small

[16] Bernanke (2016).

[17] The rules are issued by the International Accounting Standards Board (EU und UK for IFRS), and the Financial Accounting Standards Board (U.S. for GAAP).

fraction of central-bank money. Central-bank loans are usually collateralised with eligible securities, bank loans rather with pledging housing property, other assets or current income, or third-party guarantees. But this is no value coverage for the money, but credit default safeguards for the creditor in the event of a loss.

Nevertheless, to this day, still existing gold stocks of a central bank are correctly booked as *assets*, while reserves, banknotes and future CBDC, in disbursement of central-bank credit to banks, are booked as *liabilities* of the central bank. Central-bank money is thus not accounted for as sovereign base money in its own right, but continues to be represented like a promise to pay, as if it were a money surrogate, not "real" money at all, but still like a liability to pay out silver and gold.

The inconsistency for central banks is that a credit liability to disburse money is booked, but even when the credit is disbursed in notes, the liability is not booked out again, but continues to exist as the balance-sheet liability "banknotes in circulation". The same applies to reserves. They are booked as a liability to disburse money, but are not actually disbursed, at least not booked out again when the credit amount is made available on the central-bank account of a bank. The liability itself serves as the money. The same applies to bank money in the relationship between banks and non-bank customers. The courts interpret a credit entry on a customer's bank account as a completed payout. After all, the account balances represent real purchasing power. But where did the funds come? From which preceding business transaction or from which other account did the respective bank or central bank take the money from?

According to prevailing case law, a credit is deemed to be made available when the credited amount of money has left the creditor's assets and has been fully and finally added to the borrower's assets. However, such a transfer of assets only takes place when a bank disburses cash, not at all when current-account balances are credited. At the central bank an asset transfer only happens with coins, but neither with notes nor reserves, both of which continue to exist on the balance sheet as liabilities of the central bank. Central-bank money creation is hidden on the asset side behind the claim on a bank to loan-repayment, on the liability side in the false identity of central-bank credit liability and bank asset. The same applies to banks, where on the asset side the creation of bank money is hidden behind the claim on the customer to repay a respective loan, and on the liability side in the false identity of bank credit liabilities and customer account balances. The overall picture is that today's accounting practices concerning central-bank and bank credit are inconsistent. Some critics even see the practice as a kind of legalised false accounting.[18]

8.5.2 *"Debt Money" That Is Supposed Not to Be Debt*

The recent monetary reform movement has been concerned with putting sovereign money into circulation as debt-free money, preferably as genuine seigniorage. Newly created central-bank money needs not in fact be credit-and-debt money as hitherto. Instead, it can and should be a safe and secure stock of sovereign money free of interest and redemption; not a liability, but always a positive-numbered monetary asset, serving as a reliable base for extending credit and any other financial transaction, independent of the respective creditors and debtors, precisely because it is to function as a safe-stock means of payment beyond the false identity of money and credit, where the money is at risk when loans are at risk on a larger scale and banks are threatened by illiquidity and insolvency. Sovereign money—issued either by way of central-bank lending or as genuine seigniorage—is a reliable means of payment not threatened in its existence by whatever chaotic chain reactions financial markets may produce in a crisis.

To be sure, even debt-free money is not entirely for free. Expressions such as money creation "at the stroke of a pen" or "at a mouse click" fail to recognise the costs of banking operations in terms of personnel and IT. The profit from the creation of reserves or CBDC is not the full face value, rather, similar to the profit from coins, the face value minus supply costs.

Apart from that, the term debt-free money is, strictly speaking, a pleonasm. For money in and of itself, as the object of a credit agreement *is* debt-free. But according to existing accounting principles, IFRS and GAAP, money cannot be *ex nihilo*. Every credit entry is supposed to be a transaction following preceding transactions. An asset must come from somewhere or have resulted from something, and have a corresponding counter entry. This may well mean receiving money as a subsidy or donation without anything in return. But creating money by conjuring it up

[18] Cf. Schemmann (2012, pp. 37–59). A number of neo-Austrian economists, too, consider the accounting practice for credit-and-debt money on a base of fractional reserves to be fraudulent, for example Huerta de Soto (2009, chs. 2 and 3).

"out of thin air" into one's own books, that's not possible, not even for a central bank. Hence the distortion of the accounting rules in bank and central-bank money creation by hiding the entry of newly created money behind the credit claim, and circulating the money as a continued liability instead of booking it out when it is made available.

The idea of a perpetual debt that would only formally, but not really be debt, that is, the oxymoron of a debt-free debt, is a deformation of the concept of debt, just as the declaration of genuine seigniorage as profit without this resulting from business transactions means overstretching the concept of earnings or revenues.[19] D. Bezemer therefore called debt-free money the impossibility of dry water when discussing the Icelandic parliamentary initiative for sovereign money in 2015.[20] Taking the false identity of money and credit for granted, this seems to be true. However, as soon as one thinks beyond the self-contradictory and ambiguous Banking School frame of reference, perspectives of debt-free money issuance open up.

8.5.3 *Base Money as a Kind of Equity or Social Capital*

In view of the situation discussed, some authors have suggested that in the future all newly created central-bank money should be treated like the coinage of earlier times and booked as an asset.[21] This harks back to the principle of genuine seigniorage: the face value of newly minted coins minus their production costs. The coins were spent into circulation by the respective sovereign. With coins, it still seems to work that way up to the present day. The state mint produces the coins and the treasury sells them to the central bank. The difference today is that the central bank pays for the coins with a reserve entry into the government's transaction account at the central bank. The central bank now has the coins as an additional

[19] The notion of a purely formal credit to the government free of interest and redemption, not representing "real" debt, was initially, for lack of a better approach, so held in the recent monetary reform movement, but later dropped (Huber and Robertson 2000; AMI 2010; Jackson and Dyson 2012). "Modern money theory", by contrast, has so far not corrected itself and continues to hold the inconsistent view of "debt-free debt", including a distorting re-interpretation of the terms credit, debt and equity.

[20] Bezemer (2019, p. 164).

[21] In recent monetary reform concepts first proposed in Benes and Kumhof (2012, p. 6).

asset and the issued account balances as an additional liability. The coins are thus not plainly debt-free when they are put into circulation by the central bank. The central bank is left with a standing liability.

If a central bank were an industrial enterprise, the newly created money could be accounted for under "stocks" or "inventories". A bank, however, cannot account for its money creation in this way. Actually, one could introduce such a "money stock" procedure specifically for the issuance of central-bank money. This would require amending the IFRS and GAAP rules, or to introduce a special statutory rule to this effect.

The basic idea of the coin analogy is that central-bank money is to be created as an asset that is spent into circulation, or by way of an asset swap when the money is lent into circulation, both of which includes disbursement and closing-out of the money, rather than keeping it as an issuer liability, as is the case with notes and reserves today. In this context, Th. Mayer coined the terms *asset money* (which only exists and circulates as an asset) and *liability money* (which is recorded as a liability of the issuer).[22]

For a central bank, coins, notes, reserves and CBDC would first have to exist positively as assets. Then these funds can be spent, lent or invested. In the balance sheet, there is then an asset swap without liability. The respective amount is withdrawn from the assets of the central bank and added to the assets of, say, a bank, as required by prevailing legal opinion. In return, the central bank has a corresponding claim (asset) on the bank, while the bank has a liability to pay interest and repay the principal (liability). Still, however, the question arises as to how the money, as an asset, gets on the balance sheet in the first place.

On this issue, it has been suggested that central-bank money should be booked as equity. Authors include Jackson/Dyson, Sigurjonsson, Schemmann, Mayer, Bossone and Costa.[23] The base money would enter the central bank's balance sheet as a monetary asset and on the liabilities side in a special sub-account of the equity account, for instance as an item "money creation". One might think of it like this. If the money is issued, it disappears again from the balance sheet both as asset and equity. A little disadvantage is that the central-bank balance sheet would no longer

[22] Mayer (2014, pp. 22, 146–161).

[23] Jackson and Dyson (2012, pp. 210, 311–321), Sigurjonsson (2015, p. 81), Bossone (2018, 2021), and Bossone and Costa (2021).

reflect the current total stock of base money. That stock would have to be recorded in a separate statistic.

Notwithstanding, there remains a fundamental objection to the equity approach. Booking base money on the liabilities side as a new category of equity capital means a double distortion of concepts, that is, a distortion of the balance-sheet concept of profit as well as of the concept of equity capital. Newly created money is something different from liable corporate capital. Central-bank money is not equity capital of the central bank. Similarly, the gain from central-bank money creation (genuine seigniorage) is different from a profit-and-loss bottom line as in the case of profit from interest.

Kumhof et al. have followed the train of thought in a similar way.[24] According to the authors, base money should no longer be a balance-sheet liability of the central bank. In their opinion, however, it should not be an asset of the central bank either, nor should it be equity of the central bank. Rather, it should be "social equity", or "equity of the nation". Semantically, this hits the mark. For this is what central-bank money is supposed to be: the basic monetary endowment of a nation or community of nations. But how is it accounted for? There is no way getting round the fact that central-bank money must be represented on the central-bank balance sheet, and that it ought to be represented as an asset, not as a liability.

8.6 Beyond the False Identity of Money and Credit

8.6.1 *Separation of a Central Bank's Money Creation from Its Banking Operations by Means of a Currency Register*

Genuine seigniorage does not arise as profit from interest, but from a sovereign act of money creation. The money created goes—like interest-borne seigniorage and the entire central bank profit—either to the treasury, from where it is spent into circulation through current government spending, or the newly created money goes into creditary operations of the central bank. This implies distinguishable acts of money creation for one thing, and regular banking transactions for another, in contrast to today's inconsistent and unclear amalgamation of the two aspects.

[24] Kumhof et al. (2021, pp. 15, 26).

Resolving the inconsistency was sought in a number of proposals in establishing separate institutions. For example, both I. Fisher as well as S. Gesell in their time proposed a money-creating currency board separate from the treasury's budgeting and the commercial operations of the central bank. However, the accounting distinctness of money creation does not necessarily require a separate institution. Rather, coherent monetary policy would suggest all relevant decisions be taken by just one body. This does not compromise the functional distinctness of sovereign money creation and central banking.

In this sense, and with the pros and cons of the approaches discussed above in mind, an updated variety of an earlier classical approach suggests itself. That approach goes back to Ricardo's *Plan for the Establishment of a National Bank* of 1824. Ricardo was the most prominent representative of the Currency School. In accordance with his concept, the Bank of England was subdivided by the monetary reforms of 1844 into an *issue department*, responsible for issuing central-bank notes, and a *banking department*, which conducts banking business operations beyond money creation.[25]

The separation of banknote issuance and banking business operations continues at the Bank of England to this day. However, it soon proved to be of little relevance, because the separation of money and credit was not consistently implemented. For a long time, the so-called country banks could continue to issue private banknotes. The note issue was basically tied to the gold standard, but time and again the tie was relaxed or even suspended. Government bonds were to some extent counted as part of the gold base. Most importantly, it was the creation of bank money that was not given due consideration, although clearing via current accounts already played a certain role at the time and increased steadily in the further course of the nineteenth century.[26] Similarly, the issue department did not act like a sovereign money creator, but continued to act like a commercial bank, issuing notes against collateral, or redeeming notes against silver coins.[27] At the time, central banks were privileged private banks, not yet the national monetary authorities most of them have become today.

[25] O'Brian (2007, pp. 112, 152, 179) and Le Maux (2020).

[26] Lutz (1936, p. 75).

[27] O'Brian (2007, pp. 93–154).

Deficient implementation of a principle does not prove against it. Money creation separate from banking operations can be implemented coherently by having base-money creation at the central bank take place via a separate ledger. This is not a balance sheet, rather a *currency register* separate from the accounts in the central bank's *operational balance sheet*. Such a register is based on sovereign acts of fiat money creation. These are not linked to preceding business transactions. For this reason, and as explained in the previous sections, double-entry bookkeeping cannot be meaningfully applied to modern fiat money creation.

The currency register would be a separate ledger of the central bank, but there is no need for a separate body to keep it. Decisions concerning the monetary register, that is, concerning base-money creation, should fall to a central bank's governing body, in the U.S., for example, the Board of Governors and the Open Market Committee of the US Federal Reserve; in the UK, the Governors and Board of Directors of the Bank of England; and in the Eurosystem, the Governing Council and the Executive Board of the ECB. In terms of monetary policy, the currency register and the banking operations of a central bank belong together. The currency register would be published on an ongoing basis in parallel with the central bank's balance sheet.

The currency register is like a journal. It records the creation and the stock of legal tender denominated in the home currency as well as the issuing channel by which the money is put into circulation. The receipt of foreign currency continues to be included in the central bank's business balance sheet, as does the management of forex holdings. The currency register would record the relevant transactions in two accounts:

- the *currency-in-circulation* account, or *currency* account for short, which records the amounts of issued central-bank money by its form,
- the *issue account*, which records the issue channel by which the funds are put into circulation.

The currency account represents the actual central-bank money creation, in that it serves the creation and, if applicable, the deletion of a respective amount of base money. At the same time, the currency in circulation is recorded according to the monetary form, subdivided into coins, notes, conventional reserves and future CBDC. The current account and the issue account have the same total balance. This is mostly money

Table 8.1 The currency register's structure of accounts

Date	*Currency account*				*Issue account*	
	Coins	Notes	Conventional Reserves	CBDC	Genuine Seigniorage = Allocation to public purse	CB liquidity = Deposit into central-bank balance sheet

in domestic use, partly also as home currency abroad. In today's categories, the currency register's bottom line corresponds to the monetary aggregate M0.

The money comes into existence with the act of its registration. A respective amount is entered into one of the currency sub-accounts and is likewise allocated to a specific issue channel, either as genuine seigniorage to the treasury or as a deposit in the central-bank operational balance sheet (see Table 8.1).

Each entry in the currency register includes the respective amount of central-bank money simultaneously linked to one of the two issue accounts. If necessary, the accounts can be further differentiated. Coins and notes remain items as long as traditional cash is in demand and the supply of it is maintained. The material stocks of coins and notes would not be entered into the currency register prior to their issuance. As hitherto, the metal and paper pieces only become money when they are entered into the currency register and into the central bank's commercial balance sheet.[28] A backflow of funds from the banks or the treasury deletes these funds from both the issue and the currency account. As long as in circulation, the forms of central-bank money should be convertible into each other.

Together with the entry of an amount in the currency account, that amount is also entered in the issue account. The issue account has two sub-accounts:

[28] Today, the right of coinage in most cases still lies with the national treasuries, as a remnant of feudal coinage. This should long ago have been devolved upon central banks. These, in turn, should have taken over the shares of all private and corporate part-owners (banking and financial corporations, confederations and associations) where this still applies. In general, a central bank as the national monetary authority should no longer be run in the form of a joint-stock company.

- *Genuine seigniorage*, that is, allocation of newly created reserves or CBDC to the treasury as a variable contribution to government funds to be spent into circulation.
- *Central-bank liquidity*, that is, a deposit in the liquid money stock of the central bank's balance sheet for use in all types of central-bank operations.

The transfer of genuine seigniorage to the treasury contributes to financing government spending. However, this is not necessarily to be seen as monetary financing. After all, this is about seigniorage which is first and foremost due to the public purse. The central bank decides on the accruing seigniorage independently and according to monetary policy considerations. Parliament and the governing cabinet must not have a say in this and no right to issue instructions to the central bank, in particular regarding allocations of genuine seigniorage. How much new money is created in each case and how much of it is circulated by genuine seigniorage and how much by credit to banks and the financial economy beyond, is to be the sole responsibility of the central bank in fulfilment of its legal mandate—which, of course, would have to be spelled out somewhat more precisely than is the case today.

Regarding the size of seigniorage, it should be clear to everyone that this cannot be a tremendous amount of money. Depending on government expenditure and economic growth, one may expect the amounts involved to be in the order of about 1–4% of total public spending in old-industrial countries. This is not small change, but far too little to fund government spending on a larger scale or to replace the regular tax financing of public budgets. Genuine seigniorage does not release policymakers from the requirement of sound fiscal management.

Seigniorage is not earmarked. What the money is used for is decided by the government, possibly also the parliament. This corresponds to the separation of powers between monetary and budgetary-fiscal functions.

The deposits of the currency register in the commercial balance sheet of the central bank are to be understood as callable loans without specified maturity. The deposits do not need a fixed maturity date. They just need to be callable. It can be left open here what the conditions of such notice would be—for example, exceeding a certain limit of currency holdings on the central-bank's balance sheet. At the same time, redeemability enables reducing the current money supply, should this be indicated, without having to withdraw tax revenues from circulation and thus improperly conflating monetary and fiscal policy. Deposits of the currency register into the central bank's commercial balance sheet would be non-interest bearing (unlike central-bank lending to banks). For in this case, interest would have no function, since the currency register and the central bank's banking operations belong to one and the same central bank as a currency area's monetary authority.

8.6.2 *Changes to the Balance Sheets of Central Bank and Banks*

The central bank's balance sheet would continue to show the banking operations of the central bank and would remain largely unchanged. The key change is that the central bank no longer records notes, reserves and CBDC as liabilities—to banks and public bodies in the form of conventional reserve balances as well as "banknotes in circulation" and soon also "CBDC in circulation". Instead, the deposits of the currency register constitute a liquid stock of actually existing central-bank money on the asset side of the central bank's balance sheet, either in the form of cash in vault, or CBDC, or conventional reserves on central-bank account. These monetary assets are matched by corresponding liabilities on the central bank's balance sheet to the currency register. The previous items *liabilities to banks, public bodies* and *currency in circulation* become a new item position *liabilities to currency register*, non-interest-bearing and at open maturity, but callable at any time.

When the central bank lends to banks, there is an asset swap in the central-bank balance sheet (credit claims on the banks for liquid money to the banks). The same applies to the purchase of foreign exchange, securities or other assets by the central bank. More generally, funds from the item *liquid currency stocks* are exchanged for securities or other asset items, in particular claims on foreign central banks, home and foreign credit institutions, as well as claims on the government; the latter, for example, as a standing but capped overdraft facility.

As for banks, nothing changes on their balance sheets as far as bank money continues to exist in parallel with cash and CBDC. In this respect, banks remain monetary financial institutions, operating on a fractional reserve base and enjoying privileged central-bank and government support for the foreseeable future. However, dwindling cash is going to be replaced by CBDC to an increasing extent. CBDC, like cash, banks cannot create themselves. Banks must disburse CBDC transactions in full, and for being able doing so they must have fully available that CBDC, whether through repayment of principal, earnings, or borrowing CBDC from customers, on the money market and from the central bank. This is likely to be driven by customer demand for the various types of money, as well as by the banks' competition for customers. Apart from the addition of CBDC as an asset, nothing changes in the structure of the bank balance sheets. But of course the recomposition of the monetary bank assets and the shifting proportions between cash, CBDC and conventional reserves is highly significant.

Overall, using a currency register for the purpose of money creation separate from the balance sheet of the monetary authority's banking operations makes it possible to straighten out today's inconsistent accounting for money creation, by enabling double-entry bookkeeping in the central bank's balance sheet in a coherent way without the confusing and dysfunctional pseudo-identity of credit and money, and without overstretching the categories of credit, debt and liability, profit and equity. This also applies to genuine seigniorage, the issuance of which through allocation of the monetary register to the treasury need not be accounted for as a liability, or as equity capital of the central bank.

In accounting terms, the core element of the approach is the asset-only accounting of central-bank money and its circulation through direct and full asset transfer from payer to payee. In the bank-customer relationship, of course, this only applies to cash and CBDC. With cash and CBDC, customer funds exist separately from the banks' balance sheets. However, this still does not apply to traditional central-bank reserves and bank money. The public is unlikely to ever receive conventional reserves. However, it would not come as a surprise if, with the transition to pure asset money, the previous reserve economy of the central banks and the bank money privilege were seen in retrospect as a bizarre phenomenon in the historical transition from traditional to modern money.

References

AMI (American Monetary Institute). 2010. *Presenting the American Monetary Act*. Valatie, NY: American Monetary Institute. http://monetary.org/wp-content/uploads/2011/09/32-page-brochure.pdf.

Barbiero, Francesca, Miguel Boucinha, and Lorenzo Burlon. 2021. TLTRO III and bank lending conditions. *ECB Economic Bulletin*, Issue 6: 104–127.

Benes, Jaromir, and Michael Kumhof. 2012. The Chicago Plan Revisited. IMF Working Paper, 12/202 August 2012, revised draft February 2013.

Bernanke, Ben S. 2016. *What tools does the fed have left?* Part 3: Helicopter Money. The Brookings Institution.
Bezemer, Dirk. 2019. *Money and its uses*. Driebergen-Rijsenburg: Triodos Bank.
BlackRock Investment Institute. 2019. Dealing with the next downturn. *Macro and Market Perspectives*, August. Authored by Simon Wan, Elga Bartsch, Jean Boivin, Stanley Fisher and Philipp Hildebrand.
Bossone, Biagio, and Massimo Costa. 2021. Money for the issuer: Liability or equity? *Economics* 15 (1): 43–59.
Bossone, Biagio. 2018. The 'accounting view' of money: Money as equity (Parts I+II). The World Bank Blog, May 14–21. blogs.worldbank.org/allaboutfinance/accounting-view-money-money-equity-part-i/blogs.worldbank.org/allaboutfinance/accounting-view-money-money-equity-part-ii.
Bossone, Biagio. 2021. Bank Seigniorage in a Monetary Production Economy. Post-Keynesian Economics Society Working Paper, no. 2111, August.
Buiter, Willem H. 2007. How robust is the new conventional wisdom in monetary policy? Working Paper, London School of Economics/Universiteit van Amsterdam, April 15.
Buiter, Willem H. 2014a. The simple analytics of helicopter money. Why it works—Always. *Economics* 8 (28): 1–51.
Buiter, Willem H. 2014b. Central banks: Powerful, political and unaccountable? CEPR Discussion Paper, No. 10223, October.
Buiter, Willem H., and Sony Kapoor. 2020. To fight the COVID pandemic policymakers must move fast and break taboos. voxeu.org, April 6.
Crocker, Geoff. 2020. *Basic income and sovereign money. The alternative to economic crisis and austerity policy*. London: Palgrave Macmillan.
Diessner, Sebastian. 2020. *Mainstreaming monetary finance in the Covid-19 crisis*. Brussels: Positive Money Europe.
Douglas, Clifford Hugh. 1974. *Social credit*. Bloomfield Books, Reprint of the revised version of 1934. First edition in 1924.
Friedman, Milton. 1991. *Monetarist economics*. Oxford, UK and Cambridge, MA: Basil Blackwell.
Friedman, Milton. 1992. *Money mischief*. New York: Harcourt Brace Jovanovich.
Gali, Jorda. 2020. Helicopter money: The time is now. VOX/CEPR discussion paper, ox, March 17.
Goodhart, Charles A.E., and Michael Hudson. 2018. Could/Should Jubilee Debt Cancellations Be Reintroduced Today? CEPR Discussion Paper, DP12605, January.
Huber, Joseph, and James Robertson. 2000. *Creating new money. A monetary reform for the information age*. London: New Economics Foundation.
Hudson, Michael. 2018. ... *and forgive them their debts. Lending, foreclosure and redemption from bronze age finance to the jubilee year*. Dresden: ISLET Verlag.

Huerta de Soto, Jesús. 2009. *Money, bank credit, and economic cycles*, 2nd ed. (1st 2006). Auburn, AL: Ludwig von Mises Institute.

Jackson, Andrew, and Ben Dyson. 2012. *Modernising money. Why our monetary system is broken and how it can be fixed*. London: Positive Money.

Jackson, Andrew, and Ben Dyson. 2013. *Sovereign Money—Paving the way for a sustainable recovery*. London: Positive Money.

Jourdan, Stan, and Marc Beckmann. 2021. *Why green monetary policy is legal and legitimate*. Brussels: Positive Money Europe.

Jourdan, Stanislas. 2020. *Helicopter money as a response to the Covid-19 recession in the Eurozone*. Brussels: Positive Money Europe.

Jourdan, Stanislas, and Wojtek Kalinowski. 2019. Aligning Monetary Policy with the EU's Climate Targets. Working Paper Positive Money Europe, Brussels, and Veblen Institute for Economic Reforms, Paris, April.

Jourdan, Stanislas, Monique Goyens, Edoardo C. Coppola, Sébastien Godinot, and Adrian Joyce. 2021. *How the European central bank can unleash the building renovation wave*. euractiv.com/section/energy/opinion, September.

Kumhof, Michael, Jason Allen, Will Bateman, Rosa Lastra, Simon Gleeson, and Saule Omarova. 2021. Central bank money: Liability, asset, or equity of the nation? *Vanderbilt Law Review* 74 (5): 1231–1300. Reprinted as CEPR Discussion Paper 15521.

Le Maux, Laurent. 2020. Central banking and finance: The Bank of England and the Bank Act of 1844. *Revue Economique*, Presses de Sciences Po, May 2020. ffhal-02854521f.

Lennkh, Alvise, Bernhard Bartels, and Thibault Vasse. 2019. The rise and fall of central banks as sovereign debt holders. SUERF Policy Note, Issue No 109, October.

Lutz, Friedrich. 1936. *Das Grundproblem der Geldverfassung*. Stuttgart and Berlin: Kohlhammer.

Martin, Philippe, Éric Monnet, and Xavier Ragot. 2021. What else can the European central bank do? *Les notes du Conseil d'Analyse Économique*, No. 65: 1–12, June 2021.

Mayer, Thomas. 2014. *Die neue Ordnung des Geldes*. München: FinanzBuch Verlag.

Mehrling, Perry. 2011. *The New Lombard Street. How the fed became the dealer of last resort*. Princeton University Press.

O'Brien, Denis Patrick. 2007. *The development of monetary economics*. Cheltenham: Edward Elgar.

Ryan-Collins, Josh. 2015. Is monetary financing inflationary? A case study of the Canadian economy 1935–75, Levy Economics Institute of Bard College. Working Paper, No. 848, October.

Ryan-Collins, Josh, and Frank van Lerven. 2018. Bringing the helicopter to ground: a historical review of fiscal-monetary coordination to support

economic growth in the 20th century. Working Papers PKWP1810, Post Keynesian Economics Society (PKES).
Schemmann, Michael. 2012. *Accounting perversion in bank financial statements. The root cause of financial crises*. IICPA Publications.
Sigurjonsson, Frosti. 2015. *Monetary Reform. A better monetary system for Iceland*. Icelandic Parliament, submitted to the Committee on Economic Affairs and Trade, March.
Tobin, James. 1972. Inflation and unemployment. *American Economic Review* 62: 1–18.
Turner, Adair. 2016. *Between debt and the devil. Money, credit and fixing global finance*. Princeton University Press.
Van't Klooster, Jens, and Rens van Tilburg. 2020. *Targeting a sustainable recovery with Green TLTROs*, September 2020, Positive Money Europe, Brussels, and Sustainable Finance Lab, Utrecht University.

Index

J. Huber, *The Monetary Turning Point*,
https://doi.org/10.1007/978-3-031-23957-1

www.ingramcontent.com/pod-product-compliance
Ingram Content Group UK Ltd.
Pitfield, Milton Keynes, MK11 3LW, UK
UKHW020836290926
15470UKWH00004B/1371
* 9 7 8 3 0 3 1 2 3 9 5 6 4 *